Renunciation

Renunciation

*My Pilgrimage from Catholic Military Chaplain,
Hawk on Vietnam, and Medal of Honor Recipient
to Civilian Warrior for Peace*

Charles J. Liteky

ISBN-13: 978-1542932400
ISBN-10: 1542932408

First edition. March 2017, San Francisco

Cover design: Kantorski Design (www.kantorskidesign.com)
Front cover photograph: Chaplain Charles J. Liteky, undated. Credit: Florida Photographic Collection.
Back cover photograph: Charles Liteky renouncing his Medal of Honor at the Vietnam Veterans Memorial, Washington, D.C., July 29, 1986, in protest against U.S. policies in Central America. Credit: AP Photo/Ira Schwarz

Every effort was made to source and properly credit photographs used in *Renunciation*. Photographers are urged to contact the Charles J. Liteky and Judith Balch Liteky Trust if their work has not been acknowledged.

Facebook: www.facebook.com/charleslitekyrenunciation/
Website: charlieliteky.org

IN MEMORIAM

Judith Balch Liteky
May 6, 1942–August 20, 2016

Judy Liteky was a long-distance runner for peace who inspired many to resist with joy and to endure with conviction. From her days in a religious order and as a college professor, Judy developed educational programs for Latina women and worked in the sanctuary movement for refugees in Central America. Through her membership in Pax Christi and many other organizations, Judy supported the School of Americas Watch and served as a plaintiff in a lawsuit to require the U.S. government to release the names of Latin American personnel who attended the school. Her numerous contributions to the cause of justice and nonviolent resistance have inspired many through the years, including Charlie Liteky. Judy was Charlie's pillar and rock and beloved wife. She encouraged him, marched with him, inspired him, and visited him countless times in prison. Judy was to have written her own words in this book but, sadly, she took sick before it could be completed. This book simply would not have been published without Judy's cheerful and loving support. May she walk among the stars.

Charles Joseph Liteky
February 14, 1931–January 20, 2017

Charlie Liteky is a former Catholic priest and military chaplain who was awarded the Medal of Honor in Vietnam. Through all those years he never questioned the teachings of his church on war and blindly accepted his country's assertion that the war in Vietnam was fought for a good cause. In his late thirties Charlie came to form his own conscience on war after being challenged by a college student and his own experiences. Charlie found the courage to change. He left the military and the priesthood and became involved in numerous peace actions, including the Veterans Fast for Peace and nonviolent resistance at the School of the Americas, Fort Benning, Georgia. He served two prison terms for civil disobedience. While comforting the afflicted in several war-torn areas, Charlie afflicted the comfortable, from Ronald Reagan through his own church leadership, who stood in compliance or silence while war raged around them. Charlie was strongly influenced and supported by his loving wife, Judy, who was there with him every step of the way. She encouraged him to persevere in the publication of this book. May he walk among the stars.

*Those of us who knew and loved Judy and Charlie Liteky
are saddened that neither lived to see this book published.
Nevertheless, we hope the words found herein inspire young
and old alike for the first time in their lives to find the courage
to form their own consciences. May the spirit of Judy
and Charlie live in each of us.*

Contents

Citation

Medal of Honor

LITEKY, CHARLES J. (ANGELO)

Rank and organization: Chaplain (Capt.), U.S. Army, Headquarters Company, 199th Infantry Brigade
Place and date: Near Phuoc-Lac, Bien Hoa Province,
Republic of Vietnam, 6 December 1967
Entered service at: Fort Hamilton, New York
Born: 14 February 1931, Washington, D.C.

Citation

Chaplain Liteky distinguished himself by exceptional heroism while serving with Company A, 4th Battalion, 12th Infantry, 199th Light Infantry Brigade. He was participating in a search and destroy operation when Company A came under intense fire from a battalion-size enemy force. Momentarily stunned from the immediate encounter that ensued, the men hugged the ground for cover. Observing two wounded men, Chaplain Liteky moved to within fifteen meters of an enemy machine-gun position to reach them, placing himself between the enemy and the wounded men. When there was a brief respite in the fighting, he managed to drag them to the relative safety of the landing zone. Inspired by his courageous actions, the company rallied and began placing a heavy volume of fire upon the enemy's positions. In a magnificent display of courage and leadership, Chaplain Liteky began moving upright through the enemy fire, administering Last Rites to the dying and evacuating the wounded. Noticing another trapped and seriously wounded man, Chaplain Liteky crawled to his aid. Realizing that the wounded man was too heavy to carry, he rolled on his back, placed the man on his chest and through sheer determination and fortitude crawled back to the landing zone using his elbows and heels to push himself along. Pausing for breath momentarily, he returned to the action and came upon a man entangled in the dense, thorny underbrush. Once more intense enemy fire was directed at him, but Chaplain Liteky stood his ground and calmly broke the vines and carried the man to the landing zone for evacuation. On several occasions when the landing zone was under small arms and rocket fire, Chaplain Liteky stood up in the face of hostile fire and personally directed the medevac helicopters into and out of the area. With the wounded safely evacuated, Chaplain Liteky returned to the perimeter, constantly encouraging and inspiring the men. Upon the unit's relief on the morning of 7 December 1967, it was discovered that despite painful wounds in the neck and foot, Chaplain Liteky had personally carried over twenty men to the landing zone for evacuation during the savage fighting. Through his indomitable inspiration and heroic actions, Chaplain Liteky saved the lives of a number of his comrades and enabled the company to repulse the enemy. Chaplain Liteky's actions reflect great credit upon himself and were in keeping with the highest traditions of the U.S. Army.

Tributes

Roy Bourgeois

When I was in Vietnam, I met a Buddhist monk who said, "Our greatest enemy in life is ignorance." Many of us returned from the war in Vietnam seeing the truth in those words and now wanted to be peacemakers. Among them was Charlie Liteky. Charlie became a great peacemaker. He inspired and touched deeply the lives of many, including my own.

On November 16, 1989, six Jesuit priests, their coworker, and her sixteen-year-old daughter, Celina, were massacred by the military in El Salvador. A U.S. Congressional Task Force went to El Salvador to investigate and reported that those who did the killing had been trained at the U.S. Army School of the Americas (SOA) at Fort Benning, Columbus, Georgia.

As a humble act of solidarity, nine of us participated in a water-only fast for thirty-five days at the main gate of Fort Benning and called for the closing of the SOA. In our group of fasters was Charlie Liteky.

When our long and challenging fast ended, the first anniversary of the massacre of the six priests, the mother, and her daughter was approaching. I invited members of the fast to stay in town and plan an act of civil disobedience at the School of the Americas – where soldiers from El Salvador continued to be trained.

Charlie Liteky and his brother, Patrick, decided to stay. The three of us, after much reflection and discussion, decided to pour our blood at the headquarters of the School of the Americas. This blood would be a symbol of the bloodshed of thousands of people killed in El Salvador by graduates of this military school.

We were arrested, brought to trial, and sent to prison. Prison was hard, but Charlie, Patrick, and I had no regrets about what we did. It was rooted in our ignorance of the past and our determination to be peacemakers today.

S. Brian Willson

Charlie Liteky is one of a kind. He is the only recipient of the Medal of Honor to have returned that award to the government that issued it to him. Depositing it at the Vietnam Memorial Wall in 1986, he was protesting his government's murderous policies, this time in Central America. By then he understood that the U.S. war waged against the Vietnamese had been based on layers and layers of lies, and millions of innocents had died because of them. He, like so many soldiers, was dealing with a sense of deep betrayal perpetrated on us by our own government, even as he had acted heroically as a Catholic chaplain saving the lives of more than twenty U.S. soldiers in Vietnam.

Charlie's political awakening emerged in the early 1980s in San Francisco. There he was sorting out his separation from the Catholic Church. Ordained a priest in 1960, he had formally left the priesthood in 1975, when he began journeying down a path that included marrying Judy Balch, an activist former nun. While in San Francisco he was painfully exposed to the stories of *campesinos* fleeing repressive regimes in Central America financed by the United States, especially from Guatemala and El Salvador, who were on the underground railroad on their way to safer points north.

Charlie then became an intense student of the real history of the United States: its systematic policies of genocide and barbaric plunder since its origins. His activist journey has been consistent, tenacious, outspoken, and courageous. He pulled no punches as he has identified chronic injustices at home and lawless imperial policies abroad. He participated in serious water-only fasts, one of which led the FBI to identify him and three other veteran fasters (myself included) as domestic terrorist suspects. He ventured onto U.S. training bases in efforts to educate military personnel about their likely participation in unconscionable and criminal acts under orders when deployed. For these activities, he spent two different year-long sentences in federal prisons. When President George Bush II was making it known that he was going to attack Iraq, Charlie joined a small number of U.S. citizens who went to Iraq as vulnerable witnesses. He spent several months before, during, and after the 2003 shock-and-awe, in a tent adjacent to a water-treatment plant in central Baghdad. There he also addressed invading U.S. troops as they entered the city. This is Charlie.

Charlie and I first met in person in January 1986 at the Witness for Peace (WFP) house in Managua, Nicaragua, where he was completing his participation in a WFP delegation in Nicaragua's war zones. I was studying Spanish in Estelí, Nicaragua, but was visiting Managua for a day. We immediately commiserated with each other about the diabolical U.S. terrorist policies in Nicaragua and wondered what we might do in response.

What was so striking for me was that in that first meeting, we discussed three dramatic, inspiring individual examples of conscience, each of whom we knew about. I had never met anyone who could so readily discuss this detailed activist history. He knew of the immolation in 1965 of the thirty-one-year-old Quaker, Norman Morrison, outside the Pentagon window of Secretary of War Robert McNamara in protest against the U.S. war in Vietnam. He knew of the ten Irish hunger strikers, led by twenty-seven-year-old Bobby Sands, who all died in prison in 1981 while participating in open-ended, water-only fasting, for periods anywhere from forty-six to seventy-three days, in efforts to be acknowledged as political prisoners rather than common criminals in their struggle to achieve Irish independence from England. And he knew of Mitch Snyder, who at that time was a forty-three-year-old relentless activist in Washington, D.C., participating in a number of lengthy fasts to raise awareness about the chronic issue of homelessness in U.S. capitalist society. These three actions, little known or remembered by the majority of people, had inspired both Charlie and me, and here we were in our first meeting excitedly talking about them. I shall never forget.

So, naturally we discussed whether lengthy fasts, even open-ended ones, and self-immolation were expressions we might consider. We both were experiencing the intensity of egregious U.S. policies causing so much pain and suffering, believing our country was mired in a moral emergency. We wondered why more of our fellow citizens were unwilling to risk their lives to save other lives, whether at home or abroad, like the valiant WFP activists in Nicaragua. It seemed like so few really understood the diabolical nature of U.S. policies or could experience the suffering of others as their suffering too. This was something that Charlie felt deeply, and it was foundational in our mutual commitment to participate in an action that might raise consciousness and, we hoped, radically change U.S. policies.

We were quite certain we did not have the courage to participate in life-ending self-immolations, though we discussed it. But the idea of an open-ended, water-only fast was an idea we thought was worth serious discernment. So, after a 1986 spring and summer of witnessing the lawless and sickening efforts of the U.S. Congress and President Ronald Reagan to violently oust the Nicaraguan Sandinista government, either by starvation or terrorist-inflicted murders, we decided to embark on a staggered, open-ended, water-only fast, along with two other veterans who agreed to join us. We ended the fast after forty-seven days because one of our fasting veterans was approaching death.

After the Veterans Fast for Life on the steps of the U.S. Capitol, Charlie continued his bold actions for nearly thirty more years, inspiring countless people, myself included, to boldly and actively tell the truth about unspeakable U.S. policies, while advocating justice for all.

Thank you, Charlie. You are indeed one of a kind.

Chronology

1972 spring	Reality House drug rehab home opens
1973 summer	Second laicization request; withdraws request
1975	Third laicization request; accepted
1978 or 1979	Pine Island, Florida
1980 January	VA hospital in San Francisco
1981 Feb	Meets Judy Balch
1983 Oct 22	Marries Judy Balch in San Francisco
1985 Sept	Trips to El Salvador and Nicaragua
1986 Jan	Meets Brian Willson
1986 July 29	Renounces Medal of Honor
1986 Sept 1	Veterans Fast for Life; ends on October 17
1988 spring	Moves with Judy to Eden Valley farm
1990 Sept 1	Fast and actions at School of the Americas
1991 June	Sentenced to Allenwood Work Camp
1991 Dec 13	Released from Allenwood
1997 Sept	More actions at School of the Americas
2000 July 29	One-year sentence to Lompoc Prison
2001 July 27	Released from Lompoc
2002 and 2003	To Iraq with Voices in the Wilderness

In Gratitude

IN HIS LAST YEARS, Charlie Liteky spoke often of people to whom he was grateful for their love and support. His wife, Judy, was his loyal and loving companion to her death just six months before his. Charlie cherished Judy and deeply appreciated her support and forbearance through the years. Charlie and Judy's travail in the last three years of their lives was considerably lightened by Scarlett, a Pomeranian/poodle mix, who brought joy to their lives.

Father Roy Bourgeois and S. Brian Willson were Charlie's companions in many actions through the years, and he spoke often of their inspiration and support during their resistance together. He deeply respected and was grateful to both men. And there were the thousands who joined with Charlie in his actions, fasts, and arrests in the cause of justice for all. They all had a special place in Charlie's heart and he was deeply grateful to them. He also never forgot those common grunts to whom he ministered in Vietnam. He deeply admired their loyalty and courage in combat although he, and many of them, came to bitterly regret that war.

Charlie spoke often of his mother, Gertrude, and his father, Navy Chief Charlie Liteky, and his brothers, Jim and John Patrick. He loved them all.

San Francisco, which Charlie and Judy called home for so many years, was also the place where many good friends walked with Charlie during good and bad times. He deeply appreciated the joyful companionship of his friend and eventual legal guardian Bob Frank. Bob and his wife, Janie Frank, were there with Charlie to the end. Charlie was thankful for the friendship and support of his longtime coworker and final roommate, Alvaro Zunigo. Other San Francisco friends who looked after Charlie's personal and medical needs include Geralyn da Silva, Chris McCarty, Maureen Aggeler, and Angela Taylor.

Charlie was grateful to so many other friends and companions in the struggle and the mere mention of their names does not do justice to all they did for Charlie: Brooks Anderson, Judy Bierbaum, Blase and Theresa Bonpane, Kevin Brickley, Barbara Garza-Brickley, Father Tom Burns, Ken Butigan, Theresa Camaranesi, Rita Clark, Charlie Clements, Maria da Silva, Maria Eitz, Daniel Ellsberg, Jack Gilroy, Mike Hastie, Deborah Hannula, Harvey Harrison, Paul Hendrickson, Joseph Holland, Immaculate Heart Community, John Ketwig, Ed Kinane, Margaret Knapke, Sherri Maurin, Erin McCarty, Monsignor Mickey McCormick, Rick McDowell, George Mizo, Duncan Murphy, Richard Olive, Dolores Perez Priem, Sister Megan Rice, Kathleen Rumpf, Carolyn S. Scarr, Mary Trotochaud, Collette Quinn, St. John of God Catholic Church, St. John of God Sanctuary Committee, School of the Americas Watch, Sophia in Trinity, Janet Smith, Father Louis Vitale, Gloria Wilson, and Louis Wolf.

A word of thanks to Thomas P. Fenton and Mary J. Heffron for their book design and production assistance; to outreach coordinator Mike Virgintino; to cover designer Joseph Kantorski; to website creator Mark Woods; and to the photographers who contributed the images used in *Renunciation*.

Finally, Charlie was grateful to Dr. Joseph Fahey, retired professor of Religious Studies and Peace Studies at Manhattan College (Bronx, New York), whom he asked to shepherd this book through to publication.

Foreword

YOU ARE ABOUT TO READ AN ACCOUNT of the remarkable pilgrimage of an army chaplain who demonstrated courage on the battlefield and a Catholic priest who had the courage to question the values of his military subculture and to eventually reject war itself. I am honored that both Charlie and his wife, Judy, asked me to write this foreword. They did so, I think, because I was there at the beginning of Charlie's pilgrimage to peace and because they asked me see the book through to publication.

Manhattan College, 1969

I first met Charlie Liteky on March 27, 1969, when I invited him to speak to students in my Peace Studies course at Manhattan College (Bronx, New York). Since a theology of peace in the Roman Catholic tradition cannot be discussed without also talking of the church's centuries-old tradition of justifying war, it was fitting for my students in this Catholic institution to hear from a Catholic priest who had been awarded the Medal of Honor for his valor in Vietnam.

Charlie, of course, did not receive the medal because he blessed that war or because he killed people. He received it because he saved the lives of American young men. But he did wear the uniform of an American soldier and he was a commissioned officer in the U.S. Army. Make no mistake about it, chaplains who serve as military officers *do* take sides in wars and serve as de facto supporters of war. Where did Chaplain Liteky stand?

Tom Stonier, a colleague and first director of the B.A. program in Peace Studies at Manhattan College, had suggested I invite Father Liteky (then known by his religious name, Angelo) to speak to my students since we wanted to honestly explore all traditions on war and peace. We were pledged to giving a fair hearing to voices that endorsed the just war theory, which had been a Catholic tradition since the fifth century. So, I invited Charlie to speak to my students on the ambiguous topic "The Christian Chaplain in a Modern Army." I encouraged Charlie, however, to examine the war in Vietnam from the perspective of the church's just war principles.

Almost a hundred students were anxious to hear what a Catholic priest had to say about a war in which they themselves might have to fight, kill, and perhaps die in just a few months. A few wanted him to justify the war since they intended to enlist. Some, in fact, were already enrolled in the U.S. Air Force's ROTC program. Others hoped he would oppose the war so they could use his address to support their claim to conscientious objector draft status. Some backed the war wholeheartedly and wanted the United States to "nuke" Vietnam. Many were confused and torn apart about the war and didn't know what to think.

The question every young man had to ask himself in 1969 was, "Am I willing to kill and die in this war?" That is a terrible burden to place on young men who, under normal circumstances, would be looking forward to careers and loving relationships in the years ahead. Young people who had not yet begun their adult lives were already staring into the face of death.

What would U.S. Army Chaplain Father Angelo Liteky have to say to them?

Charlie arrived on campus wearing a crisp U.S. Army uniform with captain's bars and numerous military ribbons. One ribbon was for the revered Medal of Honor. This medal is the only one that merits a salute from generals to lowly privates. (I was disappointed that he did not wear the formal version of the medal draped around his neck.) His address to my students went through the just war principles that were divided into *jus ad bellum* (rules before going to war) and *jus in bello* (rules about conduct in war). On each count, he insisted, the United States was engaged in a "just war."

Chaplain Liteky never did say that Jesus himself would bless this war, but that was the message that my students took from his talk. Almost immediately he was challenged about how a Catholic priest could justify this war; students wanted to know if he had any personal doubts about the war. Charlie held politely but firmly to his support for the war. I distinctly remember the saddened look on the faces of students who had hoped that Father Liteky would offer them some way out of going to Vietnam. Some of us on a panel of faculty respondents challenged him on one or another point of the just war principles, but again he held firm.

At the end of the symposium we showed a short film, *The Soldier,* that depicted a young William Shattner being shot in slow motion. I watched Charlie as this film was being shown, and I saw him look down several times. Some people thought we shouldn't have ended with that film, but we felt it was important to remind all that war in the end comes down to killing single human beings.

After Charlie's talk, we had supper at Stella D'Oro, an Italian restaurant just off campus. This gave us an opportunity to explore the personal side of Charlie and his views on the war. Over dinner, Charlie told us that this was one of the very few times he had left the military "cocoon." He had accepted my invitation, he explained, in part because he wanted to know why young people so opposed the war. He told us that there were already some "rumblings" among the enlisted men and that even some officers had expressed doubts that the war could be won. We didn't get into much more depth than that. One thing stands out in my memory of that day at Manhattan College: Charlie Liteky was an instantly likeable and kind man. But honestly, those of us at the dinner really couldn't tell if Charlie believed what he said or not.

When I wrote to thank Charlie for his talk I wanted to tell him that he really needed to examine his conscience about the terrible war in Vietnam and his support for it. But Tom Stonier advised that I use more polite terms and ask Charlie to examine his military subculture in the light of his dominant culture as a Catholic priest. I did ask Charlie to examine the assumptions of his subculture, but I wasn't sure if he would get my real meaning. Charlie never responded to my letter, and I was not to hear of him for the next twenty years. It turns out, though, that he *did* get my meaning. I was, of course, to learn much more about Charlie in the years that followed.

In the late 1980s a colleague from the Consortium on Peace Research, Education and Development told me that he had met a former army chaplain who had renounced the Medal of Honor. He told me that the chaplain told him that a letter he received from a professor at Manhattan College many years earlier had sown some seeds of doubt that began his pilgrimage to conscience. "Do you know who wrote that letter," my friend asked me? "I do." I responded.

* * *

This book tells the story of how in the postwar years Charlie teamed up with Father Roy Bourgeois and Brian Willson and numerous other courageous women and men to oppose the training of Latin American military officers in the U.S. Army School of the Americas (SOA) at Fort Benning, Columbus, Georgia. Charlie was horrified at the murders of the four missionary women in El Salvador. He opposed the war in Iraq.

Charlie talked and walked. He protested and persuaded. He went to jail for his convictions. He engaged in a ministry of protest and his quiet voice was never so loud as when he spoke for those who had been silenced by a brutal and imperialistic U.S. foreign policy. You will hear Charlie's voice speak loudly and clearly for the silent and the silenced in this book.

Fort Benning, 1990

I finally had a chance to meet Charlie again when I accompanied Hugh Thompson and Larry Colburn in March 2000 to Fort Benning, where they gave a talk to Latin American military officers at the School of the Americas. Helicopter pilot Hugh Thompson, his gunner Larry Colburn, and crew chief Glenn Andreotta were the ones who stopped the massacre in My Lai, Vietnam, on March 16, 1968. On that fateful day, Hugh landed his scout helicopter and ordered his gunners to fire on American troops if they continued killing innocent Vietnamese civilians. (Glenn Andreotta was killed in action just three weeks after the My Lai incident. Larry Colburn passed away in January 2017. Hugh Thompson's remarkable story is told in Trent Angers, *The Forgotten Hero of My Lai: The Hugh Thompson Story*. Arcadian House Publishers, 2014, rev. ed.)

Vic Hummert, an old friend of mine, first put me in touch with Hugh in 1998 when I traveled to Lafayette, Louisiana, for Vic's wedding. When he met me at the airport Vic asked if I had ever heard of Hugh Thompson. "No," I replied. So Vic explained who he was and then took me to Hugh's office, where I left my card along with an invitation to give a lecture at Manhattan College and other universities in New York City. Hugh accepted my invitation and after he came to New York we became friends.

In January 2000, Hugh invited me to a meeting in the Harvard Club in New York City with Larry Colburn and TV journalist Mike Wallace of *60 Minutes*. Hugh and Larry were concerned that their upcoming visit to the School of the Americas would be misinterpreted as support for the U.S. Army's training program and for U.S. military policy in general in Latin America. I volunteered to draft a short introductory statement disavowing any such support. They liked the idea and surprised me by asking me to accompany them to Fort Benning to serve as a witness to their opposition. I called Father Roy Bourgeois, the Maryknoll priest who founded SOA Watch, to let him know I was coming to Fort Benning with Hugh and Larry. Roy informed me that Charlie Liteky had received permission from the Pentagon to go on base to hear Hugh and Larry. Charlie was then encamped outside the base waiting for sentencing for his protest actions against the SOA. At last I had a chance to meet Charlie again after all those years.

After Hugh and Larry finished addressing their audience of almost three hundred U.S. and Latin American military officers, the moderator asked for questions. A man in civilian clothes in the front row raised his hand and was recognized. As he rose to speak, a U.S. Army lieutenant colonel seated next to him stood up and said, "Gentlemen, this is Mr. Charles Liteky, recipient of the Medal of Honor." I then witnessed something remarkable. Everyone in the auditorium instantly sprang to attention and saluted Charlie. They all knew that Charlie had renounced the medal and recognized that his presence outside the gates was a nettlesome reminder to them of their involvement in crimes committed in South and Central America. Still they saluted him. I respected a military code of honor that continued to honor a man for his heroic battlefield deeds even when he later denounced his earlier warrior ways. I really don't remember what Charlie asked Hugh and Larry at that time, but I do remember that he praised them for their courage in saving so many lives at My Lai.

(Charlie later told me that he thought that Hugh Thompson, Roy Bourgeois, and Brian Willson were the real heroes who came out of the Vietnam War. I told him he was missing one. "Who?"

he asked me innocently.)

After the symposium ended I made my way to the front of the room and found Charlie. "Hi, Charlie," I said. "I'm Joe Fahey from Manhattan College." "Joe," said Charlie, "you wrote me that letter!" We both smiled and hugged each other. I can't tell you how happy I was at that moment. It was like I was meeting an old friend I thought I'd never see again. I felt in the presence of a saintly man who had had the courage to denounce war and seek the path of nonviolent resistance to the very forces that had sent him to Asia many years earlier.

Hermit Years, 2004–2005

After our meeting at Fort Benning, Charlie and I stayed in touch. We corresponded by phone and mail and in personal visits. Through it all I discovered that Charlie had a wonderful sense of humor, and laughter often marked our conversations. I really got to know him well when I visited him during one of his "hermit" phases in his cabin in the small mountain town of Fort Jones near Yreka in northern California.

I visited Charlie in the summers of 2004 and 2005 and we often talked for hours long into the night. We would have a drink and sit on the porch of his cabin and as it got dark we would throw Ritz crackers to foxes who darted in and out under the night sky. In the darkness, Charlie relived his war years and described the battles he had witnessed in Vietnam. He denounced the madness of that war, but consistently showed respect for the American soldiers he served. "I never saw any of them say no," he said, "when their sergeant ordered them into battle."

Regarding the Medal of Honor, Charlie said that what he did that day happened every day in Vietnam. He didn't think he deserved the medal any more than so many courageous medics and soldiers who sacrificed their lives daily for others. "Hell," he said, "I could name dozens of guys who deserved that medal more than me." He especially singled out the medics who were wounded and killed in Vietnam saving the lives of U.S. soldiers.

It was in this context that we discussed the "politics" of receiving the medal. In hindsight Charlie realized that the Lyndon Johnson administration and the Pentagon were well aware that support for the war was falling apart among Catholics at home and especially on college campuses. Already in 1966, the U.S. Catholic Bishops Conference had expressed doubts about the war in their document *Peace and Vietnam*: "There is a grave danger," the bishops wrote, "that the circumstances of the present war in Vietnam may in time diminish our moral responsibility for its evils." Translation: the war is evil, get the hell out. Although the U.S. bishops had held in 1968 that "our presence is justified" the sentiment of many bishops was clearly against the war. So was that of the scholars and theologians and a growing number of Catholics. Draft counseling had been instituted on many campuses around the country. I especially remember when Manhattan College hired a full-time draft counselor, Paul Mazur, to help our students find a way out of going to by now what was called "Nam." There were long lines all day long outside Paul's second-floor office in Manhattan Hall.

By 1971 official Catholic acceptance of the war was over. In November 1971, the U.S. Catholic bishops officially voiced their opposition to the war based on the just war principle of "proportionality":

At this point in history it seems clear to us that whatever good we hope to achieve through continued involvement in this war is now outweighed by the destruction of human life and of moral values which it inflicts. It is our firm conviction, therefore, that the speedy ending of this war is a moral imperative of the highest priority. (*Resolution on Southeast Asia*, 1971)

The response was quick and dramatic: Catholic college students who now had the support of the Catholic bishops sought conscientious objector status in droves.

In hindsight, Charlie was now convinced that he had been awarded the Medal of Honor as a political move to drum up support for the war among Catholics. He noted that the medal had also been awarded posthumously to Maryknoll Father Vincent Capodanno on January 7, 1969 (for his battlefield actions in Vietnam on September 4, 1967) and thought that that award may have been political also. In no way did Charlie intend to demean those awarded these honors, but he did begin to wonder whether at least some of the many awarded medals might have been given to put a positive shine on an unpopular war.

Charlie also discussed his utter sadness and frustration at the failure of the leadership of the Catholic Church to speak out on Vietnam and later on El Salvador and Iraq. Like Albert Camus in his speech to French Dominican Friars at Latour-Mauborg in

1948, Charlie told me he had waited for that voice but simply never heard it. He was saddened that he had to leave a church he had served and loved. As with everything Charlie did, leaving the priesthood and the church took courage too.

During our long evenings together, Charlie shared with me what happened when he learned of the My Lai massacre on March 16, 1968. After returning to Vietnam in 1969, he started hearing rumors about the slaughter in My Lai. He knew that civilians were killed every day in that war – the military calls this "collateral damage" – but the extent and nature of the atrocities in My Lai sounded different. There, U.S. infantry soldiers lined up and murdered hundreds of mostly women, children, and old people. Charlie told me he really questioned what he was doing in Vietnam after hearing about My Lai.

Just after hearing the first rumors about My Lai, Charlie was having breakfast with enlisted men (chaplains often ate with common soldiers rather than in the officer's mess) and he casually asked if any of the soldiers had heard about the incident at My Lai. He was shocked at the response of one battle-hardened soldier who told him between mouthfuls of corn flakes, "Yeah, I've heard about it. Happens every fuckin' day."

Charlie was shocked at this answer and started to wonder whether events like My Lai were being hidden from him. He had been with infantry men in battle, but had never seen anything like this. He knew that civilians were being killed in air strikes. Are these the casualties the soldier meant? Or were U.S. soldiers wantonly killing civilians on the ground every day?

Talking later on with Charlie, it occurred to me to ask if he had ever heard stories like this in confession. I knew a Catholic priest would never break the seal of confession, so my question was generic: "Did any soldiers ever confess to killing civilians like at My Lai?" "No," Charlie replied. He added that outside confession some soldiers complained to him about how useless the war was and especially how stupid they thought the senior officers were, but murdering noncombatants was never mentioned. The vast majority of confessed sins, he explained, had to do with the soldiers' sexual lives: masturbation and prostitution.

This, too, caused him to reflect on what he was doing in Vietnam as a Catholic priest. He was representing a church that taught people that sexual sins far outweighed the sinfulness of war. Following orders to kill people in a just war was not only okay, it was expected of faithful Catholics. Francis Cardinal Spellman had said so himself. This realization disgusted Charlie. Another seed of doubt was thus planted in a military chaplain's mind – or should I say heart.

VA Hospice at the Presidio, 2016

I last visited Charlie on December 10, 2016, in the VA hospice at the Presidio in San Francisco. Visiting together with another of Charlie's friends, Bob Frank, I found a man who was physically a shadow of the man I had seen just two years earlier. He looked thin and gaunt. He opened one eye slightly to greet us. Although we stayed for an hour, I wasn't sure he recognized who we were. When Bob and I told him his book was at last going to be published, he told us he didn't remember writing it. He said this several times.

At the end of the visit I made the sign of the cross on his forehead, and he said, "Someone just touched my forehead." I told him that was a blessing from me and Roy Bourgeois. Again, opening one eye, he said a quiet, "thanks." Then he put his finger to his lips and slipped back into silence.

Charlie died on January 20, 2017, the day Donald J. Trump was sworn in as president of the United States. One of Charlie's friends imagined him saying, "That's it! I'm outta here!" But Charlie isn't out of here; he is with us still. He will walk with us as we resist in this new era of injustice. Charlie Liteky, *Presente*!

***

It took a lot of convincing before Charlie agreed to the publication of this book. When I first raised this possibility with him he told me he had written it for himself, to help "exorcise some of the demons" from his past. He didn't think about having it published. I think, however, that it was his wife, Judy, who finally convinced him to publish this book. I also lobbied for publication because I knew the great value it would have if placed in the hands of college students. In the end, Judy's firm confidence in the merits of the book for others persuaded a reluctant Charlie. He wanted it self-published to preserve both the title he had chosen and the integrity of the content.

This book can be used in courses of study in which the lives of courageous people are examined. These courses can range from theological, religious, and philosophical courses to courses in history and politics. Since the United States has long been a warrior state, our young people will unfortunately be confronted with whether they can kill and die in war for some time to come. Let them read this book. Let them see that there is another form of "service" besides joining the military. They also serve who resist wars.

People in the active military, including military chaplains, will find this a challenging book. It will challenge them to examine the assumptions of their own military subculture. Charlie told me that he found that most chaplains like him did not think about the contradiction between wearing the military uniform of an aggressor state while also preaching the gospel of peace. Let Charlie's pilgrimage inspire your own.

Charlie laughed when I told him that Robert McNamara might have had a change of heart if he had read a book like his. But people in government service will find this book important if for no other reason than it is their job to understand those who oppose their foreign policy objectives. Government officials must understand that an important distinction must be made between defending the people of the United States and defending "U.S. interests." The latter, history shows, are little more than the interests of those who would have our military protect and defend those territories and raw materials that will enhance the personal and corporate wealth of a few.

Finally, this book will be of interest to anyone who enjoys a good read. It is written from the heart by a man who had the courage to change. What great truth, dear reader, stands before the door of your life that you are afraid to open? Will you, if you open that door, have the courage to act on what you see? Maybe you need to be honest with your parents, or friends, or employers. Can you do that? Albert Camus said, "I rebel; therefore, we exist." Let us take heart from Charlie's courageous rebellion. Let us exist because Charlie opened that door for us.

> *One cannot at the same time possess*
> *an open mind and a closed heart.*

– Dr. Joseph J. Fahey

Dr. Joseph J. Fahey is a retired Professor of Religious Studies and Peace Studies at Manhattan College. He is the author of *War and the Christian Conscience: Where Do You Stand?* (Orbis Books, 2005).

Introduction

THIS IS THE STORY OF MY LIFE, a so-called memoir, a memory put to words from beginning to almost end. A few names and places have been changed or omitted to save embarrassments or to protect reputations.

Two threads run through this memoir. First, there's my *military* story: growing up in a military family, becoming a Catholic military chaplain and "hawk" in Vietnam, leaving the military, and eventually becoming a civilian peace activist. This part of the story describes my personal ethical wrestling with the powerful experience of war and with the powerful institutions behind it, namely, the U.S. military and more broadly the U.S. government.

The second thread is my *church* story: growing up in a Catholic family, becoming a priest, wrestling with mandatory celibacy, marrying, and also wrestling with my religious formation in church doctrines and even with my understanding of God. This part of the story describes wrestling within myself, with sexuality, with intimate relationships, and with my images of God.

The first thread in this memoir might be called the outer institutional world, while the second one deals more with the inner personal world. But these two dimensions cannot be separated for they constitute my one life.

I share publicly my military story in the hope that young people in, or going into, the military, and believing that their country stands for freedom and democracy, may pause to investigate and reflect upon the nature and purposes of U.S. foreign and domestic policies, and perhaps take a step further to discover our country's violations of its Constitution, the United Nations Charter, and universal laws of morality.

My lifetime journey, now at eighty-one years and pressing on, began in the shadow of a professional Navy man. As such, I became an acculturated hawk and a pseudo-patriotic person. But the hawk in me flew too close to the sun of truth to remain a hawk. In Vietnam I saw too many young men die and too many wounded for life, and for a cause that I concluded was not based on truth.

1

Union of Opposites

NAVY CHIEF CHARLES LITEKY, my father, was not a big man (5'11", 185 pounds), but he had solid, large meaty hands, broad shoulders, and a thick chest. He did not go about looking for trouble, but was ever ready should it come to him.

Possessed of a hair-trigger temper, he responded to an offense with a flash of anger and no consideration for the consequences. He did not hesitate long enough for the chemistry of fear to summon caution. Flight was out of the question. The occasion could be as simple as a driver cutting him off on the road or the cashier at a supermarket reaching a grocery total other than his calculation. (Had he lived long enough, he would have questioned the results of scanning technology.) As a teenager he was big enough and bold enough to lie about his age and join the Navy at fifteen.

My mother, Gertrude, was his temperamental opposite: soft-spoken, unassuming, and even-tempered. Naturally curled, strawberry-blond hair blended with fair, lightly freckled skin. She possessed a quality uncommon to most beautiful women, unawareness of her beauty. She wore little to no makeup and maintained a model's figure until the day she died. Her speech, unlike her husband's, was free of vulgarity with one exception. She shocked him speechless. In response to one too many of his vulgar expressions, she said, "I don't want to hear any more of that crap."

In Washington, D.C., Gertrude first saw Charlie from a distance swaggering up V Street, SE, dressed in navy-blue, bell-bottomed trousers, a matched form-fitting blouse, and the white sailor's hat. She was approaching thirteen. He was eighteen.

Sitting twelve steps up from the sidewalk, on the landing in front of the family home, she could see clear to the bus stop at the end of V Street. She watched him until he drew close enough to notice her attention, then, judiciously looked away as if disinterested. It seemed as if he would pass directly below, but he turned abruptly up the stairs leading to the house next door. He noticed her watching and shocked her with a greeting, "Hello there, young lady." Embarrassed, she blushed and bolted into the house. "He was so handsome," she said to me across the kitchen table the year after his fatal heart attack, "dressed in his military blues."

Charlie dated Eunice Seaman, the girl next door, for several months. He arrived at the same time each Friday afternoon. Rarely did Gertrude miss an opportunity to watch him from a distance as he stepped off the bus and swaggered up the block to call on Eunice, an attractive brunette of Charlie's age. Gradually, Gertrude overcame her shyness and returned Charlie's greeting with a captivating teenager's smile. One day he surprised her, "I'm off to sea, young lady, but someday I'll be coming back for you." Unknowingly, he blessed the teenager with a fantasy.

Years passed without a word or the sight of the young sailor and Gertrude passed from a shy young girl to a self-possessed lovely young woman. Charlie sailed the world, visiting exotic places, fulfilling his need for adventure. He was a gifted storyteller, yet he never mentioned other women. Gertrude went to work after finishing the eighth grade, doing odd jobs, until she was seventeen, old enough to begin a career as a telephone operator. By the time the sailor who said he would return for her kept his promise, she had been promoted to supervisor. However, Charlie did not return for Gertrude. It was Eunice for whom the bell next door rang, but she was long gone.

When Charlie learned that Eunice had recently married he said, "Too bad," like Eunice had missed the opportunity of her life. Undaunted, he descended the steps and started walking back down V Street toward the bus stop. He was disappointed, but far from crushed. He was not the kind of man to put all of his social eggs in one basket.

Halfway down the street he stopped abruptly as if he had been given a military command to "halt!" Remembering his promise to the teenage girl, he did an about-face and briskly walked back to 1229 V Street. The steps were empty. Without hesitation, Charlie ascended and rang the doorbell.

A stern-looking woman of Charlie's height, in her early forties, opened the door. Suspiciously, she looked the young sailor in the eye and said in a tone of authority, "Yeees," the kind of yes that says, "What do you want?" without inflection. It was Gertrude's older sister and self-appointed guardian, Mary. She was not impressed with the sailor's "military blues." "Is Gertrude home?" inquired Charlie.

"Is she expecting you?" answered Mary.

"No."

"Then you had better go. Come back when she is expecting you."

Mary was very protective of her younger sister. She took on the responsibility of raising her after the death of their parents. She was a no-nonsense person with the chiseled facial features of a wizened frontier woman: long, coal-black hair pulled tight against her temples, wound into a bun at the back of her head.

Charlie, sensing there was no pressing this ramrod, said "thank you" and started to descend the steps when a tall, slim, strawberry blonde appeared at the front gate. No longer a petite, shy teenager, Gertrude had matured into a woman of exceptional beauty. She stopped when she saw the sailor descending the steps, with Mary looking ominously over his shoulder.

Gertrude recognized the sailor immediately, but had forgotten his promise to return for her someday. That fantasy had faded soon after his departure. Both the future bride and groom had changed, Gertrude more than Charlie. She was now a full-breasted, curvaceous young woman standing eye level with the sailor.

Charlie walked slowly down the steps, conscious of the fact that Mary was above him monitoring his every move. When he reached the bottom landing, he turned sideways to Gertrude giving Mary full view of his behavior. To Gertrude he said, "Do you remember me?" Mature beyond shyness, she replied, "Of course, I remember you. You haven't changed that much."

"You have," Charlie responded.

A year-long courtship followed and the sailor and the strawberry blonde were married in the small Catholic church a half block up from 1229 V Street. Having no home of his own and the limited income of a seaman second class, Charlie moved into the crowded house of Mary's family of six.

Four months after marriage, signs of Gertrude's pregnancy appeared and I was well on my way to hearts and flowers day for Charlie and Gertrude, February 14, 1931. Valentine's Day is a good day to be born. Friends rarely forget your birthday.

2

Hawaii & World War II

SHORTLY AFTER MY BIRTH, my father was transferred to the Naval Air Base at Pearl Harbor, Hawaii, an overseas assignment that permitted family accompaniment. Two memories of Hawaii remain. The first was seeing a seven-year-old movie star, Shirley Temple. She was wearing a blue-and-white sailing outfit, standing dockside of a sailboat moored at the yacht club, across the road from our bungalow. I don't know why I remember this distant sight of Shirley in her sailing attire. I can only guess that Mother told me how famous she was. Over the years, whenever I see her on the screen, especially as a child, Hawaii returns.

The indelibility of my second childhood memory of Hawaii is easily explained. At age three, I escaped the backyard supervision of Mother, wandered across the road, and discovered the yacht club swimming pool. Running poolside with abandon, I tripped and fell into the deep end. Seventy-one years later, I can still see the side of the pool ascending as I descended. From out of nowhere a hand appears grasping and lifting me to the surface. I don't remember the man's face, only his bronzed forearm and hand. I owe my life to a Hawaiian I'll never be able to thank.

After five years in Hawaii, we returned to Washington, D.C., to live once again with mother's older sister, Mary, and her husband, Ben. The house was a five-bedroom, three-story gray stucco, common to southeast Washington in the thirties.

Aunt Mary had three children, Jim, Joe, and Mary Lou. Jim,

the oldest, took a job with the A&P and made a managerial career
of it. Joe, the wild one, much like my father, joined the Navy in his
teens to see the world. I don't remember much about Mary Lou,
the teenager, during this phase of my life on V Street. However,
she was party to an event in my childhood that constitutes an unforgettable peak experience.

I was six, going on seven, at the time. It was late afternoon.
My father arrived home from work to join the entire household in
the living room for before-supper colloquy. Bored by adult conversation, Mary Lou motioned for me to follow her upstairs to
her bedroom, where she commenced to dress me in her clothing
and apply makeup. Then she led me downstairs where the adults
were still talking. I'm not sure what Mary Lou was expecting, but
subsequent events made it clear that she did not know my father
very well. The conversation stopped when I made my entrance.
Before any of the women could comment, the Chief reacted with
derisive, mocking remarks like, "My! What a pretty little girl.
What's your name little girl?" Blushing with shame, I ran upstairs. This is the first negative memory I have of my father. It was
the beginning of the formation of a memorial pool of emotional
pain that would deepen with each buried offense.

My formal education began at a small Catholic school two
blocks up the hill from Aunt Mary's home on V Street. The Sisters
of St. Joseph administered the school. They taught me my numbers, letters, and prayers, and about the gradation of sins and the
existence of angels, devils, and saints, and they introduced me to
basic Roman Catholic theology, a religious construct that answers all the big questions about life from beginning to end and
beyond. It never occurred to me to question Catholic theology
until the early evening of my life.

After a year or so of enjoying the hospitality of Gertrude's
sister Mary, we moved up the hill to an apartment in a section of
Washington called Congress Heights. Again we lived within
walking distance from school, the first of three public schools I
attended. In those days Catholics were obliged to send their children to parochial schools, but there were none in our neighborhood. There was no recitation of prayers in public school, but
civic indoctrination continued every day in the form of the
Pledge of Allegiance to the flag, etc. The ideals of patriotism, like
the beliefs of Roman Catholicism, were passed on to me by lay
teachers, nuns, and a military father.

The most significant events in my second school year were

an encounter with a schoolyard bully and my father's reaction to his son's failure to defend himself. "Don't you ever come crying to me again," he warned and commenced to give me my first boxing lesson. I'm not sure this is the best way to handle a child's first experience with a bully, but I know of no better way. This schoolyard scenario is not uncommon. I would like to say I met the bully again and redeemed myself, but I have no such memory. I know he did not trouble me again. I assume that my hatred for bullies of any sort is rooted in this early experience.

In November of 1938, Mother gave me my first little brother. She named him James ("Jim"). He was eight pounds, two ounces, a pound heavier and two inches longer than me at birth. I remember his numbers, but not his arrival. I don't recall Mother being big with Jim, nor do I recollect being excited over his birth. Perhaps, it was because he marked the end of my privileged, only-child status.

Shortly after Jim's birth, Dad was reassigned to Coronado Naval Air Station located on an island in San Diego Bay, southern California. He left before us to select a house in the city, since residence on the island was not available to enlisted men. Dad's daily commute to work was by the traditional Navy longboat, a sturdy, thirty-foot-long, seat-less inboard, wide enough to accommodate thirty sailors standing two abreast.

From the Coronado dock, I looked out over a mile of open water to catch the first sight of a longboat loaded with white-capped sailors, a daily thrill. The longboats motored across the bay, one behind another, forming a dotted, white, serpentine line from shore to shore. This daily ritual of longboat watching stopped when brother number three arrived. John Patrick ("Pat") weighed in at just over ten pounds. Mother's babies were coming bigger with each successive birth. Good Catholic that she was, I'm sure she would have had more children. I'm inclined to think a sister would have been good for me; girls and later women may not have been such a mystery, but Pat's birth precipitated a hysterectomy.

World War II

Residence in San Diego was abruptly cut short by an event that changed the lives of all Americans, especially military men and their families, the Japanese attack on Pearl Harbor, December 7, 1941. The next day, war with Japan was on. Three days later Germany joined the Japanese, and the United States was full bore for war. Within a month we were back on the East Coast, resettled in a government housing project in Norfolk, Virginia, built for dependents of U.S. Navy personnel called to war. I did not know it then, but dramatic changes in my life began when I waved good-bye to my father as he sailed off to war aboard a newly commissioned aircraft carrier, the U.S.S. *Hornet*. Standing dockside of this gigantic floating airfield, my father hugged and kissed us for what could have been the last time, but not before telling me I was the man of the house now, responsible for Mother, Jim, and Pat. At age eleven, I was not up to the delegated obligation, and I did not take it seriously. Along with thousands of children, mothers, spouses, and sweethearts, I became one of the first mainland civilian casualties of war. As I watched the seafaring warrior climb the gangplank, life without father began.

The *Hornet* did not immediately proceed to a war zone; first came a procedural shakedown cruise. Everyone on the *Hornet* knew they would soon be sailing into waters roamed by German submarines and the Japanese naval forces that had devastated Pearl Harbor, but few knew that an incredible military plan was in the works – one that would shatter Japanese security just as Pearl Harbor had shaken our confidence. A naval officer conceived the idea of rapidly retaliating against the Japanese just as they had surprised us. Since we had no territory close enough to Japan to use as a launching pad for a bombing attack, an aircraft carrier might be used to transport small bombers close enough to Japan to effect a U.S. version of Pearl Harbor over Tokyo. Such an attack would be a surprise blow straight to the military solar plexus of Japan, wiping out the complacency and presumed safety of distance. The newly commissioned *Hornet* was chosen for this mission and set sail westward to the Alameda Naval Air Station, across the bay from San Francisco. Sixteen B-25 bombers, small, but too large to be hidden in the belly of the carrier, were crowded onto its flight deck and lashed down for a sea voyage four to five hundred miles short of the Japanese mainland. Bombers had never before taken off from the deck of an aircraft carrier. Flattop runways were considered too short. This bold plan necessitated hours and hours of short-takeoff practice on land. The operation was a joint Army/Navy venture led by the Army's celebrated flyer, General Jimmy Doolittle, and handpicked pilots.

Once at sea, the secret of the *Hornet*'s mission was revealed to the crew, releasing a wave of patriotic jubilation. Army/Navy cooperation and a spirit of common cause camaraderie were essential. The initially unwelcome Army personnel invading Navy territory soon became royalty deserving of preferential treatment. The Army pilots were risking their lives to the extreme. It was payback time and everyone aboard the *Hornet* was ready to cash in.

The plan was for the *Hornet* to sail to within four to five hundred miles of Japan, launch the bombers, and return to Pearl Harbor. After dropping their bombs on and around Tokyo, the pilots would first fly to safe landing airfields in China, beyond Japanese control. Launch time was predicated on reaching to within four or five hundred miles of mainland Japan. Anything short of this mark would reduce the chances of a safe return. Unfortunately, reaching the ideal takeoff point was made difficult by early-warning radio-equipped picket boats that the Japanese had positioned about six hundred and fifty miles distant from the Japanese mainland. These had to be destroyed. The possibility that they would alert the mainland of an attack was too important to ignore. On April 18, 1942, just three months after the Japanese attack on Pearl Harbor, Doolittle's Raiders redeemed a rocked and wounded nation and set the United States on a long three-and-a-half–year road to victory in August of 1945.

My father's role in the Tokyo raid was significant; it was the crowning moment of his thirty-two-year-long Navy career. He was a member of the flight deck wave-off team that had to calculate the best moment for the pilots to rev their engines to the max, thrust forward at full throttle, and for the first and last time, carry out a short-distance carrier takeoff. Every one of the planes loaded with 2,000-pound bombs successfully followed General Jimmy Doolittle down the flight deck runway, into the air and off on a journey of hopeful return.

I did not learn the full story of Doolittle's raid from Dad. The interested reader can find detailed accounts in two best-selling books: *Fly Boys,* by James Bradley (Little Brown Press, 2003) and *The Ship that Held the Line,* by Lisle A. Rose (Naval Institute Press, 2012). The *Hornet* eluded Japanese discovery and returned to Pearl Harbor as planned. The bombers were not so fortunate. Their fuel supply was too low to allow them to reach the safety of interior China. Some of the flyers were captured; others escaped with help from Chinese peasants, who paid with their lives for aiding the Yanks.

The material damage done to the Japanese was minimal in comparison to what would come later, but the psychological wound, like Pearl Harbor to the United States, would be historic. The *Hornet* went on to distinguish itself in a number of sea battles, but it did not survive the war. The victim of torpedo, dive bomber, and kamikaze attacks at the Battle of Santa Cruz, October 27, 1942, the *Hornet* was sent down to the bone yard of naval wreckage, Japanese and American, at the bottom of the Santa Cruz Islands Sea. Happily, 90 percent of the crew survived, my father included. The U.S. military-industrial machine would later grind out three more *Hornet*s.

3

Virginia & Florida

THE NAVY HOUSING PROJECT where Mother, my two younger brothers and I, would await Dad's return reminds me of the low-income housing built for the poor throughout the nation. Ben Moreell was twenty acres of cleared land adjacent to the highway leading to the main gate of the naval base at Norfolk, Virginia. Six rows of two-story apartment houses arranged in precise military symmetry accommodated wives and children of men who had shipped off to war. Each four-unit apartment complex looked like a huge white box, ventilated with rectangular air holes; tasteless, colorless, but utilitarian. There were no trees, no shrubbery.

In 1942, Ben Moreell was a community without men, a place where wives waited for husbands to return or to receive news from the officer of the day that a husband would not be returning. It was a place where mothers raised children alone, a place where young boys could play at being grown men, free from male parental control. Six of us preteen males took up the adult behavior of smoking and drinking whenever we could find or steal the means to do so. Our source of booze was a storehouse behind a restaurant on the main highway. Occasionally, the door was left unlocked. We never took more than a single bottle; hence, we were never caught.

We were too young for serious womanizing, but some of us began to play on the fringes of sex with prepubescent project girls as curious as we were about physical differences that attracted us to and repelled us from one another. Most of our activity was limited to bodily contact like wrestling on a living room floor while mothers were off shopping. However, I remember well one precocious preteen girl, Lucille, who bestowed favors on teenage boys in order to become popular.

At least two years away from puberty, I had given my father no cause to discern a need for the customary father–son birds-and-bees talk before he left. Consequently, I was, at best, curious over the stories I had heard about encounters with Lucille in the privacy of a project storage facility. With no preplanning, I met her one afternoon when she was walking home after school. Half-heartedly, I suggested we meet for some fun. Her answer indicated she knew what I meant, but she quickly declined my invitation on the grounds of unlaundered panties. I was not interested enough to wait for the washing. Many more exciting diversions called to me.

Hopping streetcars, skipping school, sneaking into movies and the downtown wrestling arena satisfied my need for adventure. I especially liked waiting with Oliver Simpson outside the arena rear exit door for a glimpse of the Masked Marvel, hoping he would reveal his identity. He seemed to relish our attention, but gave us no more than a wave of appreciation, maintaining the mystery of the man shrouded in a purple mask.

To these illicit activities I added dime store shoplifting, which could have resulted in my arrest had I not escaped the grasp of a plainclothes, dime store detective and hopped a streetcar to safety with the loot of the day concealed in my pockets: two cheap smoking pipes.

Shreds of tobacco found in the pockets of my blue jeans revealed my smoking habit and notes from school teachers alerted Mother to my truancy. Fortunately, she did not discover my criminal exploits. In an effort to force my attendance, she drove me to and from school, watched me enter in the morning and exit in the afternoon, five minutes after the bell rang announcing the end of the day. I thought I had devised the perfect plan for avoiding school until teachers' notes caught up with me.

Until I began this task of autobiographical writing, I did not appreciate what Mother did for me and what I did to her. I am of the opinion that most of us go through life without acknowledging parental love, patience, and courage. We remember their faults and take their love for granted. I should use the singular rather than the plural pronoun here. Reviewing my boyhood history helps me understand why I never wanted to have children. I would not have wanted a brat like me.

By the time my father returned after two years at sea, I was an inveterate juvenile delinquent. There was no way he could have prepared himself for the conflict that lay ahead. I had tasted freedom from parental control and loved it. The warrior came home to a different kind of war, an undeclared father–son war, for which neither of us had had training. When Mother told me of his homecoming, I feigned excitement, but sensed the beginning of the end of an exciting life without father.

The day after his return, the military man did the military thing: he announced a briefing, a family briefing for my benefit. I was not surprised. I was sure Mother had shared her frustration with me with him. To his credit he did not come down hard on me. He simply informed me that we would be moving soon to Fort Lauderdale, Florida, one more geographical area unknown to me. I did not want to move. I did not want to leave the gang. I said nothing, but felt sad and angry.

When I shared the news of our impending move to Florida with the boys, a meeting was called at the clubhouse. This was serious stuff. The clubhouse was a collection of wooden crates retrieved from disposables abandoned by families' ever-moving into the project. We were able to put together a shack, a home away from home, restricted to members only. Six wooden milk crates served as chairs and an old mattress provided overnight sleeping for anyone choosing to run away from home for a day. The whole thing was sequestered in a patch of woods on the outskirts of the project.

After a brief discussion of my options, Oliver Simpson offered to accompany me on a runaway trip to his uncle's farm in Ohio. Adventure at its best, but I declined, not yet ready to leave family forever. Two years of independent, fatherless life had left me with no affection for him, but the hardest of hearts could never reject Mom's love.

The clubhouse gang voted me lifetime membership, assuring me of a place to stay if ever I chose to return. Looking back on this small band of friends, I realize we were a means of survival for one another. We were victims of war, as are all children of military wartime parents. There was no dominant one among us, no "Lord of the Flies." Without one another we would have been deprived of the essential, human need for social contact.

This need for community remains with me today, but is difficult to find in a culture that champions individuality to the extreme. "Take care of No. 1." "If you don't do for yourself, no one will." This kind of self-centered culture reminds me of the song, "The Reverend Mister Black": "You got to walk that lonesome trail; you got to walk it by yourself. Nobody else can walk it for you."

I've walked a lot of lonely trails since leaving Virginia at the age of twelve. Paradoxically, my loneliest living has been in the company of others, especially those committed to Christian love where particular friendships were discouraged in favor of universal love.

Fort Lauderdale

We moved to Fort Lauderdale in the fall of 1943, in time for my father to enroll me in the only Catholic school in town, St. Anthony. I was not happy with the forced move or return to school, especially Catholic school. Mother had removed me from parochial school in Norfolk for refusal to conform and because of a physical altercation I had had with a nun.

I don't remember what set the nun off, but it was irritating enough for her to come rushing toward me like a bull on red. Fleet of foot, I fled the classroom and ran down the hallway to the sanctuary of the boys' lavatory, assuming she would not follow. I grossly misjudged this lady. She barged into the restroom, blocked my exit, pinned my shoulders to the wall next to a urinal, and began to lecture me on unacceptable behavior. Pressing my shoulders against the wall to the point of pain, she tapped into my defensive mechanism, moving me to grab the fleshy underside of her upper left arm and squeeze with such force that she screamed and released me. Bolting from the lavatory into the hallway, I streaked through the front door like a cat fleeing a Rottweiler.

My Catholic education in Virginia was over. But this was not the end of my parochial schooling. My father was determined to remain faithful to his obligation to educate his sons in a Catholic school. Both he and a new set of nuns became a wall of authoritarian constriction impinging upon my need to be free. As life closed in, I grew restless and sullen and began to daydream about bygone days with friends in Norfolk.

On the last school day of September, 1943, Sister Mary Eleanor called me to her desk. Handing me my first report card, she said, "This is not good, Charles. I know you can do better."

I looked at the string of "Ds" glaring up at me and maintained nonchalance. Then she went to backup. "Show this to your father. I'm including a note. I want it signed. Return the note and the card to me Monday."

Ordinarily, I took the city bus home, but on this afternoon of my report card reckoning, I chose to walk the three miles to the living room site of my execution. I arrived to find my father home from work seated at the dining room table reading the evening paper. Placing the report card and the note from Sister Eleanor in front of him I started to leave, but he ordered me seated. I chose the opposite end of the table, a good six feet distant. After reading my report card and the nun's note, he exhaled a disgruntled sigh of frustration, looked directly at me and opened with a question.

"What kind of explanation can you give me for this report card?"

"It's the best I can do," I replied in a tone of independent self-assurance.

Retaining the composure of a leader of men, the chief petty officer said firmly, "I don't believe you, Bud. If this is your best, you need help, bad. From now on I want you to come directly home after school. When I come home from work I want to see you sitting at this table doing your homework. Sister Eleanor wants to see me after school Monday. That means I have to take off from work early. I don't intend to do this more than once. Do you understand?"

I nodded my head.

"Don't nod your head at me! I want to hear you say yes."

"Yes," I responded in an angry whisper.

The air grew electric. His circuitry was being tested and his wires were warming.

"I think I know what's troubling you, Bud. You haven't been right since we moved. I know you did not want to leave Norfolk. You miss your friends."

He was right. I remained silent.

"Well, you're going to have to decide where you want to be, with your friends or your family."

Grateful to be asked to unburden myself, I spoke from an angry heart, "My friends in Norfolk!"

The rapidity and tone of my response took him by surprise. Until this moment I had not known the full fury of my father's temper.

He thundered: "You smart-assed little brat."

As he shouted, he began to move from his end of the table, circling to his left. Feeling the tension of the moment, I circled left also, maintaining the buffer of the table. When we had just about exchanged table ends, I made a tactical error that cost me the only advantage I had over a stronger adversary: speed. Instead of bolting through the hallway into the kitchen and out the back door to the safety of the woods behind our house, I slipped into the bathroom and locked the door.

This was the second time in my life I took sanctuary in a lavatory. Like my experience with the nun in Norfolk, I underestimated my opponent. It did not occur to me that I was trapping myself. I expected him to knock on the door and order me out, but there was no knock, no voice of any kind, assuring me not to be afraid.

A quick try at the door knob immediately followed by a powerful kick tore the lock from its casing and sent me flying backwards, falling head over heels into the bottom of the tub. Before I could move, I felt a heavy, meaty hand pressing against my chest and saw a huge fist cocked and ready to strike. He must have felt me trembling, because he released his hold, dropped his fist, and stood beside the tub looking down at me as if he was lost.

Cradling me like an infant, he carried me into my bedroom and gently lowered me onto my bed. He said nothing until he reached the door. Silhouetted against the hallway light he looked back at me and said in a tone of resigned sadness, "Anytime you want to leave, let me know and I'll help you pack your bags." He closed the door, leaving me alone in the darkness of a warm Florida evening. I feel sorry for him now, but I did not then. I was too angry to feel anything but rage.

4

Running Away

I LAY UPON MY BED, unconcerned that the early evening light was fading, that I would soon be alone in the dark. I had my share of childhood phobias, but darkness was not fearsome as long as there was as much as a pinhead of light, a single point of reference. A sky devoid of heavenly bodies would frighten me. The sliver of light comforting me squeezed through the crack at the bottom of the bedroom door.

Plans to leave were unfolding. They did not include help packing my bags. I would take no bags. I would wait until all movement in the house ceased. Two hours passed before the bedroom door opened wide enough for my father to look in on me. Through slits of eyelids not quite closed, I saw his huge silhouette. Looking down at me, he paused long enough to convince me that I had fooled him into believing I was asleep. Perhaps he wanted to say something like "I'm sorry for being so rough on you," but he just stood there, looking. Slowly, he closed the door, taking away the light and enveloping the bedroom in darkness, save a sliver of illumination at the bottom of the door.

An hour passed before I dared move. Plans completed, I dressed in the dark for the journey, feeling my way for the best of what I owned: a beige Palm Beach suit that breathed (allowed body heat to escape), a dress shirt, but no tie. Holding my brown penny loafers, I stood with my ear to the bedroom door for five minutes, listening.

Satisfied that Mom and Dad were down for the night, I tiptoed into the living room and with the help of a penlight, located Mom's purse atop the china cabinet. Using a dining room chair, I reached the purse, removed thirty dollars, and ever so carefully stepped down and walked softly to the front door. Once outside, I eased the door shut, slipped into my loafers, and began the two-hour walk through dimly lit residential neighborhoods to the bus station.

After our conversation about where I would prefer to be, at home or Norfolk with friends, I reasoned that the bus station was the first place Dad would check. Consequently, I purchased a ticket to Jacksonville, Florida, one-third the distance to Norfolk. The bus was scheduled to leave at 1:30 a.m. The clock over the ticket agent's window read 12:30. "May I check your baggage, son?" said the ticket agent. "No, sir," I replied and took a seat in the empty waiting room on an unoccupied wooden bench running along a brick wall. The ticket agent showed no signs of suspicion. I had an hour to wait.

Reflecting on my sudden choice of Jacksonville over Norfolk, I felt satisfied I would not be immediately traced. I began to feel excited about the trip, like I was pulling off some great escape. I did not think of Mother, but gleefully imagined my father peeking in on me in the middle of the night. But why should he check on me? Perhaps, he wanted to apologize. This was wishful thinking.

I wanted him to say he was sorry. Suppose he does go into the bedroom, pulls down the covers, and finds bunched-up bed clothing. Would he call the police? What will I do if the police come? Run, damn it. I'll run. Fear was beginning to creep over me like a cold breeze. I began to fidget, but afraid the ticket agent might notice. I walked outside and paused beyond the limits of the bus station lights. The streets were dark, desolate, and silent.

To ease tension, I began to pace back and forth in front of the bus station. When my back was turned, the headlights of a car approaching the ticket office shone past me to the end of the block. I turned to see a police cruiser parked in front of the station and an officer entering the building. He left the cruiser lights on and the motor running. His hurried pace fired my imagination. Dad *did* check on me; he called the police. I walked around the corner and waited, daring not to be seen by the police officer who surely was asking the ticket agent about me. Expecting to see the officer dash out the door to cruise around the block in search of me, I readied for flight.

The distance from the police car to the corner where I stood was about fifty yards, close enough for me to hear the cruiser's radio. Suddenly, the static was broken by a high-pitched voice: "Deputy Eggert, Deputy Eggert, come in please." The deputy came bursting from the station and answered, "What's up, Doris?" "Trouble, we have a tripped alarm at the La Solas and Fifth jewelry store. Can you check it out?" "I'm on my way. Over and out." Within seconds the officer disappeared, leaving behind the scent of exhaust fumes and burned rubber.

I returned to the waiting room anxious about the nature of the lawman's visit. I was relieved when the agent announced the imminent arrival of the bus and cautioned me against taking any more walks. "The driver is not going to wait. He is running late. He should be here in five minutes."

I boarded the bus, took an aisle seat near the back, next to an elderly lady who was leaning against the window, sound asleep. It was hours past my bedtime. Exhausted from tension and lack of sleep, I quickly joined my seatmate in slumber. Both of us woke to the sight of a sunny day and one another. In a kind, grand motherly way, she began to question me about my home, destination, and age. She seemed satisfied with my answers, but concerned that a twelve-year-old boy was traveling alone over a distance of a thousand miles.

I assured her that I was capable of caring for myself and directed her attention to the passing scenery of the Florida coast.

I was two hundred miles away from home – feeling no remorse over my departure. On the contrary, I was elated over what I imagined lay ahead of me, mainly reunion with friends not seen in over a year, friends who cared about me, with whom I had shared the freedom of fatherless life. I was drawn to the warmth of the gang and repelled by the cold, calculated discipline of a military father. After several stops along the coast, the bus arrived in Jacksonville around noon on Saturday.

It was a cool but not uncomfortable late October day. By this time my father would have missed me and possibly alerted the police. I was relieved and aglow with satisfaction when I found the law nowhere in sight. I went immediately to the ticket window and purchased a ticket for the next bus to Norfolk, due to leave at 1:45 a.m. The expense left me with eleven dollars and fifty cents for survival. I never worried about money. I had more than enough to make it to friends who would help.

The bus to Norfolk was express and only half full, leaving a seat for me to stretch out and enjoy some needed sleep. However, I could not avoid more conversations with elderly women who were curious and concerned about a young boy traveling alone. They complimented me on my gentlemanly behavior and self-assurance, unaware that I was a fox in lamb's clothing, traveling on money stolen from my mother, and that I would just as easily relieve them of any cash they might carelessly have left about.

I felt no remorse whatsoever over lifting the money from Mother's purse. There was so much and I took so little. Stealing was a prohibition of Catholic morality that never touched me. Missing Mass on Sunday, however, was another matter. This was a serious offense, a matter of conscience, mortal sin material, and a death blow to the soul that resulted in the loss of sanctifying grace, which sends Catholics rushing to confession for forgiveness. I never missed Mass without a serious reason. It never occurred to me that running away from home was serious.

After two days of bus riding, the Greyhound lumbered into Norfolk at 3:30 a.m., that eerie, silent hour when no thing or person is moving, save a stray starving dog scrounging for scraps. Fortunately, street cars to the naval base were still running, carrying young sailors back to their barracks or ships after a night on the town. The line ran right by Ben Moreell, my final destination.

After an hour in the shivering cold, I boarded the streetcar behind three sailors, envying their heavy wool pea coats, lamenting the fact that I had failed to consider the climate difference between Norfolk and Fort Lauderdale. Clearly, I did not need a suit that breathed. The heated trolley felt so good that I considered riding till daylight, but feared interrogation by the conductor. It was too late to contact friends. I thought of the clubhouse. I knew I could find it even in the dark.

The ride to the Navy housing project was just long enough to warm and prepare me for the half-hour walk to the clubhouse. Passing my former home on Randolph Street, I paused to reminisce for a moment, but it was too cold to tarry. I walked to where the project ended and the woods began.

The territory had not changed. The night was clear and a three-quarter moon illumined the still-worn path leading to the clubhouse. It was no more than a hundred yards into the woods and far enough off the path to go unnoticed by a casual hiker. I found the clubhouse unchanged, but it was padlocked. My Palm Beach suit was working, but not for its intended purpose, breathing in cold air and exhaling body heat, gradually refrigerating me. A brief memory scan brought up the image of the project gym.

I took to running again, back through the project to the street leading to ten acres of cleared land around the gym. It loomed huge and ghostly white in the moonlight.

All doors were locked and the large windows on the sides of the building were out of reach. By jumping, I was able to grasp the edge of the windowsill and pull myself onto the narrow ledge of the first south-side window. Standing on the ledge I pushed against the frame of the window, moving it enough for a hand-hold beneath the bottom sash and creating enough space to enter.

Sitting precariously on the inside sill, I faced almost total darkness, but for the night light of the moon filtering through the window to give some relief from what I feared most, total darkness. I could not see the floor of the gym nor the wrestling mat in the left-hand corner of the front of the building. According to my calculations it was directly across from where I was perched. I also remembered that the floor of the gym was at least six feet beneath me.

Not about to leap into darkness, I grasped the inside sill and lowered my body to its full length, but my feet were still short of the floor. With no place to go but down, I let go of the sill and fell only about a foot onto a hardwood floor, shattering the silence of the morning with a base-drum-like sound that echoed off the floor and walls of the empty gym like a clap of thunder.

Rolling onto my back, I lay flat on the floor listening to the deafening sounds of silence and the rhythmic, rapid hissing of my breathing. After a brief pause I stood up and began to walk cautiously toward the estimated place of the mats. Even though I assumed the absence of anyone in the gym, the sound of my leather-healed loafers on the hardwood floor unnerved me.

Removing my shoes, I continued to walk silently through the darkness until my toe touched the soft edge of the canvas-covered wrestling mat. Dropping knee first onto the mat, I rolled into a fetal position, exhaled a sigh of relief, and began an overdue descent into slumber.

But, just before leaving reality, I was shocked into a state of sharp alert by the sound of an interior door at the far end of the building opening and closing. Step by echoing step, someone, unseen, was walking toward me. I could see nothing, but I could feel my heart pounding as if it were trying to beat its way through my chest.

Walking alongside the wall, I felt my way to the exit doors, grasped both push bars, and pressed outward, exploding into the cold morning air and running the fastest dash I'd ever run. About a hundred yards distant, I turned around, dropped chest down, and looked back at the black hole from which I had erupted.

A tall, shadowed figure behind a flashlight appeared in the doorway. Slowly, he moved the beam in a semicircular sweep. Initially, the light passed over me, but quickly returned and covered me in a blanket of illuminated exposure. It was time to flee again. "Stop or I'll shoot," I heard the man shout, but no shot was fired. He must have concluded that I was just a kid.

I continued running until I outdistanced the beam. Cold again, I ran back to the project, entered the hallway of the first apartment building, curled up in a corner at the bottom of the stairs, and fell asleep too exhausted to reflect on my first close call.

The cry of a baby coming from an upstairs apartment awoke me to a new morning. It was refreshing to see daylight after a night of restless sleep. I was still tired, but also excited over the possibility of a reunion with friends. As I walked the streets of the project, pondering my next move, the quest was resolved by the sight of well-dressed women with children in tow leaving their apartments. They reminded me that it was Sunday, church time. Ironically, Mass was celebrated in the same building I had entered a few hours earlier.

My Palm Beach suit breathing in cold morning air was wrinkled and soiled from the trip and subsequent activities, but I was unconcerned about my appearance. The important thing on this Sunday morning was attendance at Mass. Casually, I walked toward the gym, a different-looking building in the sunlight. I arrived late and took a seat in the back to avoid recognition by adults who knew me via my parents.

Just before the end of Mass I left and briskly walked toward the project, satisfied that I had fulfilled my Sunday obligation. I was on the edge of the project when I heard footsteps behind me, closing fast. "Curly, it's me, Oliver. Hold up!" He had seen me on his way back from communion. We embraced eagerly like friends, longtime parted, and Oliver exclaimed, "You did it, Curly. You ran away from home." He was ecstatic, exuding a spirit of adventure and firing questions about the trip. "Let's go to the clubhouse," he said. "Okay, Oliver, but first I need something to eat. I'm awful hungry, and I remember, Mr. Plummer doesn't open until twelve on Sunday." "Curly, you leave the food to me. I can beat my Mom home from church. I'll meet you at the clubhouse. Here's the key."

Oliver returned carrying a bag full of our favorite food: bread, baloney, peanut butter, and a large bottle of Pepsi-Cola. Seated on milk crates we shared the banquet. I told him the story of my life from the time I left Ben Moreell to the moment he first saw me on his return from communion.

Entranced, he said, "Wow! That's great, Curly," and excitedly continued, "you did the right thing, Curly. Let's go to Ohio. I know we can work on my uncle's farm, and I know where we can hop a train." Neither one of us had ever hopped a train. "I'm ready, Ollie, but first I want to see the other guys and have some fun. Is everyone still here?"

"Everyone, except Joe Seager. His Dad was killed. They moved back to California. I know Joe would go with us." I did not react to the bad news. "I wish I could have seen Joe. Maybe someday we can go to California. I used to live there." Oliver responded, "If trains go there, we can go there."

"Oliver, have you ever hopped a train?" I asked. "No, but I've seen it in the movies. You just have to be able to run fast. Anyway, we hop streetcars, don't we? No big deal, Curly." Not as self-assured as Ollie, I responded, "Well, we can give it try."

Still animated, Oliver continued, "Everyone else is here: Henry, Louie, George, and one new guy, Tony. He came two months ago."

"How come you put a lock on the clubhouse, Ollie? I near froze last night."

"Little kids found the place and made a mess, so we decided to lock it up. Everyone has a key. You can use mine. You can sleep here until we move on. I'll bring another blanket."

Gradually, word of my return and need for essentials spread to the rest of the gang and each member arrived with a contribution of food, clothing, and small change. After hearing the details of my runaway story and plans to move on to Ohio with Oliver, the boys agreed that I did the right thing, but expressed no enthusiasm for the Ohio trip.

We shared stories of past adventures until late afternoon and resolved once again to be for one another. Before leaving, each club member swore to the secret of my presence and promised to help with needs. No one volunteered to move on to Ohio with Oliver and me. Neither did anyone try to dissuade us.

5

Returning Home

TWO WEEKS OF ACTIVITY, reminiscent of bygone days (sneaking into movies, hopping street cars, etc.) were abruptly interrupted by an exchange of phone calls between Oliver Simpson's mother and my mother and father. Surmising that I may have returned to friends in Norfolk, Mother shared her suspicions with Mrs. Simpson. She may also have finally missed the thirty dollars lifted from her purse and put two and two and a bus ticket together. I'm guessing. Mother never mentioned the theft to me, nor I to her.

After pumping Oliver to no avail, Mrs. Simpson began to do her own detective work. Missing food and blankets led her to believe that Oliver was lying, but she wisely chose not to confront him. Instead, she told Oliver my folks had called with inquiries about me, and that I had been missing for two weeks. Confident of Oliver's complicity, she told him to be on the alert for my presence and to tell me my mother was sick and wanted me to call right away. I could use the Simpson phone.

This was news I did not want to hear. Oliver and I were readying to move on to Ohio. I'd been away from home for a little over two weeks without once feeling remorse over leaving, concern for parents and little brothers, or anxiety for the future.

Unexpectedly, feelings for Mother I did not know I had, were surfacing. She had tried to discipline me, but she never said or did a mean thing to me. If she had, I might not be writing this book. Had Dad been the sick party, I think I would have said,

"Too bad, he'll get over it." I was caught between the horns of a dilemma: one horn freedom, the other, affection.

Sensing a need to share my problem, I asked Oliver to call a clubhouse meeting. At four thirty on a Friday afternoon, exactly two weeks after leaving home, I sat in a circle of five preteens, seeking their advice on a decision that would affect the rest of my life. The argument for returning was simple: sick mother. Father was not a part of the equation. Paternal alienation had not abated. The case for going on to Ohio was supported by two factors: my initial intent to escape father and the excitement of a new adventure.

Beginning with Louie Francisco, I asked my circle of companions for opinions.

"If it were my mother, I'd go home," Louie said.

Anthony Palucci agreed.

"Send her a letter. Tell her you're sorry she's sick and go on," replied Henry Meeker.

"I know what you think, Oliver. How about you, George?"

George was a quiet person. When he spoke, everyone listened.

Laconically, he opined, "Go home."

Three to two in favor of returning. Not surprising, given no one but Oliver was for new life in Ohio. I decided to call home.

Oliver's mother embraced me as if I were her own and promised my favorite fried chicken meal after the phone call. My father answered the phone.

"This is Bud. I want to talk to Mom."

"Your mother is too sick to come to the phone. If I send the money for a train ticket will you come home?" His voice was soft and deep, free of anger.

I hesitated. "I want to talk to Mom," I insisted.

"Hold on. I'll see if she's awake." Within seconds he returned. "Your mother is sleeping, Bud. I don't want to disturb her. She's been restless since you left. If I send the money," he repeated, "will you come home?"

I hesitated again. My answer was my life. Sensing my difficulty, Mrs. Simpson looked sympathetically at me. Oliver, sitting in the living room, head in hands, said nothing.

Finally, I said yes and turned the phone over to Mrs. Simpson.

I slept for most of the thousand-mile train ride from Norfolk to Fort Lauderdale. When I wasn't sleeping I was brooding over my loss of freedom and the end of an odyssey. I wondered if I would ever see my friends again.

"Wake up, son," I heard the black porter say as he gently nudged me on the shoulder. "We're coming into Fort Lauderdale. I'll help you with your baggage."

"I don't have any baggage."

"Looks like you're the only one getting off here, boy. We should be there in ten minutes. I'll be back for you."

He walked up the aisle illumined by small footlights at the base of each seat, his head and hands disappearing in the darkness, creating the illusion of a floating white coat. As the train shifted and slowed to a halt, I saw the white coat coming toward me, announcing a moment of truth. In a few minutes I would be face to face with the man I had run away from, the man I had last seen standing at my bedroom door, the man I never expected to see again. As anxiety increased, my heart rate rose.

"Fort Lauderdale, son! Is someone going to meet you?"

"My father will be here," I said with dispassionate certitude.

"You take care of yourself, son," the porter urged, as I stepped off the train. His tone was deep, soft, and reassuring, as if he sensed the gravity of the moment. I looked at the gray-templed black man and replied, "I will." As the train pulled away, he waved and I waved back. I wonder now what he was thinking.

Turning, I found myself standing alone on a long, dimly lit, wooden platform. As I walked toward the station, the door opened and there he was, wearing the work clothes of his profession, navy-blue denim dungarees and a white T-shirt, looking very much like the powerful man I remembered. I was wearing my getaway Palm Beach suit, doing what it was made for, inhaling and exhaling warm tropical air. We stopped cold when we met, he in the doorway, I on the platform, a few feet distant. Seconds, like hours, of silence followed; no familial hugs. He was searching for the right words, and I had nothing to say.

He looked exhausted, his face no longer the red, contorted image indelibly imprinted on my memory. He was nonplussed, all his physical strength, all his experience as a leader of men of no use. My sudden departure and reticent return had shocked him into a new parental reality of relating to a son he loved, who was now beyond physical discipline. At this critical junction, a wrong word could have sent me fleeing again and he knew it. The balance of power had shifted from father to son, though I did not know it. I did, however, know I would not remain for long around anyone or anything that hurt or constricted me.

I broke the silence. "How's Mom?"

"She's still under the weather, but much better since I told her you were coming home. She's anxious to see you."

I followed him to the car.

In 1943, the Seaboard Railway Station was fifteen miles from downtown Fort Lauderdale in the middle of open-range cow country, an illumined oasis in a desert of darkness. My return followed my departure by two weeks and two days, approximately the same time of morning, 1:35 a.m.

The ride home was like a trip through a long tunnel: darkness, except for the dashboard lights. We were not inclined to speak beyond the necessary. We needed one another, but neither of us could say so. The day never came when we could say "I'm sorry" to one another. He died before either of us was able to apologize. We were a proud, stubborn pair who missed one of life's great moments. Contrary to the movie theme, I do not think love is "never having to say you're sorry."

When we arrived at the house, Mom was in bed, but awake and waiting. Entering her bedroom alone, I stood by her bedside and asked, "Mom, are you okay?"

Extending her arms, she drew me close. Sobbing, she said, "I'm all right, Bud, now that you are home safe. You had me worried sick." Shaking her head in disbelief and holding back tears, she continued, "And all you took was your Palm Beach suit." I almost replied, "and thirty dollars," but decided to let it rest. Neither Mom nor Dad ever mentioned the theft or the reasons for my leaving. I sensed they understood that I would leave again unless home became a place where I wanted to *be*, more than *be from*.

Back in my bedroom, I could not sleep for remembering my runaway experience, the entire round trip from start to finish, and I wondered if I had made a mistake by returning. Mom did not seem all that sick. "Well, I can always leave again," I said to myself. "But where would I go? I can't go back to Norfolk; that's the first place he would look." The prospects of a trip to nowhere were not inviting. With the recollection of Oliver Simpson waving me off, I slipped sadly into a state of restless slumber.

I woke to a late Sunday morning and went to church with the family as usual, as if I'd never been away, and resumed the ritual. I had nothing special to say to God. My prayer was the unspoken prayer of my presence: here I am again, God, just like I'm supposed to be.

Bonding and Forgiveness

Church over, my father asked me if I wanted to take a ride. He said he had a surprise for me. I was skeptical, but curious. On the way west he explained that we were going to visit an old Navy buddy, Harry L. Spike, a retired mess chief. I was puzzled. Why would I want to meet one of Dad's Navy shipmates? We turned off the asphalt onto a dirt road that ended in the front yard of a rambling ranch house, with a wide front porch and a lonesome rocking chair. "Wait here, Bud; I'll only be a minute. I want to check on the dog."

"I'm not afraid of dogs," I replied, in a tone of teenage bravado.

"Wait till you see this one," he cautioned. Dad knocked on the screen door, someone answered and he disappeared. After five minutes I tired of waiting and began walking toward the house. Halfway there, the watch dog came tearing around the corner of the porch in pursuit of a jackrabbit. He saw me and changed victims. There was no time to return to the car. I froze, but the dog kept bounding toward me. Six feet from me the beast went airborne. It was then that I discovered it was a male, a full-grown, fawn-colored Great Dane.

He landed forepaws first in the middle of my chest and before I could recover he pinned me with his front paws. Then, out came his wet, shiny, pink penis searching for a port of entry, undulating as if he were mating with a bitch in heat. Before receiving a semen shower, I was rescued from this attempted canine rape by Harry Spike. "No, Duke, no," Harry shouted. But, Duke was focused. It took a swift kick from Harry to end Duke's encounter with his imaginary mate.

The blow sent the dog yelping away. I needed no help getting to my feet and running to the car. Harry was right behind me, full of apologies and assurances that Duke would never molest me again. As far as I was concerned Harry L. Spike and his dog could go to hell and I could go to Ohio.

I sat within the safety of the locked car watching Duke, now resting on the front porch of the ranch house as if nothing had happened. Harry and Dad were standing nearby. I could see that they were trying to control their laughter. This event could have spoiled my father's first attempt to bond with me, had it not been for the surprise. When they parted, Harry walked back behind the house and Dad came toward me. Seated behind the steering wheel, he made no effort to start the car. "Are you okay, Bud?"

"I want to go home," I mumbled.

"Okay, but you haven't seen your surprise."

"No more surprises. I just want to get out of here. I saw you and Harry laughing. It wouldn't be so funny if it was you."

As my father started the car, Harry came around the side of the house leading a huge gray stallion. "That's your surprise, Bud. Harry says he's the fastest horse in the whole county and he's yours to ride whenever you want to."

"Wait," I said, unlocking the door. I had never been on a horse, but I had ridden many a range and caught many an outlaw across the borders of my imagination. I was awestruck by the size and beauty of the animal. Forgetting about Duke, I left Dad in the car and walked directly to the horse.

"This is Tidge, Bud," Harry said. I reached up to pet him on the nose and he jerked his head away.

"Not so friendly is he?"

"He's just a little shy with strangers. He'll be fine, once he gets to know you. Have you ever ridden a horse?"

"No, but I can learn."

"Good. My son, Harry Jr., will teach you. He rides in rodeos. Tidge is too high strung for beginners. When you're ready, we'll start you out on Ben"

"I'm ready now."

After a few lessons on gentle Ben, I was astride Tidge, riding the Florida flatlands throughout the summer of 1943, playing out my cowboy fantasies. Tidge ran with the abandon of a horse without a rider. The big gray was a stroke of genius on my father's part. Through Tidge, we were gradually able to relate to one another. Dad praised my riding progress. I loved the praise as much as the riding.

Doing fun things together, we became companions, filling the vacuum of bygone clubhouse friends. He taught me to play tennis and introduced me to deep-sea fishing. Life was looking up at home and at school. I began to live to please him.

He woke up to my teenage needs; however, he failed to do one important thing. I did not reflect or expect it at the time. He failed to say he was sorry for scaring me half to death. I wasn't waiting for him to apologize. I thought I had forgotten about the incident in the bathroom. I was twelve years old at the time. The event buried itself in my subconscious where it lay smoldering for thirty-two years.

I doubt I would have unearthed it had it not been for the diligence of a friend who told me one day that he could hear anger in my voice, like I was "chewing on some old bones." Once surfaced and relived, I was able to forgive him in absentia, review the good times we spent together, and enjoy the warm memories of a father's love.

Vocation?

The nuns noticed the change in my behavior. One Sister in particular divined that I might have a vocation to the priesthood. She planted a seed and watered it with caution. A call from God to serve him was not to be taken lightly; one's eternal salvation might be at stake. Despite the serious nature of God's calling impressed on me by this pious nun, another call to action coming from within my teenage loins was shouting for attention. It was the pubescent chemical call of attraction to the opposite sex. This physical call, with its emotional overtones, sent the supposed spiritual calling deep into the vault of my memory bank where it remained for six years.

High school introduced me to athletics, a love that prevails to the present day. Big inherited hands made passing a football and handling a basketball easy. I never achieved stellar status, but it was fun. Athletics gave me two years of collegiate education before the vocational seed that Sister had planted sprouted through the crust of my resistance and demanded attention.

The decision to terminate college education and enter a seminary for the Roman Catholic priesthood happened in a way that mystifies me to this day. I feel like I entered the seminary through the back door. It was an angry, sour-faced priest who nudged me to give the priesthood a try.

In the darkness and anonymity of the confessional I admitted almost breaching the moral limits of premarital sex. I had not gone all the way, thanks to the resolve of the college girl in question. Just when the heat of our petting reached the point of no return for me, she cooled me down with a statement I had to honor, "I'm saving that for my husband."

When I confessed this interrupted incident of sexual intercourse to the disgruntled priest, he lost his cool and excoriated me. I did no more than digitally explore the topography of my collegiate date. You would think I had approached the gates of hell. Perhaps I shouldn't be so hard on him. Petting fell into the category of mortal sin, and it was his duty to help me avoid hell and make it to heaven.

I left the confessional fuming over the browbeating I'd been given, but when I calmed down, I said to myself "Hell, I could do better than him," and took my first intentional step up the steep mountain of time that led to the priesthood.

6

Seminary Training

$\mathbf{Y}$ears ago, when I began this memoir, trying to write about nine years of seminary life, I drew a blank at the first page. I wondered what I had gained or lost in exchange for the investment of so much of my lifetime, the years when most college students are on their way to acquiring the credentials necessary to do what they wanted to do.

What would I have done with those nine years had I not gone to the seminary? I suspect I would have continued playing football at any college that offered me a scholarship and graduated with a BA in physical education. Further, I may have married a childhood sweetheart and had some kids. Nine years lost was all I could think of when my mind took me back in time to 1951. Feelings of anger, puzzlement, and resentment surfaced, but words eluded me. Disinclined to write under the influence of negative emotions, I shelved this seminary chapter with the intention of returning to it when recollection was less emotionally charged. Twenty years later, that day has dawned.

Minor Seminary

I arrived at the minor seminary of a religious community called the Missionary Servants of the Most Holy Trinity on September 1, 1951. I chose this particular community because of an association with a Missionary Servant priest who provided religious services for Catholics attending a summer camp atop Lookout Mountain, Mentone, Alabama, where I was then working. He was different from any priest I had ever met, free of clerical hubris, just an ordinary man with the attractive gift of humility. When I shared my feelings about the priesthood, he encouraged me to honor them and give the seminary a try. "Better to be sure," he counseled, "than go through life wondering." Shortly thereafter, I took his advice.

I was delivered to the doorsteps of the seminary by the same man who predicted I would not last for more than six months, my father. I proved him wrong by completing two years of minor seminary, six years of major, and one year of intense spiritual training called the novitiate. No doubt my father's negative attitude toward my choice of profession or vocation, requiring celibacy, helped my determination to stay the marathon course to ordination and beyond. I think his reticence was related to his observation of my active high school and college social life, which included several romantic relationships, the last one, just a week before he drove me to the seminary door.

As I stepped from the car in front of the little white wood-framed chapel at the end of a tree-lined, one-lane dirt road, a quarter mile up from a two-lane dirt road, midway between Phoenix City and Eufaula, Alabama, a gray-haired man, dressed in black trousers and a short-sleeved white shirt approached me. Smiling and extending his hand, he surprised me with an out-of-context question, immediately putting me at ease. "Do you play basketball?" Basketball had been the love of my life, a way of being an important person in a small community of high school athletes. "Yes, I do," I replied with enthusiasm and the confidence of an experienced athlete. He was the rector of the seminary.

I had never been a good student, one who was motivated by a desire to make above-average grades. Family academic accomplishments were without history. Neither my father nor mother finished high school. Dad was Navy all the way since age fifteen. Mother was intellectually gifted, but born too soon to enjoy the feminist revolution. Once married to the sailor, she entered the world of the housewife: washing and ironing clothes and cooking for three sons and a husband in "military blues," who had captured her heart. She had little time for intellectual pursuits.

Remaining eligible to play sports had been the motivation behind my scholastic efforts in high school and college. Bs, Cs, and an occasional D were good enough grades for sports. Grade A would have been a pleasant surprise, but I and my father took more pride in my making the team. Consequently, meeting the scholastic requirements necessary for becoming a priest meant entering a whole new scholastic world.

Even though I had had two years of basic college courses, this was not enough to begin the philosophy and theology studies required for the priesthood. French, Latin, and Greek, plus a practical introduction into the spiritual life of prayer, meditation, spiritual reading, and Mass were now to be my daily fare. In addition I was assigned to a specific spiritual director, a priest presumably experienced in matters spiritual, who would serve as guide along my spiritual way. His advice was to be preferred over one's own sense of direction. I vividly remember the admonition, "The man who follows his own way has a blind man for a guide." To my good fortune, I was assigned to the same priest who had first attracted me to the priesthood.

Spiritual Life

The concept of a spiritual life involving a personal relationship with God was at once new and attractive. Prior to entering the seminary I was, at best, a Sunday-obligation Catholic, with a conscience that stung like an angry wasp when I sinned, especially when the sin exceeded the clearly defined limits of sexual morality. Exploration of the geography and topography of female anatomy, real or imagined, was taboo, a serious sin that qualified as mortal. Going all the way (premarital sex) was out of the question. This is not a complete list of forbidden sinful territory, but it represents the major material of my confessional matter prior to the seminary, with the exception of going all the way.

The spiritual life as I perceived it was an individual journey toward union with God preceded by the eradication of sin and the illumination of the mind with transcendental truths, like the Incarnation, the Trinity, and a host of mysteries beyond human comprehension. Once achieved, union with God promised a state of bliss this side of heaven and the possibility of receiving special favors from God. Governing behavior and controlling one's emotions, desires, and fantasies were essential to spiritual growth.

For the next nine years I studied subjects I had never heard of, prayed more than I ever dreamed possible, and lived an isolated, for-men-only life. Involvement with a woman was impossible since there were no women around. They were out of sight, but never out of mind. Sexual activity was imaginary except with one's self. Masturbation was a problematic serious sin for some, but not for me, thanks or no thanks to my father. He strictly forbade the practice and frightened me into strict restraint. When I reached puberty, he threatened to make me sleep with my hands above the covers and further neutralized by boxing gloves. In addition, he cautioned, "Masturbation results in deep circles under your eyes and warts on your hands." He never had to invoke his threat. I can only assume that the origin of this unusual admonition dated back to his childhood experience with his father.

The extent of my seminary sexual activity was, to be sure, imaginary with one notable exception, the coveted wet dream. Since dreaming was involuntary, there was no sin, no guilt, no need to confess, just pure satisfying explosive pleasure, with a woman of my dreams, always young, always beautiful, always mysterious, never a woman I knew. In my case this nocturnal event occurred about once a month following the natural accumulation of seminal fluid.

At one point, two years into the journey, despite my newfound spiritual life of daily Mass, meditation, spiritual reading, and Stations of the Cross, I grew weary of life without women and decided I had had enough. Rushing to my spiritual director, I announced, "I'm going home to marry my old girlfriend, Father." (I gave no thought to whether she would have anything to do with me.) For all I knew she could have already married) As if the good priest had anticipated my announcement, he laconically responded, "I think you should give the novitiate a try first." This was not what I wanted to hear; furthermore, I resented the fact that God was speaking to me via a third person. Why did he not speak to me directly? But I did not have the spiritual maturity to disagree with the director nor the courage to honor my freedom and say No to God without fear of eternal doom.

Novitiate

The spiritual director was right, the novitiate proved to be the time and place to decide if I wanted to continue the journey to the priesthood, profess temporary vows after the conclusion of one year, accept a new first name, and study for six more years. The decision to continue came toward the end of my obligatory novitiate year. A new love entered my life, a nonsexual spiritual love of God, nurtured by the pervasive spiritual environment of the novitiate. This could have been a dry, abstract relationship had I not accepted the Catholic belief that God became man in the person of Jesus Christ. The God-man crucified became very real to me. Even though I had seen porcelain or wooden figures of Christ nailed to a cross many times, the idea that Christ had suffered and died for my sins never took root in my consciousness. Neither had it ever occurred to me that I was in any way responsible for his suffering and death. Reading and reflecting on the painful death of Christ I developed a compassionate love of gratitude toward a God who could assume my humanity, suffer, and die. The scriptural account of his suffering and death touched me deeply. Replicas of his bloodied body, head crowned by thorns and feet nailed to a large wooden cross, fired my imagination and carried me mentally to the scene of his crucifixion. There, on a hill outside Jerusalem, I stood with his mother, Mary, and the apostle John and heard Jesus cry out, "Father, forgive them for they know not what they do," and "I thirst," and finally, to his heavenly Father, "Into your hands I commend my spirit." Without question, I accepted the notion that this Jewish God-man named Jesus Christ died for my sins. But he did not just die. Crucifixion ranks high among the most barbaric and tortuous methods of execution. Stripped naked, nailed to a wooden cross, and raised perpendicular to the ground, the victim hangs by nails piercing his hands until death. Christ's agony is thought to have lasted three hours.

So intense was my meditation on the wounds of Christ that I felt occasional pain in my hands and feet, unaware at the time of the power of mind over matter, exemplified in psychosomatic phenomena. Experience would one day reveal what the mind can do to and for the body. Fear of embarrassment inhibited me from mentioning the pain associated with meditating on the crucifixion to the novice master.

After completing the novitiate, I professed temporary vows of poverty, the renunciation of ownership, chastity, the abnegation of sexual pleasure in or out of marriage, and obedience, the submission of one's will to a legitimate superior. Three years of temporary vows were required before professing perpetual vows for life.

For the first time since beginning down the spiritual and educational path to the priesthood I was happy with my decision. I no longer felt that I was reluctantly answering God's call, backing into the priesthood, so to speak. The novitiate had given me a new, exciting life of striving for perfection and growing in a love of God, in particular, the Son of God, Jesus Christ.

Following my profession of vows and the taking of Angelo

as my new first name, symbolizing a break with my former life, I studied the philosophy of Thomas Aquinas, a brilliant thirteenth-century Italian Dominican monk who was the Church's principal philosopher and theologian of his day and thereafter. As for the new name, I was permitted to submit the names of three saints. From this list the major superior of the community would select the one he judged appropriate for me. From the three names I submitted, he selected Angelo, which was my third choice after Jonathan and Dismas. Jonathan is a derivative of John, the apostle. I liked John because of his closeness to Christ and his courage in following Jesus to Calvary when the rest of the apostles ran away and hid. Dismas, a criminal, sometimes called the "good thief," crucified alongside Jesus, appealed to my sense of unworthiness for I too was once a thief. All I knew about St. Angelo, an early-century martyr, was his martyrdom by way of crucifixion. Some names lend themselves to nicknames like Joey for Joe and Johnny for John. Angelo became Angie to friends in the Order. I didn't care for it since it could also be short for Angela. Also, to the consternation of Italians, Angelo did not match with Liteky, an anglicized version of Litecky, a Slovak name. I wished I'd been given the name Dismas until I realized I would then have been nicknamed Dizzy. If you finish this memoir you may agree with my first choice of Dismas.

7

Major Seminary

THE NOVITIATE FINISHED, six years of studies lay ahead of me – two years of philosophy and four of theology. The subject matter was, generally speaking, boring. Some of it I do not understand to this day, for instance, the philosophical definition of the principle of individuation. Just by way of curiosity, I had always wondered what gives us our individuality, what makes us unique, one of a kind. One of the few times I remember being intellectually stimulated in the seminary was when the professor announced that the material for the next class would be the principle of individuation. Excited to be so close to satisfying my curiosity, I arrived at the 9:00 a.m. class expecting something along the lines of a concrete explanation. Instead, the professor propelled me into the ethereal realm of philosophical gibberish with the definition "matter signed by quantity," which makes about as much sense to me as quantum physics.

Philosophy was followed by a study of the doctrines and moral principles of the Church from its beginning to the present. When doctrines beyond comprehension were presented, like the Trinity (three persons in one God), the Incarnation (the union of the divine and human in the person Jesus Christ), the virgin birth of Mary (conception and birth without human involvement), and Transubstantiation, which accounts for the substantial presence of Christ in the accidents of bread and wine, the special category of faith was employed. The inexplicable was to be accepted in faith. This was no problem for me, since I had the unquestioning faith of a person born to the Catholic Church and its teaching authority. Supposedly, I received this so-called gift of faith at Baptism. Furthermore, I was raised by Catholic parents and educated in the faith by Catholic nuns; consequently, I never seriously questioned the validity of the Catholic faith. Like most children raised to believe in one faith or another, I simply accepted what Mom, Dad, the nuns, and, occasionally a priest said. This faith in the Church prevailed throughout most of my life until the day I felt free to think for myself rather than think with the Church. This freedom came gradually, like a blade of grass sprouting its way through concrete in search of sunlight.

Despite the bland, incomprehensible, and sometimes weird nature of Catholic doctrine and morals, like purgatory and indulgences that freed poor souls imprisoned there until temporal punishment for their sins was satisfied or an indulgence set them free, I did find a subject engrossing enough to capture my attention and imagination: mystical theology, which is closely allied to ascetical theology. Through ascetics like prayer, fasting, and a multitude of other self-denying exercises, the body and soul of an aspirant to perfection is chastened to receive expressions of God's love in many forms.

Mystical Theology

My first assignment in mystical theology was to write a paper on the life of a mystic. Perusing books in the seminary library on the lives of saints and holy people, I chose Therese Neumann, a simple peasant woman with a big heart from a little village in Bavaria, a state in southeastern Germany. Super-sensitive to suffering humanity, inclusive of Christ crucified, Therese not only prayed for sick people in her village, she asked God to transfer their suffering to her. It is written that her prayers were answered and she suffered everything from the rheumatism of her father, the throat problem of a local priest, and a multitude of maladies suffered by others in her village. She felt it was her duty as a devotee of Christ to take on the suffering of others. Her compassion for the crucified Christ and his death was rewarded by the gift of the stigmata, the wounds Christ endured at his crucifixion on Calvary.

Aiding my choice of Therese Neumann as the subject for my paper was the fact that she was still alive at the date of my writing, 1956. She died six years later. One day, a priest, a World War

II army chaplain, visited the seminary and shared the experience of his brief interview with Therese, while on duty in Germany. He was one of many in a line of visitors curious to see the woman afflicted with wounds similar to those of a crucified person: hands, feet, head, and side. Once a week she bled profusely from the wounds as she lay in her bed. Also, from the time she received the stigmata she refrained from eating or drinking anything but Holy Communion until the day she died in 1962.

Though the priest was not wearing his clerical garb, Therese greeted him as "Father," followed by her offer to tell him something about himself. "No thanks," he replied and moved on. He laughed as he shared with us this story about his reluctance to have his inner secrets revealed.

I was deeply impressed by all of this mystical stuff. It settled well with my growing devotion to the crucified Christ. Throughout the many years of studying for the priesthood, isolated from the world, I spent many prayerful moments in the chapel feeling sentiments of gratitude and sadness, while kneeling before a life-sized replica of the crucifixion.

Final Vows

I professed final vows in 1957, closing the gap to ordination to three years. The year before ordination to the priesthood, I was ordained a deacon and thereby empowered to preach, distribute communion, and do almost everything a priest could do except hear confessions and celebrate Mass. The diaconate is the last step before the final step, the priesthood. The diaconate year was one of anticipatory excitement over what would soon be the beginning of a new way of life in a world from which I had been almost totally removed for almost nine years. I would also be called by the title "Father," rather than my personal name.

* * *

My diaconate year was moving along nicely until a fall day in early October. Leaves were falling from the trees around the old southern hotel that was now our seminary, announcing the coming of winter. Before the beginning of morning classes, I was summoned to the superior's office, unaware that I had done anything to merit a visit with the head man. The superior was a tall, middle-aged man with a face and voice that commanded respect while exuding gentility. I had known him for three years and had never heard him say a harsh word to anyone. He bade me sit down, looked at me solemnly from his seat behind his desk and said, "Brother Angelo, I have sad news for you." Since my father had been a bedridden patient for the past five years, I was not immediately shocked. I expected to hear of a heart attack or his death, but my father wasn't mentioned. It was Jim, my younger brother by seven years. I haven't said much about Jim in this memoir, because I knew him only as a child. His teens and college years were hidden from me in the isolation of my seminary days. I heard he was a superb basketball player, but I never saw him play.

When death came to Jim, he had recently graduated from Florida State University, taken a job as teacher and coach at a local high school in Jacksonville, and captured the fancy of a beautiful young woman, recently crowned Miss Jacksonville. He was an excellent swimmer. I heard that he bet someone he could swim underwater from dockside to the point of a marshy island a hundred yards down river. To do so, he would have had to cross part of the Santa Fe River, which ran two or three miles per hour. After diving into the darkness of the river, he failed to surface. Volunteer scuba divers from Jacksonville crisscrossed the river, holding on to ropes strung along the bottom, plotting the river bottom as if they were on an archeological dig.

I arrived at the site on the second day of the search for his body. Limited visibility made it necessary to feel for Jim's body. With no scuba diving experience, I wasn't able to join the divers combing the bottom of the river. Pacing anxiously on the bank, I waited and prayed for signs of discovery. After three days of relentless searching the divers had to leave for jobs at home. Their entire effort was voluntary. I remained with a friend who had a rowboat and an idea. Someone had mentioned that a submerged body would rise to the water's surface after seventy-two hours due to gases released by a decaying body. It was thus possible that Jim's body would surface after three days, provided he was not trapped beneath a sunken log. My friend suggested that we board a rowboat and drift with the flow of the river, as Jim's body might float after surfacing. It was now dark enough to require flash lights. Within minutes, a crosscurrent carried us to the left of the tip of the island.

Our route and timing were fortuitously perfect. As soon as we passed the point of the island, Jim's body rose to the surface, immediately in front of the boat, face down with hands stretched upward, as if he wanted to climb in our boat. Cold water had kept his body in perfect condition except for a deep, clean gash over his left eyebrow. He had evidently stroked himself headlong into a log or stone and knocked himself unconscious. From here to eternity in a flash. That's the way I like to think of his last mini-second of life. At that time of my life I was brimming with a faith that assured me of his happiness in heaven. Had we not been at the exact place at the exact time of his surfacing, the current might have carried him into underbrush along the riverbanks or as far away as the sea, and this story would have been tragically different. It was sheer accident, coincidence, or maybe even providence that we were at the right place at the right time to receive Jim when he surfaced.

By the time we rowed back to the dock, the grim side of nature had begun to take its course: his body was decomposing with its unique, unforgettable scent. An ambulance arrived within an hour to take Jim's body to a funeral home in Jacksonville where an undertaker would prepare him for viewing, funeral, and burial. He was the only son of three of us still living at home. Both Pat, the youngest, and I were in the seminary. Dad's remark upon Jim's death was, "God took two of my sons to his service. Now he has the third." Mom's sorrow remained internal.

The sudden, unexpected death of a loved one creates the void of a lifetime, due in part to the unique nature of every life. I cannot help wondering what life would have been like for Jim and what he would have meant in the lives of those who knew him. Silly perhaps, but I wish I could have seen him play basketball. As a deacon, I was permitted to preach at Jim's funeral Mass, my first public sermon. I cannot, at this writing recall a single word, but sixty years later, I still feel his absence and I guess I always will until we meet in heaven, if there is such a place.

8

Ordination & Mission

IT WAS A BIG DAY in the lives of ten young men who had studied for nine years to become priests in the Roman Catholic Church. At the end of an era marked by hours, days, and years of studious preparation, we felt we were stepping out of a time warp back into real time and the real world – a place that included women as well as men. Throughout our lengthy seminary life we were repeatedly reminded of the threefold enemies of the spirit: the world, the flesh, and the devil. Fortunately, we were equipped with the tools to help people live lives in conformity with the moral and theological doctrines of the Roman Catholic Church, the one and only true church established by Christ. (It was so taught.) Family, relatives, and friends, some traveling from afar, came to witness the event, a historical Catholic rite called Ordination at which only a bishop can officiate. It was May 5, 1960.

The bishop laid his hands upon our heads one by one, said a consecration prayer, and thus ushered us into a new way of life where we would enjoy the respected title of "Father." Following Ordination came First Mass in one's hometown parish and first assignment to a specific mission of the Community. I was assigned to the Shrine of St. Joseph, a small chapel on a mini-mountain ridge, above the little village of Sterling, New Jersey. To the west lay a vast wildlife preserve, an easy hike down the mountain, a sanctuary for deer, ducks, and a variety of birds. St. Francis would have loved the place. It was idyllic for prayer and contemplation, radiating peace over the valleys on either side of the mountain.

In addition to founding a religious community for men, a missionary congregation of women named Missionary Servants of the Most Blessed Trinity was also established. The nuns staffed a retreat house a half mile south of the Shrine, but their main mission was to be the embodiment of Christ's love among economically depressed people regardless of location. They served in a variety of ways, initially in the South and eventually throughout the United States and Puerto Rico. I arrived at the Shrine in June of 1960 to join three Missionary Servant priests in an effort to lend spiritual support to small groups of laypeople, largely women who the Missionary Servant nuns had organized. The groups, known as Missionary Cenacles, engaged in what was called the Missionary Cenacle Apostolate. Once a week, I drove alone all over New England, New Jersey, New York, and Pennsylvania celebrating Mass, preaching sermons, and hearing confessions for Cenacles, or circles of nuns and laywomen. The nuns and the women were a gracious lot possessed of great respect for priests. Unlike the nuns of ancient orders, the Missionary Servant Sisters wore plain black dresses, equally plain black stockings and shoes, no veil, or hairstyles and makeup that might attract men. Most of the time I lodged in the rectories of local parish priests, whose camaraderie I enjoyed. My work was simple in comparison to shepherding hundreds of parishioners.

After three years of this itinerant life, I was reassigned to mission parish work in the northern neck of Virginia. I did not ask for the change, but neither did it come as a surprise. I was having problems, strangely enough, with a spiritual renewal movement called the Cursillo (Spanish for "little course"). My behavior began to trouble others.

Begun on the island of Majorca off the eastern coast of Spain after World War II, the Cursillo movement was an effort by a small group of men to revitalize their faith. Over the years this little course has grown into a worldwide movement popular in a variety of religious denominations. The movement came to the United States in 1957 and so it was still young when I participated in a Cursillo in 1963 in Cincinnati, Ohio.

The renewal intent of the Cursillo worked for me, giving me a release of emotional inhibitions integral to the expression of my faith. I sometimes refer to it as the movement that blew the lid off of my pent-up emotions and allowed me to speak and pray publicly from the heart rather than voicing standard, canned prayers devoid of feeling. I enjoyed the experience, but failed to realize the negative effect of free-flowing prayer upon others who knew little of the Cursillo movement. The intensity and freewheeling nature of my public prayers at Catholic liturgical functions alarmed some Cenacle nuns and moved them to inform my superiors about my unusual behavior.

While circuit-driving in New England from one Cenacle to another, my trip was abruptly terminated by an immediate superior who surprised me after a liturgical function and said simply, "Let's go, Charlie. I've been sent to pick you up. The custodian general wants to see you at the Shrine." The man called general was the top man in our Community. (I've never understood why the head of a religious group would be designated in militarist terminology.)

"What about?" I asked.

"I don't know." said the priest sent to rope me in. "The Sisters reported you."

"For what?" I said indignantly. Again, no answer.

The trip from a small town in New England to the Shrine in New Jersey was six hours; this afforded me time for reflective silence, six hours of time to allow anger to grow from a spark of indignation to an internal firestorm. It was the first time in my adult life that I was feeling abused by authority, and it was the first time my vow of obedience was being tested. I had been ordered in without explanation. I understood the nuns' anxieties, but I could not appreciate the general's lack of consideration.

Superiors in religious life shoulder a heavy burden of responsibility for those avowed to obey them. I am talking here about adults obligated by a vow to obey another adult, as if the superior were speaking for God. Throughout my religious life, I would often hear, "it seems to be the will of God" that I do this or that or go here or there. To give another by way of a vow the power to order you here or there or do this or that takes a hefty dose of faith. At the time I had such faith. Some regard the vow of obedience to be more difficult than that of poverty or chastity. (Chastity, I have to confess, became the heaviest of the three for me.) That test was yet to come. I never failed the vow of obedience, though neither have I ever failed to confront abusive authority, but not because of bravery. It is the sense of injustice that incenses me. In my opinion, if there be such a thing as sin, abuse of authority, especially when that authority rests on faith, ranks among the greatest violations of human dignity.

After arriving back at the Shrine, I had a week to wait for a session with the general. Without solace I retreated to the inner sanctum of my thoughts and wounded feelings. Praying alone before the crucifix over the altar in the chapel, I focused, as I had often done in the novitiate, on the wounded Christ who had suffered so much for me. My pain was so much less than his, but I was too proud to suffer in silence. Christ did not cry out against His abusers. On the contrary, he asked for their forgiveness. "Father, forgive them for they know not what they do." But not me; I was a long way from that kind of love and understanding. I needed vindication for the validity of my behavior and an apology for being the victim of abusive authority.

Stigmata

On the second day of my introspective journey, a Tuesday, I began to experience pain in my hands and feet identical to what I had felt in the novitiate. This led me to believe that I might receive the wounds of Christ, the stigmata, as a sign of God's defense of my rectitude. On the third day, the pain increased, and my belief in the support and favor of God grew. By the fourth day I was moving toward certitude and fending off impulses to doubt the reality of my experience. On the fifth day, an unusual event occurred that I interpreted as a sign of God's willingness to use me as an instrument in the struggle of good versus evil, in this case evil personified, the devil.

As I entered, the chapel was empty but for a middle-aged man mumbling feebly in the back pew. He was obviously distressed. Dressed in my black habit and thereby immediately recognizable as one of the Shine's resident priests, I stopped to offer help. He responded with a plaintive request for me to rid him of his demonic infestation. He claimed that devils were forcing him to utter obscenities and he had come to the Shrine to be exorcised.

Official ecclesiastical exorcists are selected from known holy priests and appointed by bishops to perform the rite of exorcism. I had no such appointment, but I had received the minor order of exorcist in the course of my seminary training. Given the immediacy of the situation, a person in extreme distress, I decided to forget proper procedure and try to help the man. Using the name and power of the blood of Jesus I cast out all and any devils tormenting the man. No response from the devil, thank God, but the man was relieved. Becalming himself, he thanked me and left. I felt important, useful, and ready to be used again for God's purposes. I never saw the man again, but I frequently reflected on the incident and my accidental if not providential presence; one of those right-time, right-place happenings. These days I do not believe in the existence of devils, but in those days they were as real as rain to me. These days, I no longer believe in much of anything. Negative experience with faith has led me to live with a conviction based upon rational evidence rather than faith.

The day following this event was Friday, my day with the general. We were to meet at three o'clock in an office on the second floor of the building where I lodged. I was to await his summons in the recreation room, down the hall from the office. The night before our meeting I lay awake, thinking about how to remain calm and say what I had to say without displaying what I thought was my justified anger over the callous way the general had treated me. Pain in my hands and feet began to suggest that the stigmata was on its way and would appropriately appear at the auspicious hour of 3:00 p.m. on Friday, just before meeting with the general. At this time, the storied time of Christ's death, the gift of Christ's wounds would be inflicted on my hands, feet, and side, resulting in my vindication and setting me on the unknown path of a stigmatic, suffering as Therese Neumann had done. Doubts over the reality of my expectations were dispelled as quickly as they came. I refused to be a doubting Thomas. I retired somewhat anxious over the pain involved in a virtual crucifixion, but I was confident that God would help me bear it. In any event I was about to begin a new phase of my relationship with Christ.

I spent Friday morning in the chapel, praying for strength and meditating on the suffering of Christ, particularly on the abandonment he must have felt over the absence of his apostles, who had fled in fear when he was taken away, tried, and crucified. I arrived in the recreation room an hour early to wait out the hour alone. Before doing so, however, I felt bound to inform the local superior of what was about to happen. He graciously listened, and as I recall, commented that having a stigmatic at the Shrine would be a good thing. He did not seem to be humoring me, nor did he probe me for an explanation. He was a lighthearted, jovial man who must have been thinking, "I'd better let this play out."

Sitting in the recreation room waiting for the hour to pass

and the face-to-face meeting to begin, I grew weary of the silence and decided to play a record. With no selective forethought, I chose one of my favorites, *West Side Story*. I was immediately moved by the opening lyrics ("Could be! Who knows?"), which struck me as a perfect preface for what was soon to happen.

Listening to the lyrics, I shifted into interpretation mode. The song's "something due any day" was my coming stigmata at three o'clock. "Cannon balling down through the sky" was a good metaphor for the entire meeting.

As the song went on, the black minute hand on the white-faced recreation room clock ticked toward three, and I prepared myself for pain and blood, but felt too privileged to be afraid. At this point, I was absolutely certain "something great" was about to happen. The music faded at five to three, leaving me with a brief spell of peace and silence before my stigmatic "high noon."

When nothing happened by three o'clock, I checked my watch and the clock on the wall before falling into an emotional state of total befuddlement followed by a wave of anger directed at God, whom I blamed for deluding me. It did not immediately occur to me that I had deluded myself and I was not familiar at that time with psychosomatics and its influence on the body of a person under stress.

No one was around to witness my expected moment of truth and my despondency. Feeling the need for help, but with no one in mind to turn to, I left the recreation room, avoided the office where I was scheduled to meet with the general, and walked outside as if I knew where I was going. Still wearing my black religious habit, I walked down the road leading away from the Shrine and down the mountain. Walking along the road, I cared nothing about where I was going or what I looked like. I allowed thoughts about this strange happening to come and go on their own.

Sensing a need for help, the name of an allergist in nearby Plainfield came to mind. I had gone to him several times for allergy shots. My visits always included conversations about life and religion. He was a good man, Jewish, with liberal views about the religious beliefs of others. I was not looking for explanations, just a sympathetic ear and possibly financial help to go home, because I was finished with the hocus-pocus of religious life.

With the help of a stranger in a Volkswagen who stopped when he spotted my outstretched thumb, I arrived at the doctor's office around four o'clock. He was just finishing up and preparing to leave for the weekend when I knocked on his door. As cordial as ever, he greeted me like he was expecting me. He made no mention of my religious attire.

"May I talk with you?" I asked.

"Of course. Please come in." The doctor was just the person I needed: kind, intelligent, and ready to help however he could. After listening at length from start to finish, he agreed that I should go home, but he counseled, "I don't want to see you leave your priesthood behind. Let me call the Shrine and ask for someone to pick you up. I'll feel better if you make your decision to leave from there."

This is not what I wanted to hear. I wanted him to loan me the plane fare home. He left the room, giving me time to think things over. When he returned, I said, "Okay, I'll return to the Shrine, but I want the general himself to pick me up." I wanted this man, this bright intellectual man, whom I thought needed a lesson on basic human values, to hear in person from a subject he had abused.

The general acceded to my request. On the way home we talked, rather I talked and he listened without admitting fault or chastening me. When I finished admonishing him, he said, "I think you should go home. Take a vacation, as much time as you want, but before going I want you to see a psychiatrist, Doctor Anderson." I had no objection; I was as interested as the general in the origin and nature of my experience.

9

A Needed Break

<hr>

As HE LISTENED TO THE STORY of my stigmata fantasy, Doctor Anderson, the psychiatrist, had very little to say. I was expecting some kind of medical explanation. It was I who asked the question, "Did I have a nervous breakdown?" He did not answer yes, no, or maybe. He told me I was in an advantageous position as far as breakdowns were concerned, because now I knew what it felt like to be close to the edge. In other words, if I started doing the signs-and-wonder thing again, I knew to back off. This knowledge would serve me well in cases of future stress. He prescribed no medication nor did he insist on additional counseling. He did agree with the general, however, that I should take a vacation. How nice!

The general told me to take as much time as I wanted. Again, how nice! So, I set out for home for a fully funded, open-ended stay. It was several months before my scheduled vacation, so my parents were not expecting me. They deserved an explanation, but I saw no point in sharing with them what had turned out to be a fantasy that had left me bewildered and would have caused them to worry. A needed rest was sufficient to satisfy their curiosity about my untimely homecoming.

I did take the opportunity, however, to pull a joke on my father. He was a jokester's joker. One of his favorite lines to visitors – delivered from the stage of his hospital bed, in which he was then confined – was, "Did I tell you about the time I fought the bull in Tijuana wearing pink tights and a rusty sword?"

(Dad was a victim of arthritis in his right hip. He had hip re-placement surgery at a time when the prosthesis used was a heavy stainless-steel ball and socket. The surgery failed before succeeding, leaving an open wound that failed to heal due to osteomyelitis. He was a bed patient at home for eleven years and Mom, his in-house nurse, attended to his every need.)

As mentioned earlier, my father doubted I would persevere through the seminary training for the priesthood (with its rules requiring celibacy), but once ordained, he deferred to me respect-fully, as if I were his father. When I arrived home wearing a sport shirt and slacks, a wardrobe he had not seen me wear since col-lege days, he was surprised, but said nothing other than to ask, "What's the occasion, Bud?"

"I had a run-in with my major superior, Dad. He pissed me off and I hit him." The old Navy chief nodded his head in approval. This was the kind of language and behavior he could appreciate. His Navy career was filled with stories of such spon-taneous altercations.

"Just kidding, Dad. I'm taking an early vacation."

* * *

My anger with God dissipated once I acknowledged my self-de-lusion, but it was still difficult to let go. Reflection on such a trau-matic happening was natural but the chronic (though waning) pain in my hands and feet would not allow me to completely for-get the event. The memory of the man in the chapel who believed he was possessed and the lyrics from the musical, *West Side Story* did not help. I resolved, though, to live by reason and concrete evidence and be forever done with symbolic interpretation. But, as they say, "Easier said than done."

Whenever I was home, I said daily Mass for the nuns at the local Catholic school. After Mass they served breakfast in their convent dining room. Giving me preferential priest treatment – seating me at the head of the table – they could not have been more deferential to Christ himself. Of course, I never mentioned I was home for anything other than vacation. After breakfast and congenial conversation, a nun who had been out of the dining room walked in with the gift of a holy card for me. I was still seated. Placing it on the table face down in front of me, she said something like, "Just a little prayer for you, Father." Picking up the card and rising from the table in one motion, I said, "Thank you, Sister," turning the card over as I spoke. I was shocked by the image on the card, but said nothing. The image was of the flesh-colored, pierced hand of the crucified Christ vividly portrayed with blood dripping from His wounds. My resolve to avoid interpretation was being severely tested, and I thought that perhaps my timing was off, and the words of the song from *West Side Story* came rolling out of my memory: "Maybe just out of reach, down a block, on a beach, it'll be there," but I quickly recalled the counsel of the doctor, "You will know when you are close to the edge." I was not about to drift toward that chasm again.

Feeling the need to be alone and allow the reality of my fantasy rather than the fantasy itself teach me, I spent most of my time walking the beach, listening to the sounds of waves crashing and receding and of the sea gulls begging for handouts. Easter was coming, with Good Friday to remind all Christians of the suffering and death of Christ. Also, Passion Week called to mind my own weighty experience, still intriguing enough for me to wonder. Despite my resolve not to interpret coincidences like the nun's gift of a holy card, I was still somewhat apprehensive. When Good Friday passed without incident, I felt liberated from wondering or anticipating, but another challenge soon came my way.

Again, it was a nun who was the stimulus. When I dropped into the convent to say goodbye before returning to the Shrine, the nun greeted me a little sadly, "Too bad you're leaving. You'll miss the school play."

"What's the name of the play, Sister?"

"*Come Out of Your Coma*," she replied.

I smiled and said, "Goodbye." As I reflect now, why the coma in the first place? I've learned that some of life's best lessons come hard. This particular one set my feet firmly on the solid ground of reason rather than the ephemeral turf of faith. I'm not saying that faith has no place in my life but it remains subordinate to reason.

Reassignment

The general reassigned me to a new mission under a superior whom I knew by reputation to be a man with a wide-open personality, a good sense of humor, and a gift for hospitality. (For privacy reasons, I have not ordinarily mentioned names in this memoir, but I am duty bound to reveal the real name of one of the kindest men I've ever known, Father Leonard Bachman, for he was pivotal in my life.) I'm sure the general informed him about my recent history and asked if he would accept me as one of his assistants. He was the pastor of five mission churches spread over thousands of square miles in the northern neck of Virginia, a two-hour drive south of Washington, D.C. Leonard did not wait for me to arrive. He called me at the Shrine to confirm my appointment and welcome me to a team of three priests responsible for serving this territorially vast parish.

I worked with this man and two other priests for nearly three years, traveling from church to church, doing the things that parish priests ordinarily do: celebrate Mass, hear confessions, perform baptisms, witness marriages, visit the sick, and bury the dead. Never did Leonard mention my earlier experience, nor did he express any apprehension about my ability to accept responsibility. Most of our parishioners were middle-class whites, plus a smattering of blacks who, by choice, sat in the back of the church, following the separatist, cultural law of the South.

Civil Rights

This was the civil rights era when blacks and concerned whites were challenging racial discrimination in the South, where African Americans were prohibited from registering to vote. While there were never any serious incidents in our territorial parish, the media made us aware of protests in Mississippi and Alabama. Even though I was raised in the South, I never accepted southern white superiority. I was touched by the plight of blacks and I wanted to be a part of the march in Selma, Alabama. Priests, nuns, and ministers nationwide were participating, but my new superior refused permission on the grounds that my participation would alienate members of the parish. The principle of "prudence" being the "better part of valor" applied. Again, my vow of obedience was tested. Again, I passed, but did not like the constriction and chafed under his direction. Obedience is easy until it conflicts with one's own desire or perceived need.

While I did not go to Selma, I did preach about racial injustice in one of our mission churches and thus alienated at least one parishioner, who complained to Leonard. He felt that church was no place to preach civil rights and he stated that he would no longer be attending. I was sad, but not sorry; Leonard was sad and sorry. He had the heart of a pastor. I was thinking only of injustice and feeling the need to address it. Perhaps Leonard was right. Had I gone to Selma, we may have lost more parishioners, but it would have given them an opportunity to face the immorality of discrimination. Immorality left unaddressed festers like an infected wound.

Following this event, I began to feel constricted by the religious vow of obedience and decided to leave the religious community and petition to enter a diocese as others had done. I would still be under the jurisdiction of a superior, in the person of a bishop, but I would no longer be vowed to obey him. Somehow that seemed easier to me.

10

Joining the Military

THE VIETNAM WAR WAS HEATING UP and thousands of young men were being drafted. The Army was short three hundred Catholic chaplains. I regarded the chaplaincy as an opportunity to serve my country in an hour of conflict and to enjoy independence from religious superiors.

When I broached the subject to my major superior, he surprised me by encouraging me to join the military as a chaplain. Looking back, I wonder if he may have wanted to get rid of me. I agreed and began to make preparations to live a totally new way of life, which indeed it was.

I had no problem justifying the war. I swallowed whole President Lyndon B. Johnson's lie about the Gulf of Tonkin incident and the domino theory of communist aggression throughout Southeast Asia. In addition, having been raised in a military culture, I felt very comfortable around military people. At the time, I took the general's suggestion to enter the military as a vote of confidence.

Meanwhile, back home, Dad had a heart attack on March 17, 1966, while standing naked at the bathroom sink. He died on the cold tile floor, his last words shouted loud enough for Mom to hear: "I hit my goddamn arm." Mom was with him in seconds, but seconds were too long. She held him, just as she had once held his mother in a moment of peaceful passage.

On July 5, 1966, I officially joined the U.S. Army, four months after the Navy chief died at age sixty-three. It may be just as well that he left this world before I put on the Army uniform. The shock might have caused a stroke, especially if I had insisted he salute a first lieutenant.

Each branch of military service has its Chaplain School. The school for U.S. Army chaplains was located in Brooklyn, New York, ten driving minutes away from the Verrazano Narrows Bridge and twenty minutes from downtown Manhattan.

In September of 1966, I arrived at the school to join over a hundred Protestant ministers, Jewish rabbis, and Catholic priests in a two-month-long officer's indoctrination course: how to dress, salute superior officers, return salutes of enlisted personnel, and handle an automatic weapon, the M-16.

From the start I resisted the temptation to become a clerical soldier, but I had no problem with using a weapon for the protection of self or others, if needed. Primarily, I was there to serve Catholics, but secondarily, I was expected to be available to everyone, irrespective of rank or religion. The chaplaincy expanded the field of people I could serve and I enjoyed it. I also enjoyed the freedom to live alone or with others. Throughout my military service I did both.

Fort Benning

After completing Chaplain School in October of 1966, I was assigned to a U.S. Army post, Fort Benning, Georgia, known as the Home of the Infantry. Fort Benning is one of the largest military posts in the world, 280 square miles of Georgia pines, rolling hills, and dense forests. It is also home to a variety of reptiles, including rattlesnakes and water moccasins.

I could have been sent to any one of a myriad of Army posts situated around the country. It was just by happenstance that the administrative branch of the Chaplain Corps selected Fort Benning for me, a post fifteen miles northeast of the place where I began my academic and spiritual preparation for the priesthood in 1951. I knew the general area well.

I was assigned to a basic training battalion commanded by a lieutenant colonel who expected his chaplains to help carry out his military mission, namely, convert civilians into soldiers. I knew nothing about the making of a soldier. I was there to provide for his spiritual needs. On the occasion of my first obligatory orientation, the colonel gave me the impression that he had had problems in the past with independent-minded chaplains who did not share his military priorities. At the outset, he wanted me to understand his interpretation of my duties. His arrogant, pompous behavior exceeded my tolerance quotient and moved me to speak without thinking.

"I don't think we will have any problems, Colonel. As long as people are nice to me, I'm nice to them." Fortunately, I had no investment in the military, no intention of making it a career. I joined the Army to help fulfill the Army's need for Catholic chaplains at a critical junction of U.S. involvement in Vietnam. This freed me from fear of a superior-ranking officer's negative efficiency report.

My duties were clear-cut: provide religious services and counseling and lend an ear to young men less than enthusiastic over military life. Most were draftees, young men, eighteen and over, called to military service to fight in a country thirteen thousand miles away. They could answer the call or be sent to prison for desertion, go to Canada, or any place that would have them.

Throughout the six months I served as a chaplain to basic trainees at Fort Benning, I never encouraged a soldier to remain in the Army if he was excessively afraid, homosexual, or opposed to war for reasons of conscience. At the time, I had a biased, negative opinion of homosexuals and was as opposed as most to their presence in the military. Time and experience would change my cultural assumptions of the nature of homosexuality.

Company commanders were obliged to send a soldier who claimed to be homosexual to the chaplain for evaluation, and I was obliged to render an opinion. How I was supposed to know the validity of a man's claim to be gay, I don't know. On one occasion a young man who sensed I doubted his orientation said, "What do I have to do to convince you that I am homosexual?" I did not need proof. His question was enough to convince me.

Others were apprehensive about committing themselves to a cause that clearly was not related to national security. Vietnam was not invading us. We were invading them. As I would one day hear a young black soldier say, "No Vietnamese has done anything to hurt me." I would come to appreciate the plight of the black man forced to fight under the banner of "freedom and democracy," when his people were fighting for the same at home. An appeal to patriotism with people historically oppressed was useless.

I did not try to convince anyone of the need to remain in the Army if they wanted to leave, but I felt obliged to point out the consequences of doing so: a dishonorable discharge – a lifetime record of negativity on paper that might discourage potential employers.

However, one young man left his mark on me. His conviction about nonviolent action was unshakable. Punishments for refusing to serve did not deter this Midwesterner. He was a draftee who initially thought he could handle the duties of a soldier until the "kill, kill, kill" bayonet course. The possibility that he might one day be screaming at a human being as he plunged a bayonet into his chest changed his mind about soldiering.

Bad discharge, prison, and the label "coward" did not influence his newfound sensibility. All the dishonorable discharge cards were stacked against him since he did not come from a church that officially sanctioned nonviolence, like the Quakers or the Mennonites. A personal claim of conscientious objection was not enough.

I felt sad for him, but I admired him as much as I later admired the men who fought and died in front of me in Vietnam. He was risking his life in a different way, the rest of his life. I had nowhere near the respect for human life this young man, half my age, possessed. It would take twenty years of walking an uphill rocky road of violent events before I could even think about embracing nonviolence as a way of life. I don't remember the young man's name, but I can still hear him saying, "I will not continue my military training regardless of what they do to me."

Recalling this interview with a committed pacifist, I appreciate the power of example. I tried, to no avail, to convince him with cautionary words, but without saying a word it was he who began to convince me of the power of nonviolence. He planted a seed that others would water. When he walked out of my office, I never saw him again, yet he has a permanent place in my memory.

Nonviolence, or pacifism, was the Christian way of life for its first three centuries, but when Christianity became the religion of the Roman Empire under Emperor Constantine, pacifism became an ideal rather than a practice. Theologians of the era developed a way for Christians to join the military and kill for peace: the just war theory. One twentieth-century bishop, Bishop Carroll Dozier, disagreed and stated publicly, "We must lock away the just war theory in the same drawer as the flat earth theory."

Most basic trainees were young enough to be my sons. Consequently, I regarded them with paternal concern. I watched them respond to training in the military arts, lose their individuality, and meld into units of destruction. After eight weeks of basic training they moved on to eight more weeks of advanced training in specialties chosen for them: cooks, clerks, mechanics, truck drivers, medics, artillery, and infantrymen.

It took at least six specialty men to support one infantryman. It was well known and accepted that the infantryman was the most likely to be killed. He was the one who fought the enemy directly in the jungle, sometimes face to face, sometimes hand to hand, but most frequently, unseen in the camouflage of jungle foliage or the dark of night.

* * *

A month before my assignment to Vietnam, an onerous duty fell to me at Fort Benning. My turn to be the officer of the day rolled around. Like hospital doctors, chaplains were expected to deliver news of active duty deaths to dependents who lived on or around the post.

I did not know John McCormick personally, but I had visited with his wife and five children many times after Sunday Mass. He was a helicopter pilot, one of Vietnam's highest casualty-rated professions. His wife, Ann, was a gracious woman, possessed of a quiet, serene disposition, devoted to husband, children, and church. Whenever I visited, I arrived at the front door alone, relaxed, and attired in civilian clothes.

On the day of John's death notification, I was militarily stiff, dressed in my military best, and, by Army regulation, accompanied by another officer. The minute Ann opened the door and saw me dressed like an officer, she knew immediately that she was a widow and called for her children to come to the living room. We knelt as one and prayed the rosary with Ann leading. Beyond the announcement, there was little need for me to say anything to this incredible family of faith and courage. This was my first experience with the long-term effects of war.

A month later I was in Vietnam, but I maintained contact with Ann, all the while wondering how she would make it alone with five children below the age of thirteen. Two years later, I was in Vietnam again; and once more I received a letter from Ann. The improbable had become reality. Another good man had come into her life, ready to be husband to her and father to her children.

11

Vietnam

───────────────────────────────

I ARRIVED IN VIETNAM IN MARCH OF 1967, to begin a year-long tour of duty as one of four chaplains assigned to the 199th Light Infantry Brigade, based in Long Binh.

I was picked up at the Ninetieth Replacement Center by Nick, a young private first class from New York driving an open jeep beneath a cloudless sky in heat and humidity reminiscent of South Florida in August. Southern boyhood weather conditioning made adaptation easy. Nick would be my military companion for a year, driving me wherever I wanted to go without question, looking for U.S. infantry units on the move. He positioned his M-16 at ready reach, especially on the less-traveled roads in the environs of villages ringing Saigon.

The main base camp of the 199th was located twenty miles from Saigon on the east side of a north–south, recently paved, blacktop highway. It was the last of a vast concentration of military units forming a complex that included a makeshift hospital, morgue, brig, Post Exchange (PX), and multiple helicopter pads.

Like the tributaries of a wide river, dirt roads led west to small villages and east to U.S. military compounds surrounded by rolls of concertina wire (sharp-pointed barbed wire rolled into four-foot-wide coils that expand and contract like an accordion). The road to the 199th was the last entrance to a military post before the main highway curved east through the village of Ho Nai.

A sign reading Camp Frenzell-Jones marked the checkpoint entrance. Frenzell and Jones were the family names of the first two men of the 199th killed in action, January 21, 1967. A memorial plaque at the base of the sign read:

> Specialist Billy C. Jones and Private First Class Herbert
> E. Frenzell were on an Eagle Flight on 21 January 1967
> when their unit met a well-entrenched Viet Cong (VC)
> force. The unit, caught in the open and without cover,
> was in a desperate situation. PFC Frenzell, who was
> not at the time directly involved in the ambush and was
> in a safe location, chose to open fire on the enemy,
> thereby drawing fire away from the exposed positions.
> After everyone had withdrawn, PFC Frenzell started
> his attempt to move back to rejoin his squad. As he left
> his concealed position, he was shot and killed. Specialist Four Jones crawled through the mud and enemy fire
> to recover Frenzell's body. After contact was broken, SP
> Four Jones carried PFC Frenzell's body for over two
> hours through thick jungle growth and hazardous
> swamps to place PFC Frenzell on the waiting helicopter. However, when he saw another man hit and fall, he
> lowered PFC Frenzell's body to the ground and rushed
> to assist the newly wounded soldier. It was at this time
> that he was fatally wounded. His final words were, "I
> tried, I did all I could do. I couldn't do any more."

For about a mile, the land on either side of the road was cleared of flora, rendering the terrain a desert of dirt reduced to powder by the perpetual pounding of heavy truck tires, tank tracks, and the boots of soldiers walking and running about. The land was also dotted with blacktopped pads, designed to receive and send helicopter supply ships to and from forward units.

Helicopters were the flying workhorses of the Vietnam conflict. They usually ferried something good, like food, beer, and soda, but too often they served as ambulances, carrying away the dead and the wounded to a field hospital in Saigon. Whenever they landed or took off a dust storm followed, blurring vision and covering everyone and everything within a fifty-yard circle. While there was no foliage around, the color green was everywhere; green drained of light, the dull, lifeless hue of olive green.

By the time Nick dropped me off at brigade headquarters to meet the commanding general, the 199th had been in Vietnam for six months and had created a tent city large enough to house over two thousand men. The general made me feel welcome and needed immediately by assigning me to a specific battalion of five hundred men.

Having no experience serving combat units, I spent the first month observing the behavior of fellow chaplains. Duties were much the same as they had been at Fort Benning with a few significant additions: visiting the wounded in a nearby temporary hospital, anointing the dead in an adjacent morgue, counseling soldiers reluctant to return to combat, riding in jeeps and helicopters to units in forward areas around Saigon and nearby villages, conducting funeral services for soldiers killed in action, and writing letters to surviving spouses and parents.

Memorial services for young men in the bloom of youth never became routine, even though I rarely knew the dead soldiers personally. The burden of death fell hardest on those who dared to make friends.

Chaplains were responsible for finding transportation to and from forward areas to provide religious services for troops scattered around Saigon and adjacent small villages. Few of the units were accessible by road. This meant hitchhiking on helicopters that usually served as supply and mail ships. Most of the time we arrived during daylight hours, held services, and returned safely to the rear before sunset as the men walked off, single file, in small units to set ambushes along streams and trails likely to be used by Viet Cong forces.

At times, I had observed chaplains remaining overnight with a forward unit, a company, or platoon, and traveling with the same on a search-and-destroy mission the following day or days. Explanation: this practice gives a noncombatant support person an appreciation of the daily life of a soldier in the field – the hardship of weather and terrain, the fear of one's injury or death, and worst of all the loss of a fellow soldier, possibly a friend.

The accompaniment practice struck me as a valuable way to experience and appreciate a measure of the soldier's life. Consequently, I adopted the practice. The officers in command did not object to a chaplain going along on an operation. It was good for morale to see someone voluntarily expose himself to danger out of concern or compassion.

Occasionally, a group of soldiers would attend Mass in a forward base camp just before an evening operation like an ambush. They would stack their weapons nearby, teepee fashion, and somehow retrieve their own M-16 when I stretched out my arms at the end of Mass and announced, "The Mass is ended. Go in peace to love and serve the Lord."

I did this for a year without reflecting on the incongruity or the absurdity of what I was saying. They were going out to ambush and possibly kill someone and I was saying "Go in peace to love and serve the Lord." Had I been born a millennium earlier I may have been a Crusades chaplain, setting out with a group of Christian soldiers to slaughter the infidel enemy.

Accompanying men young enough to have been my sons was an energizing experience. Never have I felt more like the name they called me, "Father." I often wonder how I would have behaved in their shoes. I know, even as a "man of God," I would have taken up a weapon and killed, given the right circumstances. Had I done so, I wonder how I would feel about it today.

Of the many veterans I know now, none will talk about the experience of killing another person, even a person called an enemy. Wounding? Yes! Even helping the wounded adversary, usually a young person like one's self. Despite its horror, the war I've seen has not been without its expressions of selfless concern, not only for one's own, but for the wounded enemy as well.

One special case comes to mind, that of Sergeant Cavalo, who in an effort to spare the life of a wounded enemy almost lost his own. When ordered to do so at gunpoint, the enemy soldier feigned release of his weapon, turned quickly on Cavalo, and raked the sergeant across his midsection with bullets from his Russian-made AK-47. Fortunately, the bullets entered tender flesh rather than bone, enabling the sergeant to return fire and send the man he initially tried to save into oblivion. Cavalo's wounds merited an unscheduled trip home.

For the next several months I included operational, potential combat trips with soldiers in my weekly schedule, never once seeing the illusive enemy, only barely visible signs of his presence: booby traps crudely made from old tin cans crammed with rusty nails and bolts and an explosive charge connected to a trip wire. These applied-technology traps – designed to wound rather than kill – became the bane of the infantry soldier, forcing search-and-destroy missions to slow down in order to evacuate one wounded man via helicopter.

You could not help but respect the ingenuity of the enemy soldier who was using every possible resource to fight for his homeland. We knew very little of his historic struggle for freedom.

12

Under Hostile Fire

THROUGHOUT THE WEEK PRECEDING DECEMBER 6, 1967, the 199th Light Infantry Brigade had been receiving intelligence reports of enemy activity about thirty-five miles northwest of Saigon.

A decision was made to insert an entire battalion into the area. A helicopter insertion of around five hundred soldiers went on from dawn to dusk on December 5. By nightfall, a quarter-of-a-mile–square forward base camp, called Nashua, was built in the middle of a clearing in a thickly wooded area. A perimeter of bunkers and razor-sharp coils of concertina wire surrounded the camp. Two-hundred-yard fields of fire stretched from our perimeter over three-foot-tall elephant grass to the edge of a dense forest.

The entire base camp was open to attack on all sides. However, our defense was formidable: artillery, mortars, fifty-caliber guns mounted on armored personal carriers, thirty-caliber machine guns, and helicopter gunships on call from Long Binh, ten airtime minutes away. Just after sundown, I heard the unmistakable sound of incoming mortars exploding nearby. I was unaware at the time that two men had been wounded and helicoptered away.

In a matter of ten seconds, at least ten mortars landed in a straight line within our perimeter at ten- to twenty-yard intervals. Intelligence was correct. "Unfriendlies" were in the area. Firing mortars in rapid succession without moving the tube from side to side is like sending the recipient your return address. It was as if the VC wanted us to come looking for them, which is exactly what we did.

The next morning, December 6, 1967, around 10:00 a.m., a platoon (about thirty men) from A Company (Fourth Battalion, Twelfth Infantry, 199th Light Infantry Brigade) set out to find the mortar site. I decided to go along, as did our company commander, Captain Drees.

I was the battalion chaplain, one of a few Army personnel who could choose his combat missions under the aegis of morally supporting the men. Most of the time, I asked permission from the officer in command. I was never refused. At this point in time I had been in Vietnam for eight months. In a sense I was a veteran of combat missions, none of which had resulted in contact with large numbers of the enemy. Most of the casualties I witnessed on operations before December 6, 1967, were the result of wounds from booby traps.

Once into the woods, we discovered a footpath in line with the azimuth we were following. It would have been a gentle walk through the woods had we not been mortared the night before. We had ten good reasons to suspect that Charlie (a euphemistic name given to South Vietnamese guerrillas) was around.

I was smack in the middle of a line of thirty heavily armed men, the safest place a support person could be. Ambushes usually targeted the front or rear of a column. By choice I did not carry a weapon. I could have. I had been trained to use the M-16 in Chaplain School. I reasoned that if an occasion serious enough arose, an abundance of weapons would be available.

Even though I was traveling in the middle, I could see to the point man and beyond. I have a sharp recollection of seeing two shadowy figures clad in black outfits cross the path about a hundred yards in front of the point man. Once alerted, we double-timed it to the juncture where the two figures, presumed by their attire to be VC, had entered the woods.

Captain Drees ordered half the platoon to spread out five yards apart and enter the wooded area with weapons ready. Visibility was about ten to fifteen feet. The rest of us remained on the path, assuming prone positions, facing the area of possible contact. I stayed on the path, body pressed to the ground, close to Captain Drees.

Around fifteen feet into the woods, the first assault group was baptized with blood and the unholy spirit of war. Machine-gun fire, AK-47 automatic reports, mortars, and rudely constructed antipersonnel mines loaded with a variety of metallic junk (nuts, bolts, screws, nails) exploded on cue in a cacophony of discordant thunder. Bullets and shrapnel were flying everywhere: over our heads, snapping tree leaves, and entering the bodies of the men on the first assault. The romance of combat was over.

Conscious of honoring the chain of command principle, I went immediately to Captain Drees's side and offered help. He was on a wireless field phone strapped to the back of a soldier, too focused on reporting contact to firebase Nashua to attend to me.

The radioman was the beast of a most important burden, a heavy cumbersome contraption capable of sending and receiving messages to and from a recipient miles away. The man who carried the radio had the distinction of being the most valuable person on the mission. By way of the radio, the person in command had access to rapid, ready, and incredible firepower. The enemy knew this and cherished the chance to wipe out radio and carrier.

I left the path and entered the woods, employing the low-profile combat crawl of belly to ground, head and rear end down, eyes open and forward. I don't remember feeling signs of fear like shaking or temporary paralysis. This was not due to any personal courage, indifference to danger, or composure under pressure. I simply had no time to reflect. Responding to the obvious needs of wounded men blocked out every other emotion. In my experience when you forget yourself, there is no room for fear in the house.

Snake-like, I inched my way forward, beneath a hailstorm of flying metal, the sight and scent of gun smoke, and the muffled groans of wounded soldiers. The first person I came upon was a fair-skinned, freckle-faced, red-haired youth lying on his back gasping for air, his eyes wide open, but glazed and unresponsive. Instinctively, I eased my hand behind his neck and pulled him up to a half-sitting position. It was then that I discovered the reason for his lassitude. In the middle of his back was a deep dark hole the size of my fist. His fatigue shirt was soaked with blood.

Mortally wounded, he faded away in my arms, a first for me, a first and last for him; no time to dwell upon the queasy feeling that began to creep into the pit of my stomach. There was no dramatic last exhalation of life nor final words of comfort for me to write to his family. He just slipped away as I anointed him, and his blood anointed my thumb and the cotton pressed into the small cylindrical vile that contained the oil used in dispensing Last Rites. Gently, I laid his bloodied back to the ground and continued crawling in search of the next wounded soldier.

To my left, ten yards back toward the path, I saw a young man familiar to me. Only yesterday, we had talked about what awaited his homecoming. Enthusiastically, he told me about his band and his plans to resume playing when he returned to the world. He was sitting calmly, leaning back on his elbows, his right leg severed midway between thigh and knee. It looked as if it had been completely torn away. As in a drawing in an anatomy coloring book, I could see the cross section of muscle, bone, and tendons.

He was not shouting for a medic, as many wounded instinctively do. He *was* the medic. He knew better than anyone not to cry "medic" and thereby bring enemy fire on himself and an attending medic. Perhaps, he had already given himself a shot of morphine.

About this time, I was surprised to find myself sliding into a five-foot-deep Z-shaped trench, formerly used by the VC as a forward lookout and warning position. In the trench were three or four U.S. soldiers, one of whom was Sergeant Garrison. They were not huddled in fear. They were simply waiting for the metallic storm to cease.

My own respite was interrupted by the explosion of a mortar round twenty feet to my right forward. A soldier flew two feet off the ground and came down with a face full of blood, his identity gone. Two other men were wounded as well. I began to crawl out of the trench immediately, intending to reach the wounded men, but I felt someone holding my foot, telling me to stay put. I don't remember saying anything to the soldier, but something made him release me and I began crawling to the wounded men.

Three yards away from the trench, however, I came upon another man lying face down, motionless, his M-16 resting by his side, as if he had placed it at ready reach while he slept. He was gone, but I anointed him anyway. I grabbed his weapon and started to move on. Then the thought struck me, "This would be a hell of a way for a priest to die." Releasing the weapon, I continued crawling toward the man who had been sent airborne by the mortar round.

I was only fifteen to twenty feet from him when I clearly heard the order to withdraw. Gunships had arrived and were about to begin their firing runs close enough to warrant evacuation. I was caught between the proverbial rock and a hard place, go to the aid of the wounded and possibly disrupt a military move ordered by the captain or withdraw as ordered.

Torn internally, I returned to the relative safety of the path as the gunships commenced to fire rockets into the area very close to the wounded men I left behind. When I reached the path I did a stupid thing. I stood up just in time to see a gunship approaching for its first rocket run. I hit the ground at the very moment a rocket was released. As my head went down, my heels went up in time to catch a sliver of metal in my right foot where bunions grow. It was unfriendly friendly fire, not intended for me. It was not a serious wound, but a wound, nevertheless. It stung, but did not inhibit movement.

Wounded

I was not inclined to mention my wound to anyone at the time, given the lethal level of injury all around me. It appeared to me that the gunship runs were dangerously close to the wounded soldiers who had been unable to withdraw when the order was given. I feared for their safety, thought about cautioning Captain Drees, but opted to leave the responsibility of friendly fire casualties to him. My mission was not military, I told myself.

This decision haunts me to the moment of this writing. What troubles me is that I was willing to sacrifice these men for the good of the mission rather than speak up for their lives.

The rocket runs continued for time interminable. As soon as they stopped, I was on my way back to the men I had left behind. It would take time for the enemy to respond to the pounding he had just received from the rocket attack. I moved to the side of one wounded soldier in a matter of minutes, elated to find him still alive; dazed and grossly wounded in the face, but alive and on his way home if we could make it to a clearing prepared for "dust offs" (a term used to describe the dusting effects of whirling helicopter blades).

The area immediately in front of us, that is, in the direction of the enemy entrenchment, was sparsely dotted with trees and bushes. I was able to clearly see a makeshift, rusty VC version of a claymore mine resting against an iron tripod. Two black wires attached to terminals on top of the mine told me it was live and it could blow in a mini-second. I hastened to get on with the effort to remove the first, most seriously wounded soldier from the area. He was conscious and responsive enough to hear and do what I told him.

Recovered from the helicopter assault, the enemy resumed his defensive firing from camouflaged bunkers with 6x12–inch firing ports. There was no way I could carry the soldier and make it to the dust-off clearing without putting the two of us in further danger. We were about to invent a combat exit move that I had not been taught in Chaplain School. Spontaneously, I lay beside him and pulled the wounded soldier onto my chest, hooked my arms under his, dug my heels into the dirt, and repeatedly pushed the both of us away from immediate danger. He was aware enough to help and I urged him to push with his feet. He did, and with his help, we inched our way back to where he could be carried to the dust-off clearing.

Throughout this unorthodox exit maneuver, I was conscious of the fact that without intending to do so, this poor fellow was shielding me against falling shrapnel. Thank God, enemy fire at this point was horizontal and at least a foot over our heads.

After he was taken from my chest and airlifted off, I thought I'd seen the last of this soldier, but two days later, I ran into him again in the Long Binh surgical hospital. His face was a map of intersecting stitches, but cleaned of blood and recognizable. He could even smile. (The reconstruction of lacerated bodies by teams of doctors and nurses always impressed me as a medical miracle.) He would be in Japan in a few days and soon on his way back to the world, a fact I enjoyed telling him and other wounded soldiers.

Evacuating the wounded and anointing the dead and dying continued on the battlefield until dark. Another company joined us in the battle, along with armored personnel carriers used as moving platforms for fifty-caliber machine guns.

Finally, the light of day faded, along with the noise of battle. It was as if the buzzer sounded for the end of the game. We withdrew to the dust-off clearing where we spent the night in a protective circle, each soldier in a prone position facing outward, peering into an eerie darkness that possibly concealed enemy soldiers who were elusive and adept at night fighting.

I helped with the loading of the wounded and dead into airborne ambulances, directing them in, as if I knew what I was doing. I had seen it done many times, so I simply imitated. I must say I felt rather important standing up straight, arms and hands stretched skyward, then gradually lowering my hands as this awesome flying machine descended, its huge overhead prop blowing away everything not tied or held down.

Throughout my two-and-a-half years in Vietnam, I repeatedly marveled at the courage and dedication not only of the infantry men, but of all the soldiers in support, especially the dust-off helicopter pilots.

All night long a ring of steel created by round after artillery round fired from base camp Nashua, a mile away, protected us against a possible enemy counterattack. A slight error in judgment by the men behind the big guns would have resulted in our extermination by friendly fire. This happened more than once in the dense jungles of Vietnam.

While the men were lying on the ground facing the possibility of an attack, I visited one soldier after another with a "How's it goin'?" greeting and the offer of a cigarette. I just happened to bring along a whole carton. At such high-tension moments a cigarette can be a calming luxury even if you don't smoke, but most of us did, unconcerned then about cancer.

The night passed ever so slowly with little sleep. The sound of incoming artillery passing overhead, landing as close as fifty yards away was not music for relaxing, but we knew it was our safety wall. At first light we were told to prepare to move back into the area of conflict.

Aerial reconnaissance reported no enemy movement. Slightly wounded and exhausted, I chose to return to Nashua on the next helicopter out. It happened to be the chopper of the battalion commander, Lieutenant Colonel Bill Schroeder.

He greeted me heartily, like a father who had found his long-lost son. I did not understand his exuberance until he told me that he thought I was dead when he saw my name-tagged shirt draped over the face of a dead soldier. Without thinking, I had used my shirt to cover the soldier's face when we placed him in the dust-off chopper.

An after-action report included captured operational papers that revealed that we had accidentally encountered a battalion of North Vietnamese regulars staging for the countrywide Tet Offensive of January of 1968. They were a tough bunch, hardened by years of fighting Chinese, French, and Japanese colonialists. To them the United States was just another in a long line of colonial powers. Had they known how few we were when the battle began, they could have easily overrun and annihilated us.

The day after the action, I conducted funeral services for

twenty-five young men killed in action. Everyone at that service, including me, knew that the taps of finality could have been blowing for any one of us. The mystery of who dies and who does not in a firefight or battle awaits revelation.

They were so young. I had experienced twice their lifetimes. Why them and not me? Sometimes when I reflect upon my life since Vietnam, I wish I had been one of the December 6th fatalities. You will understand as this story proceeds.

We had no way of knowing exactly how much damage we did to this particular NVA battalion. The Vietnamese had the noble practice of not leaving their wounded and dead. Our losses were the greatest we had suffered since the arrival of the 199th in Vietnam: eighty wounded and twenty-five dead. The NVA losses reduced the effectiveness of this particular unit in the soon-to-come Tet Offensive.

Zimmerman

A week after December 6, I joined another company on a search-and-destroy mission about five miles west of base camp Nashua. It was a rapid helicopter insertion of approximately a hundred men into a dried-up rice paddy fifty yards from a dense wood line.

I never grew accustomed to the few tense moments preceding the touchdown and deplaning of a helicopter landing in an area suspected of having an enemy presence. It was not uncommon for "Charlie" to be hiding in the wood line or tall elephant grass, waiting for those special moments of extreme vulnerability when a helicopter approaches and leaves a landing zone. Occasionally, we were alerted in advance of the likelihood of enemy forces near the landing zone (LZ), referred to as a Hot LZ: bad news and tense moments for everyone en route to the designated area.

Just before touching down the door gunners opened up with M-60 machine guns, spraying thirty-caliber bullets by the hundreds over the LZ and into the surrounding wood line. Deplaning without incident, we hurried to the wood line.

The memory of the previous week had unnerved me. Once again, we discovered a well-traveled path and proceeded cautiously to walk west with flankers ten yards out on both sides of the point man. If enemy forces were in the area, the sound of helicopters, machine-gun fire, and flankers breaking bush would alert them to our arrival and they would be ready and waiting.

A half hour into following the path, our point man was dropped by a burst of automatic fire from a camouflaged position. The sharp, crackling sound of the AK-47 announced the presence of VC and the possible death of the point man. The men behind him proceeded to saturate the area with grenades and M-16 fire. I lay flat, one with the ground, like everyone else not actively engaged in this exchange.

When the noise abated I heard someone shout, "Zimmerman!" The soldier lying next to me responded and began to crawl in the direction of the felled point man. Turning to me as he moved, he said softly, "I guess I'm next, Father."

Zimmerman took point and in a matter of minutes his prophecy was fulfilled. Once again, the suspected origin of enemy fire was saturated with automatic rifle fire and grenades. Zimmerman had drawn the fire of the concealed Vietnamese soldier, exposing his position.

This was among the weirdest episodes of death I had ever experienced. Makes you wonder if there is such a thing as Spirits of Death that warn a person just before it happens.

The soldier who killed Zimmerman and the point man before him was found dead after the second barrage of fire. He was as young as the men who killed him, a lone outpost sentry who had sacrificed his life to warn his comrades. As was my custom, I anointed him and moved on with the column.

A green communication wire in plain sight ran from his trench to the path we were following and continued westward. Following a "como wire" in an area of known NVA occupation was an invitation to disaster. Whoever was at the point of origin of this wire knew exactly where and how many we were and chose rather than attack to fight from a hidden position, no more than a small hole in the ground.

Before going much farther, the captain, a young, green West Pointer, decided to call for helicopter recon. The overflight revealed that we were approaching a large enemy base camp of undetermined size. He called for artillery and we waited while shells whistled overhead, exploding close enough for shrapnel to fall within a few feet of us. A half hour of continuous artillery fire calculated to soften up the enemy passed quickly.

Few on this particular operation had seen the kind of action that awaited us. One who had seen a lot more was a professional soldier, the first sergeant, a veteran of the Korean War. I was lying on the side of the path ten feet behind him. With artillery shells passing overhead followed by repetitious, ground-shaking explosions and shrapnel falling close by, this veteran of the Korean War, turned to us and said with a smile, "Relax gentlemen! When this is over, the shit is going to hit the fan."

I knew exactly what he meant. Relaxing was out of the question for me, but I did my best to mask my apprehension. After a half hour of artillery volleys and gunship rocket runs, the seasoned sergeant shouted, "saddle up, move out," and a green group of first-time heavy-contact soldiers formed a line, five yards apart, perpendicular to the path, and cautiously moved toward the known but invisible enemy.

I stayed on the path and waited for what I knew was coming, the sound of combat thunder and lighting. I hoped the men would crawl rather than stand upright, but they did not and the result was more wounded and dead. From the beginning of our assault I wanted to shout, "get down, crawl, stay low," but I did not have the power of command. I thought I was in for another December 6, but the captain wisely ordered withdrawal immediately after the initial contact. Several men had been killed outright; a few had been wounded.

By now the sun was fading. I could hear choppers landing in the nearby rice paddies. An order had been given for extraction. It was time to get the wounded, dead, and myself out of there.

A foreboding silence followed our initial assault and I went looking for the wounded and dead. I found a husky young man, lying face down, motionless, but saw no apparent wound. There was, however, the perfumed scent of fresh blood, a sweet-smelling odor that is unique to blood before it putrefies, the kind of odor that is unforgettable. When I turned him over, the origin of the scent revealed itself: a lethal chest wound still oozing blood. He was warm, but lifeless.

Employing the firefighter's carry, I hoisted him over my shoulder and headed for the waiting helicopters. No sooner had I positioned him on my back than I felt the warm, moist flow of his blood seeping into my shirt, marking me with another lifetime memory.

Ten to fifteen choppers were lined up on the dry, rock-hard rice paddy waiting for the command to lift off. I loaded my burden into the crowded chopper and boarded behind him, my legs hanging over the open door next to the gunner.

My eyes were glued to the wood line, just fifty paces away, looking for shadowy images of enemy pointing automatic weapons our way and waiting to hear that god-awful, crackling sound of the AK-47. Rotors turning in neutral, we idled there in this valley of lethal vulnerability until every last soldier from Company D was accounted for. Finally, the choppers, filled with dead and wounded men, lifted off in unison. The silhouettes of the trees melted into the black of night.

Just as I was ready to heave a sigh of relief, the door gunners opened up with deafening M-60 machine-gun fire in the direction of the vanishing wood line. The sudden sound of machine-gun rounds exploding from the barrel of a gun that I could almost touch startled me. For a second or two I could not distinguish between outgoing and incoming fire. Breathing was heavy until we banked away from what could have been my last helicopter ride.

The NVA base camp was regimental size, large enough to warrant a B-52 airstrike. We returned the following morning to find a moonscape, bomb craters fifty feet in diameter, but not a trace of bunkers or bodies or parts of bodies. It was surreal.

This was my last combat mission before the thirty-day leave I had been given as a bonus for extending my tour of duty by six months. My leave began in mid January of 1968 and ended around Valentine's Day. Thus, I missed the most significant battle of the Vietnam War, the Tet Offensive.

On my leave, I could have gone anywhere military transport flew, but there was no more important place for me than Jacksonville, Florida, my hometown and the home of my mother, Gertrude.

13

Medal of Honor & Home

AFTER THIRTY DAYS AT HOME, I began the return to Vietnam and the 199th, with a stop first in San Francisco, an enchanting city of hills and valleys. I thought it would be a perfect place for a romantic interlude: scenic vistas of the Pacific, the Golden Gate Bridge, and a bay speckled with sailboats tilting in the wind that was rushing in from the ocean.

I heard about a demonstration against the war organized by University of San Francisco students to be held the day before my flight to Vietnam. Curiosity moved me to attend and see for myself the young collegiate protesters I had heard about. I did not wear my chaplain's uniform or Roman collar. I felt like a spy. I *was* a spy.

The demonstration was not well attended. A group of twenty to thirty students met in a small, dimly lit basement room of the university. Animated, inflammatory speeches and sixties-movement music filled the room: "All we are saying is give peace a chance" and the old faithful, "We shall overcome."

Despite feeling some discomfort, I remained for most of the demonstration, standing on the fringe of the group, quietly observing young men and women express their anger over the war. Unpatriotic is a mild word for the opinion I then had of them. I thought of them as cowardly, privileged kids, lacking the courage to put their lives on the line for their country. How easy it is to criticize and judge others, especially when I did not even have the courage to stand up in front of this the group and state my position.

Their main issue about the war was not their objections to the government's stated explanation for U.S. involvement – fighting communism – but the killing of innocents and sending innocents halfway across the globe to do the killing. At the time, I did not reflect on my reluctance to share openly my reasons for supporting the war.

I remained anonymous and left mumbling. I thought, "They just did not understand. Freedom is not free." It did not occur to me that it was I who did not understand the foreign policy goals behind U.S. intervention in Vietnam, nor did I know the checkered history of the people of Vietnam, who had endured invasion, occupation, and oppression by foreign powers for centuries.

To the Vietnamese, the United States was just one more foreign power to be driven from their homeland. It would be years before the propagandistic programming of my youth would give way to a very different version of U.S. foreign military intervention.

Back in Vietnam

When the Pan Am 747 carrying me and newly assigned soldiers touched down on the runway of Tan Son Nhat Airport in Saigon, I felt glad to be back, actively participating in a noble cause. I was ready to continue the effort to stop communism before it enveloped all of Southeast Asia.

Once back at Camp Frenzell–Jones, the rear area base camp of the 199th, I listened intently to stories about the Tet Offensive battle I had missed. The military operation had begun with a surprise attack at a time when Vietnamese were celebrating the beginning of a New Year. It was a sacred time for all of Vietnam, north and south, the beginning of a New Year, a time to begin life anew. Tet is every bit as sacred to the Vietnamese as Christmas and New Year's is to Americans. In previous years, we had honored the Vietnamese Tet holiday with a ceasefire just as they had respected our Christmas. However, in February 1968 North Vietnamese soldiers sacrificed their observance of Tet for the sake of a surprise attack. War has a way of dishonoring anything and everything: don't bother mentioning the Geneva Convention to a warrior as a legal deterrent to human rights violations.

After the initial shock, the American military and the South Vietnamese Army retaliated with unmatched firepower and quickly quelled the misconceived uprising. Though the Tet Offensive of 1968 was a military disaster for our enemy in terms of lives lost and territory gained, it was a pivotal political success. The fact that the enemy could mount a countrywide offensive that included the temporary occupation of the U.S. Embassy in Saigon showed the American public and the military that the war was not winnable.

A temporary holiday truce had been broken. Over a hundred towns and cities, including Saigon, awakened to the sounds of exploding grenades, mortar shells, machine-gun and automatic weapons fire. Tet marked the beginning of the end of a war that would grind on for seven more years of death, injury, and suffering for everyone involved. U.S. soldiers were killed and wounded by the thousands. Vietnamese casualties, mostly civilians, numbered in the tens of thousands.

* * *

After fulfilling an eighteen-month extended tour in Vietnam, I was assigned to a basic training unit at Fort Bragg, North Carolina, to finish the last six months of my voluntary three-year commitment.

Medal of Honor

The return trip to stateside service at Fort Bragg included a layover in Hawaii, where I learned through a friend that I had been recommended for the Medal of Honor (MOH) for my participation in the battle of December 6, 1967. The presentation of the medal by President Lyndon B. Johnson was scheduled for November 19, 1968, two weeks shy of a year from the day of my combat baptism into the cold, terrifying reality of war.

I was awarded the medal along with four other recipients. Present were my mother, my brother Pat, friends, and members of my religious community, the Missionary Servants of the Most Holy Trinity. As we walked down the hallway to the East Room of the White House, President Johnson directed me to his left side. I supposed some protocol reserved his right side for a person of importance or perhaps no one is allowed to walk on his right.

One by one, each recipient stood before President Johnson, listening to the citation that merited the MOH. I was too mesmerized to register a mental note of anything, but I cannot forget

Johnson's eyes: small, steely, and piercing. A reception line that began with the MOH recipients and ended with the president followed the ceremony.

Everyone present was gifted with the once-in-a-lifetime opportunity to shake the hand of four recipients of the Medal of Honor and the president of the United States. When my mother's turn came, she held on to Johnson's hand, and said, "We have finally met." She told me this years after the event. I do not know what possessed her. I wish now that I had asked for an explanation. I know she had a good sense of humor.

At this time my father was two years buried in the coveted resting place of U.S. military, Arlington cemetery, only a mile away from the White House. Had he been present for the presentation of the MOH to his first-born son, he would have been the proudest man alive.

I reported for duty at Fort Bragg, North Carolina, in December 1968 and was ordered to a basic training battalion, as I had been during my first assignment to Fort Bragg. I was in no hurry to leave the Army. Stateside duty was a bore after Vietnam and I had no desire to resume the practice of the civilian ministry. Consequently, I reenlisted for another year and volunteered to return once again to Vietnam.

14

Manhattan College

WHILE WAITING TO RETURN TO VIETNAM, I received an invitation from Professor Joseph Fahey to speak on March 27, 1969, at Manhattan College (Bronx, New York), where he taught a peace studies course on nonviolence as an effective, humane, and truly Christian way of resolving conflict.

Initially, the Catholic Church was pacifist. Christians were not permitted to serve in the military. They were obligated to live the mandate of Christ to "love one another" (Mk. 10:22). This did not allow for killing anyone for any reason. All of this changed in the fourth century when Constantine, the Roman emperor, converted to Christianity and the Christian religion became the official religion of the empire. A fourth-century bishop of the Church, Augustine (later canonized a saint), formulated the "just war theory," which some trace back to the great Greek philosopher Plato. Ever since the fourth-century introduction of this doctrine into Catholic morality, the Catholic Church has not only sanctioned wars; it has actively promoted what it called "holy wars."

At the time I received Professor Fahey's invitation I was definitely not of a nonviolent persuasion. Moreover, one of the Church's principal ecclesiastical proponents of the war was Francis Cardinal Spellman, the titular head of all Catholic priests in the military, called the Military Ordinariate. He supported the Vietnam conflict and even visited the troops. The cardinal is reputed to have remarked, "Anything but victory in Vietnam is unthinkable."

I am a product of a Catholic education that included the just war theory. In regard to Vietnam, not only was I not opposed to the war; I was 100 percent behind it. Communism had to be stopped. Given my stance I'm not sure why Professor Fahey asked me to address his class. He may have wanted his students to hear a point of view other than the nonviolent position he was teaching. Perhaps he wondered how a so-called man of God could countenance the slaughter of innocents in our saturation bombing attacks in North Vietnam, the creation of free-fire zones in the South, and the forced relocation of thousands of families into "safe hamlets"?

Dressed to the military "nines" in Army greens and wearing my ribbons for bravery (worn over the heart), I walked onto a Manhattan College stage and stood proudly before a small group of Professor Fahey's students. Also attending were three priest-professors. Not being an academic, I felt a bit outclassed, but not intimidated. I was too committed to the cause of justice to allow fear-induced enervation to influence my presentation.

The principles of freedom, democracy, and patriotism were so deeply ingrained in my psyche that it never occurred to me to question my country's effort to stop communism, which the Catholic Church had condemned severely. So I defended my support for the war in Vietnam on the basis of the Catholic Church's long-held just war theory. My seminary training had never included the study of nonviolence. Pacifism received no more than honorable mention as a one-time position of the early Church, but it was hardly seen to be a practical response to the pervasive, lethal violence of the twentieth century.

The just war theory allows for a violent response against an unjust aggressor, and the North Vietnamese – after having defeated the French at Dien Bien Phu – were judged to be aggressive against the South. In this they were following the leadership of a dedicated, charismatic Vietnamese intellectual named Ho Chi Minh. Ho chose communism as the economic and political system best suited to address the maldistribution of wealth that French imperial colonialism and the systems imposed by the other foreign powers that preceded the French had all ignored.

I had a reasonably respectful dialogue with Professor Fahey's students, with the exception of one young man who challenged me with a relevant, but cynical question: "How many bombs do we have to drop or how many people do we kill before it's enough?" I heard his anger louder than I heard his question and responded to his passion rather than his inquiry. "Look!" I said in a firm, moderately angry voice. "If we can't have a civil, respectful dialogue, there is no point in my continuing."

There were no more questions from the students or attending professors. No doubt they noted that I was nearing the end of my tolerance tether. Out of charity, they may not have wanted to embarrass me.

Shortly after returning to Fort Bragg, I received a letter from Professor Fahey, thanking me for speaking and congratulating me on a peaceful dialogue with the students. (Well, it was relatively peaceful.) This was very kind of him. Then he added, "However, before you solve your dilemma, I think you need to rise above the assumptions of your subculture."

Subculture

I was not familiar with the term subculture, nor was I aware that I was living a dilemma. At the time I just shrugged my shoulders, gave little thought to the professor's advice, crumpled his letter, and sent it flying into the circular file. But truth, like daisies pushing upwards through concrete, has a way of squeezing through the labyrinth of ignorance and denial to illuminate the darkness of lies and deceit.

I can't say exactly when I began to take Professor Fahey's advice to rise above the assumptions of my subculture. I know it was well after Vietnam. Once begun, however, the examination process became an integral part of my life. Little by ever so little, I have examined the assumptions of every subculture that has influenced me.

The noted definer of words Noah Webster gives us several definitions for the word "culture." The one I like best and that applies here is: "The sum total of ways of living built up by a group of human beings and transmitted from one generation to another."

Clear enough, but what about subculture? This term does not arise in ordinary conversation. Again Webster can help us. Subculture, the dictionary says, is "a group having social, economic, ethnic or other traits distinctive enough to distinguish it from others within the same culture or society." Before this story of my life is over, I hope to share my journey from assumptions to truth.

I continued my ministry to the soldiers and families at Fort Bragg until it was time for me to return to Vietnam. Sixteen years later, by pure chance, I encountered a young man who had attended my lecture at Manhattan College. At the invitation of an Irish activist group, I was touring the country speaking out against U.S. foreign policy in Central America. He said he was present the night I defended the Vietnam War. He thought I was ridiculous. I agreed with him.

15

Back in Vietnam

SOON I WAS AGAIN EN ROUTE BACK TO VIETNAM, headed for my assigned unit, the 199th Light Infantry Brigade, the same one I had left six months prior. Once there, I took up the chaplain's obligatory tasks of providing spiritual and moral support for the soldiers, especially those facing death daily, the infantry men.

I felt no guilt over continuing my chaplain's duties, even though at this point I was planning to leave the priesthood when my tour of duty was over. In addition, confusion about the Vietnam War was slowly beginning to seep into my consciousness, like fog descending over a highway. Despite my unsettled state I continued saying Mass, visiting the wounded, hearing confessions, and going along on patrols and ambushes.

At that time there was a growing administrative emphasis on body counts as an exclusive measure of military effectiveness. From where I sat, there seemed to be more concern for the number of enemy killed than the number of U.S. KIAs (killed in action) and wounded. Too frequently, the bodies counted were Vietnamese civilians, including women, children, and old men. An unidentified body was, "of course," an enemy soldier. This body count fixation troubled me, but I did not reveal my concern until I accidentally discovered a brigade policy of rewards for kills.

On a late afternoon in the summer of 1969, I was visiting a battalion-sized forward base camp located on the outskirts of Saigon. Around four hundred men were bivouacked there in a deserted, bombed-out furniture factory. Happy to have a roof over their heads in a relatively secure area, the men were in good spirits, scattered about in small groups, some cleaning weapons, dining on C-rations, or playing poker. Smart players got rich; I made back my five-dollar contribution and moved on.

Leaving the card game, I walked over to a young soldier sitting on an empty ammunition box, shining his boots to a mirror-like luster. "Going home or taking your R&R?" I asked.

"R&R," he replied with a wide smile.

"Where to?" I continued.

"Oh, it's just a three-day in-country R&R to Vung Tau. I got three kills." He said it so casually. I was shocked speechless. This was my first experience with rewards for killing. I said nothing to the young man, did an abrupt about-face, and walked briskly to the command bunker.

The battalion commander was sitting at his desk going over an area map. We were new to each other. I was so angry, I forgot to introduce myself or apologize for intruding. In a tone of authoritative, righteous indignation I blurted, "Colonel, are you aware of a policy granting three-day R&Rs at Vung Tau for three kills?" Calmly, with no loss of composure, he looked up at me, recognized me as a chaplain and responded matter of factly, "It's not my policy. It came down from brigade."

"Then I'm off to see the general," I replied.

"Good luck," he grinned. He couldn't have cared less. He was just implementing brigade policy.

It was twilight when my assistant and I left the forward base camp, not the best of times to be traveling the roads of Vietnam, but I was on a self-imposed mission that began the moment I heard the young soldier's enthusiastic explanation for shining his shoes. Ordinarily, my assistant drove the jeep assigned to me, but my adrenalin was on overload and I needed to drive myself and vent the feelings that were urging me on. Also he was a better shotgun rider. We arrived at the rear area of the 199th without incident, but it was too late then to go another thirty miles north to Xuan Loc, the new headquarters location.

Before descending into an uneasy sleep, I penned a letter to the chief of chaplains in Washington, D.C., explaining my opposition to the brigade policy of awarding R&Rs for enemy KIAs. I closed the letter with a question, "What the hell are we doing here?" The following morning my assistant and I were on the road to Xuan Loc. This time he drove while I mulled over what I would say to the general. I did not try to make an appointment. As far as I was concerned, the gravity of the matter to be discussed superseded military protocol. Unfortunately, I had not simmered down enough. Looking back on this chapter in my military life, I wish I had been more courteous and respectful to the general. I'm not sure I would have been as bold and brassy had I not been a recipient of the Medal of Honor, an award that commands the respect of every military person from the lowest to the highest rank.

It did not take much convincing for the general's secretary to announce my presence and need to see the general immediately. He was alone, sitting behind a dark wooden office desk in a twenty-square-foot room appointed with a plethora of military trappings, the most prominent being flags and wall maps. I walked in alone and stood about ten feet directly in front of him. He did not stand. I don't remember saluting nor do I remember any perfunctory greetings.

Standing on the pinnacle of moral high ground, I got right to the point. "General, I'm here for very serious reasons. As recently as last night I stumbled on the existence of what I am told is a brigade policy of granting in-country R&Rs, three days at Vung Tau, for three confirmed enemy kills. Also, I'm concerned about the excessive emphasis placed on body counts. We seem more concerned about the number of enemy dead than we are about the number of our men killed or wounded."

As if someone had scripted this encounter with the general, a stocky, full-bird colonel trotted into the room unannounced, ignored me, and blurted out his message of supreme import, "Sir, we have contact! Three enemy dead."

He obviously thought his announcement would please the general, who responded judiciously (I suspect for my benefit), "How many casualties for us?"

"None, sir."

"Good."

The colonel bounced out of the room as abruptly as he had entered and I continued, "General, if this R&R-for-kill's policy is not abrogated immediately, I will offer my resignation. If it is not honored, I will send a copy to every paper in the United States explaining why."

My attitude was too much for the general to think over before he spoke. Who the hell was I to tell him how to run his brigade? He rose from his seat and exploded: "I'll be goddamned if I'll sit here and allow you to threaten me!!!"

Feeling I was in the right from a moral standpoint, I was not intimidated by the manner or the rank of the man. I had nothing to lose. The Army was not my chosen career. A sense of calm came over me and I responded blandly, "Sir, I'm not threatening you. I'm just telling you what I'm prepared to do if this policy is not rescinded immediately. I came to Vietnam to support our brave young men not bounty hunters."

The general calmed down and I excused myself. That night, for the first and last time in my life, I was invited to attend a brigade officers briefing. I cannot remember the exact words of the abrogation of the "three kills for three days R&R" policy, but it *was* rescinded.

At the time, I felt good about the results of my complaint. No one ever told me that I was out of order or that I should stay out of the business of war. I did deprive soldiers of a chance to have a few days off in a little seacoast town populated with beautiful young Vietnamese women trying to make a living selling their bodies. I'm not sorry for that, but I do regret being so abrupt with the general.

Lunch with the General

I thought the bounty-hunter issue was now safely behind me, but I had forgotten about my irate letter to the chief of chaplains that closed with the line, "What the hell are we doing here?" Chaplain Sampson was not a man to avoid conflict. He immediately informed the number one chaplain in Vietnam, who was stationed at Military Assistance Command Vietnam (MACV) in Saigon.

A week after my interview with the general of the 199th I received a phone call from Saigon from the number one chaplain. He graciously invited me to dine with him and General Creighton Abrams at the general's private quarters in Saigon. I was honored. The chaplain informed me that General Abrams was concerned over the subject matter of my letter to the chief of chaplains.

Protocol demanded that I inform the general of the 199th about this invitation. I needed his permission to leave the brigade. He granted permission without hesitation and asked me to give General Abrams his regards.

I was beginning to appreciate the power of a chaplain in matters moral. The Medal of Honor helped, of course, but it was not essential. What is integral to the influence of a military chaplain is that he stands firmly on moral ground.

I felt like a VIP when the helicopter from MACV landed on the 199th helipad to "heli-taxi" me to Saigon for lunch with the military commander of all Vietnam. The chief of chaplains met my chopper and escorted me to a triple-size, heavily sandbagged, steel-framed Quonset hut, the private living quarters of General Abrams. The general's official residence could have passed easily for a warehouse.

We, "Number One" and I, were met at the door by General Abrams himself, who led us to a spacious dining room and a long rectangular table set for three. I imagined mahogany beneath the immaculate white tablecloth. The two of us sat opposite the general as he opened the conversation with a warm, smiling welcome.

He was unlike any military man I had ever met. There was no rigidity in his bearing, no strident dictatorial tone in his voice and no aura of importance contorting his face. He was below average height and slightly on the portly side, but with no bulging protrusions. I had met him before, briefly, when he pinned the Distinguished Service Cross on my chest at a forward base camp award ceremony, but, of course, he did not remember me.

Before the food arrived, the general surprised me by asking for my choice of background music. He was proud of his collection and confident that he could fill my request. My musical appreciation was plebeian, to say the least. I felt that the general was expecting a classical selection like Bach, Beethoven, or Mozart, whose names I knew, but whose music I would not have recognized. He had to be disappointed when I mentioned Broadway musicals as my preferred musical genre. "Do you have a favorite?" he asked. I couldn't think of one that I was sure he would have, so I chose three of my favorites: "My Fair Lady," "Music Man," and "The Sound of Music." He played the latter followed by his choice of something classical.

The meal was sumptuous, what you would expect of military royalty, served by a Filipino cook and waiter dressed in a white waistcoat and trousers. I had never dined more elegantly anywhere. I don't remember our chitchat over the chicken entrée. The heavy conversation began as the waiter was removing the china.

Looking directly at me, the general began: "Chaplain, the situation that motivated you to write to the chief of chaplains: I know some of the details, but I need to hear your version."

I proceeded to tell General Abrams what I had told the general of the 199th, with emphasis at the end on the bounty-hunter nature of the reward-for-kills policy. He leaned back in his chair, heaved heavily, and said, "This is not my policy, but I understand how such policies evolve."

"General," I interjected. "I need to tell you that this policy was abrogated the very evening of the day I reported it. I was told that it came down from the Ninth Division. It did not originate in the 199th."

"Thank you, Chaplain. Be assured that I will attend to this matter. I deplore such policies, but as I said, I understand how they evolve. Everyone must answer to someone above him, me included."

I was not interested in the origin of the policy, but I appreciated the general's frank admission of his frustration with the misguided efforts of subordinates to please their superiors. Awards for kills were one way of increasing the body count, then the principal means of measuring success. What politicians and military leaders did not appreciate was that counting dead bodies as a measure of success could easily lead to killing innocents and counting them as enemies.

I returned to the 199th satisfied that I had done my duty, feeling honored to have met the most powerful American in Vietnam.

16

Sharon & Vietnam Again

In THE SUMMER OF 1969, I was returning to Vietnam by way of the West Coast. A college friend suggested that I stop to visit his sister. Sharon lived and worked in San Diego, one of the cities of my childhood. I allotted myself three days for the visit and planned to lodge in a downtown hotel. I knew very little about Sharon. Her brother, Greg, told me she was single, in her late twenties, working for an advertisement agency, fiercely independent, making her way on her own. She was romantically unattached, but still smarting from a relationship that had gone sour. Greg told her that I was a war hero and a nice guy who needed to see some beautiful sights for memory's sake when things got rough in Vietnam. It did not occur to Greg that Sharon might become one of those memories. Neither did it occur to me. He also told her that I was a Catholic chaplain.

As I write about this significant event in my life, I'm puzzled over following through on Greg's suggestion that I visit Sharon. I'm also questioning her willingness to play host to a man she did not know. Perhaps my motivation to meet Sharon involved a desire for an involvement I was unwilling to admit. Perhaps her willingness to accommodate me was based on her brother's inflated estimation of me.

Sharon had lived in San Diego for nine years, knew the city well, and loved to show it off to visitors. She met me at the airport on a late Thursday afternoon holding a black-on-white welcome sign with my name on it. She stood at the arrival gate, her eyes panning the line of deplaning passengers for a uniformed Army officer in summer dress slacks with small gold crosses pinned to his collar. I wore the uniform proudly in those days of political ignorance. I was a hawk, worse yet, a hawk dressed in clerical clothing. As I approached, she broke into an engaging smile and in a tone of unshakable confidence said, "Charlie! Welcome! You must be tired," she said. "It's a long flight from Florida. Are you hungry?"

"Not very. I ate on the plane, but I could do with a snack."

"We can have that at my place. I'm only thirty minutes away."

"I'm ready, but if you don't mind I'd like to book reservations at a nearby hotel. I'm due to fly to San Francisco early Monday morning. From there, I bus up to Travis Air Force Base for a military flight to Saigon."

"No need for the hotel." she replied. "Very expensive! If you don't mind sleeping on a couch, you can stay at my place."

I was feeling a tad apprehensive about spending three nights in the seclusion of a young woman's apartment.

"Sharon, I don't mind sleeping on the couch, but…."

She interrupted! "It's settled then. Let's go." I did not object. My internal caution light began to blink, warning me to be careful. Shouldering my canvas duffle bag I walked with Sharon to her daisy-colored Volkswagen bug.

Greg had told me little about Sharon's history or her physical appearance, assuming that her size, shape, hair and eye color would be of no interest to me. Greg was right about Sharon's history, but wrong about my appreciation of her physical attributes, which were alluring. The vow of chastity did not inhibit my appreciation for feminine beauty; in fact, it enhanced it, like the mystical attraction of secret and forbidden knowledge. However, it did impose specific limitations related to my association with women. I could look, but not touch, admire, but not lust. Warm feelings were permissible as long as they were monitored and controlled. Admiration of and warm feelings for Sharon were there from the moment we met. I questioned the prudence of placing myself in what could qualify as an occasion of sin. She gave me no reason whatsoever to suspect seduction. However, an internal moral casuistry was going on as we walked to her car. Nine years of isolated seminary training with little to no female contact had educated me in the art of emotional control. This served me well in the first six years of a ministry that included almost daily association with women, some of whom were nuns. The "custody of the eyes" practice that my seminary spiritual advisors had inculcated in us – be careful where you look and on what you focus – was an effective defense against the sexual magnetism unconsciously emitted by some attractive women and seductively employed by others. Even nuns dressed in clothing of another century, plain black-and-white habits that covered their bodies from head to toe, could present a problem. Imagination blurs reality. Perfunctory courtesy hugs, associated with greetings and goodbyes, were about as close as I had come to a woman's body since my college days. I had also forgotten the intoxicating scent of female closeness. My control quotient was in line for testing.

Sharon lived on the ground floor of a one-bedroom apartment in a complex of four, a short walk to Mission Beach. Her place was cozy, artfully appointed, warm, and friendly, but two would be a crowd in a hurry if they were anything but lovers. Sensing some rigidity and apprehension on my part as I surveyed her modest living room furnished with one easy chair, a comfortable couch, and a small coffee table and lamp.

She said, "Relax, Charlie. Take your shoes off and change into something comfortable. You look so stiff in that uniform."

I smiled and thanked her. "I have some civilian clothes," I explained, "but nothing formal."

"Can I fix you a drink? Greg says you are a martini man. On his advice I bought this especially for you. I hear it's good stuff." With the agility of a bartender she put together a five-to-one Beefeater martini, straight up with three stuffed green olives on a toothpick. She poured herself a glass of white wine. I raised my drink of the gods and toasted, "Here's to Greg."

We sat, I on the couch and Sharon in an easy chair facing me. We began sharing personal histories backwards from the present. She opened the first page of my memoir with a question: "How did you and Greg become friends?"

"We met while working as counselors at a summer camp for rich kids."

"I remember, Camp Cloudland."

"You're close. Camp Cloudmont atop Lookout Mountain in Alabama. That's also where I met a visiting priest who told me I might have a vocation to the priesthood and encouraged me to give it a try."

"And you did, of course."

"Yes, but not right away. I was not ready to give up women for life. The question of a vocation to the priesthood, though haunting me, remained unanswered until I finished my second year of college."

"What was it that enabled you to overcome your desire for women or a woman in your life?"

"Well, I don't know that I've ever overcome the desire, Sharon. It's always present. You just have to control it. My decision to give the priesthood a try is a rather strange, convoluted story. Can I save it for another time?"

"Of course," she replied.

The martini, a powerful drink, is sometimes referred to as "truth serum" as it tends to relax the body, squelch inhibitions, dampen caution, and loosen the tongue. As I was expounding on the merits of the martini, I began to feel the effects I was describing. Fortunately, I stopped on the edge of the monologue and sent the conversation ball into Sharon's court.

"Sharon, why did you move from Florida to San Diego?"

Without hesitation she said, "Romance. I followed my college lover to San Diego. Listening to him describe his city, I fell in love with San Diego. We got here and Jim left. I'm still in love with the city, but I'm over Jim. At least the heavy part is over. It's the anger and dishonesty that hangs on. We were very happy until he began to lose interest in me and attend to an attractive blonde, a former friend and coworker of mine. Ironically, I introduced them at a Christmas office party."

"How many Christmases ago?"

"Last Christmas," she answered. "Jim simply exchanged lovers. That's the long and short of it. I was brokenhearted at first, angry, but not bitter. It's not my nature to nurture hurt. There's a tough side to me that I get from my mother, who's had more than her fill of unfaithful men. In a way, I feel sorry for Jim, knowing his new friend as I do. Also I'm glad we never married; nothing legal to settle. And I'm even happier that we did not have children. However, I need not have worried. A recent medical exam revealed that I will never have my own children. I'm not seeing anyone right now, and to tell the truth, I'm not interested. I'm a little man shy."

Sensing sadness in her tone, I rose from the couch, stepped to the side of her chair, placed my hand on her shoulder, and said, "I'm sorry, Sharon." It was a genuine expression of compassion. I had no intention of making a romantic move, no conscious seductive plans.

She accepted the gesture gracefully by placing her hand delicately on mine saying, "Thank you."

This was the first time we touched. Without intending it to be so, it was the beginning. I returned to the couch. She went to the kitchen to prepare a snack: cheddar cheese and crackers. She made no apologies, but she did tell me to look forward to a big California breakfast at her favorite coffee shop by the bay. "My treat. Unfortunately, we have to go early, because I must work tomorrow; however, I'm free Saturday and Sunday and I can take Monday off to drive you to the airport."

It was midnight on the East Coast and Sharon could see that I was laboring at conversation. Jet lag and the martini were creeping up on me. She made the couch into a bed, said "Pleasant dreams," and disappeared into the bedroom. I was completely relaxed, no caution light blinking, just enjoying the free-falling feeling of the moment, past and future blocked. There was nothing yet to feel guilty about. Vietnam was a lifetime away.

The California breakfast of waffles, eggs, and bacon garnished with wedges of avocado and orange was good and plenty, enough to carry me through to an evening meal at a Japanese restaurant of Sharon's recommendation. While Sharon worked, I walked Mission Beach, listening to the symphony of the waves gently embracing the shore, disappearing into the sand, foaming and hissing as they retreated. I've always had an affinity for the sea. Rarely have I lived between East and West coasts.

As I walked, I could not help but reflect on the way I was feeling about Sharon. Body chemistry was at work. I was looking forward to being with her again. How good it would be if we could walk the beach together. I said to myself, "I wonder if I'm falling in love. This is silly. Be careful. You have no idea of her feelings. Don't make a fool of yourself; you have no right to fall in love." I walked, rested, and walked some more, about six miles all told.

Before I knew it, morning had morphed into noon and noon into afternoon. When I arrived in Sharon's neighborhood, the yellow VW bug parked close to her apartment told me she was already home from work. I was about to knock on the front door when it opened, magically framing Sharon in the opening. She was still in her work outfit. In a fleeting bit of fantasy, I imagined her greeting me with open arms, but she didn't, and I returned to reality.

"We're going out for supper. Remember?"

"Yes, but I'll need a shower first."

"Check my closet. You'll find some clothing left behind by Jim and Greg. Greg's coat and Jim's dress pants should fit you nicely."

In a potpourri of borrowed evening attire, I set off to the restaurant, looking and feeling unlike my military or clerical self, except for short-cropped hair. Sharon requested a seat by the window overlooking the bay. The sun looked like a golden haystack sinking into the sea.

"This is one of my favorite places, Charlie, great views and wonderful seafood."

"It is beautiful, Sharon. Do you come here often?"

"Only on special occasions," she replied.

I smiled and offered, "Thank you. I'm so glad Greg suggested that I visit his sister in San Diego."

"Me too."

The waiter arrived and Sharon took charge.

"Remember, Charlie! This is my treat, so don't look on the right side of the menu. It's something I'd like to do for a soldier on his way to Vietnam."

"Sharon, I don't think of myself as a soldier."

"Well, you must have done something to receive that medal. Greg said you are a hero."

I changed the subject.

"I'm hungry, Sharon. Can we order? I haven't eaten since breakfast."

We had the works: cocktails, a mixed seafood platter for two, dessert, and after-dinner drinks. It was around nine o'clock when we left the restaurant. At Sharon's suggestion we walked along the dimly lit promenade by the bay. Now and then our fingers touched as if by accident. A cool wind was picking up and neither of us was dressed for it. Instinctively, I slipped my arm around her shoulder and drew her close. She did not resist. I felt wonderful, sharing in the warmth of our closeness. It was the kind of sensation I had not experienced in sixteen years. For about fifteen minutes we walked in silence except for the rhythmic sounds of the sea. When it grew too chilly to continue, we returned to her VW. We were falling in love, without a care for the consequences. I didn't want to think. I just wanted to be and let be.

The bucket-seated VW was not the best of places for continued expressions of feelings, so I reluctantly released her hand as Sharon drove the stick-shift vehicle back to her apartment. I thanked her for an evening I would never forget. I entered the apartment first at her invitation and waited for her to close and lock the door. She turned away from the door and into my arms. We embraced with peaked passion that had been building from the time we met.

It was our first kiss, mine in sixteen years, and our first chest to breast embrace. I lifted her easily and took her to the couch without disturbing the fusion of our bodies. It did not occur to me to take a left at her bedroom. Once on the couch, we lay entwined but did not disrobe. Sharon invited me to join her in bed for the rest of the night, saying we would be more comfortable, but I declined. I needed to reflect before risking continuance.

Despite what she had said earlier about not being able to have children, in the light of my uncertain future, I could not chance pregnancy. In addition, clouds of guilt were beginning to gather on the perimeter of my conscience. However, they were not dark clouds of remorse nor heavy enough to quell the feelings of a beautiful encounter. The hands on the living room clock joined at twelve. Physically and emotionally spent, reeling with feelings suppressed for a little less than half my lifetime, I descended uneasily into the unconscious.

I awoke Sunday morning to the scent and sound of bacon frying. Sharon was in the kitchen cooking breakfast, still in her nightgown. I was in a T-shirt that covered my jockey shorts. I remained on the couch enjoying the excitement of watching her move gracefully about the kitchen.

We sat opposite one another at a dinette table for two, hands joined across the abyss that separated us, saying not a word, half smiling, looking directly into one another's eyes. She spoke first.

"How do you feel about last night, Charlie? Do you feel bad? Guilty? What?"

"Sharon, I can't say that I wish it had never happened. It was wonderful. I'm on the edge of guilt, which is nothing new for me. Something is happening to me now and I'm not sure what it is. I need time to think. What about you? How are you feeling?"

Half smiling, she replied: "Well, I'm not feeling bad or guilty. I'm happy. I may be falling in love with you. I know what love feels like. It's exhilarating. I tingle all over. On the other hand, I'm concerned for you. I don't think this is the best way for you to be returning to Vietnam, but what can I do? I can't help the way I feel. Neither of us planned this. Can we just part, accept what happened gratefully as an incredible moment in time, be glad we did not go further, and move on? I can do that, Charlie. Can you? I've learned the hard way not to hold on to anything or anyone."

I marveled at the way she expressed herself, so calmly, so directly, so clearly. I wasn't ready to respond.

"Sharon, will you walk the beach with me? I think better with the surf in the background."

"Let's go," she said excitedly.

"I'd better change into something less comfortable."

"Me too," she laughed.

It was an ideal day for beach walking. The Pacific was pacific. We removed our shoes and walked on the edge of the receding tide, listening to the gentle voice of the waves disappearing at the end of their journey from afar. It was my turn to answer Sharon's questions.

"Sharon, this may be a good time to answer the question you asked yesterday about what enabled me to overcome my desire for a woman in my life. Do you remember?"

"Oh yes."

"I think I said I never lost the desire. I just have to control it."

"Is that what happened last night? You just lost control?"

"Not exactly. Control never entered my mind. I was under your influence."

"So, it's my fault?"

"No, Sharon. Your influence on me is not a fault. It's a fact, a fantastic, magnetic fact that I had no inclination to resist last night or for that matter right now."

"Then maybe we should go back to the apartment – *now!*"

"No, not until I try to explain what finally moved me to enter the seminary and train for the priesthood."

"Okay, I'm listening."

My Story

Here is the long explanation I gave Sharon: The decision to test the validity of my vocation came after a chance encounter with a young woman after a college football game. In the rear seat of a friend's car we necked and petted beyond my moral limits. While our sexual activity did not include intercourse as such, it did qualify as sinful, confessional material. The next morning found me feeling the need to go to confession.

Most confessors tended to be kind and understanding, yet I still found it tedious to admit that I had allowed myself to go beyond the limits of Catholic premarital sexual boundaries. On a Saturday afternoon that spring, I took my reluctant but needy self to the local Catholic Church. Confessions began at three o'clock. The pastor of the church was on duty. We did not know one another, but I had heard him preach and concluded that he was not the sort of man I would have sought out for confession. He was a stern dictatorial man of unhappy countenance, given to tirades in the pulpit about the gravity of missing Mass on Sunday and the obligation to support the church financially. I felt a bit uneasy, but I had to get cleaned up, back on good terms with God, so to speak.

"Bless me, Father, for I have sinned. My last confession was a month ago. I entertained bad thoughts about three times. I missed Mass once. I kissed and petted with my girlfriend one time."

The priest replied in a not-so-tender tone: "Is that all?" he asked.

"Yes."

"What do you mean by bad thoughts? Be specific!"

"I imagined myself with my girlfriend in an intimate way."

"Go on."

"We were making love."

"You mean you were engaged in sexual intercourse?"

"Not exactly. We were fully clothed."

I was ready to bolt the confessional, but he was just warming up. I think he would have made a good torturer.

"Clothes or no clothes, son, you were having sexual intercourse and sexual intercourse is for the married only. Outside of marriage, it's a mortal sin. Do you understand?"

"Yes, but...."

"No buts about it. You must control your thoughts as well as your actions; keep your hands to yourself."

The confessor continued, "You have committed some grave sins, son. For your penance say one rosary. Now make a sincere Act of Contrition."

From the depths of my being, with all the sorrow I could muster, I began, "O my God I'm heartily sorry for having offended thee...."

I left the confessional feeling humiliated and angry rather

than relieved. As I walked to the bus stop, humiliation faded, but anger grew. Rather than curse the priest and thus have to make another confession, I imagined myself as a priest and thought, "I can do better than that." Thus my journey to the seminary began. Nine years later, I was ordained.

Sharon listened without interruption throughout this lengthy explanation, then responded, "If I understand you correctly, Charlie, you became a priest because you thought you could do a better job or be a better priest than the one who was mean to you in the confessional."

I continued with my explanation: Actually, he wasn't the reason I became a priest. He was the reason I decided to give the priesthood a try. The seed of a vocation was planted in my mind or heart or soul, whatever, when I was fourteen by a Catholic nun. She impressed upon me the importance of responding to a call from God to serve him. If I refused to answer the call, I would go through life restlessly wondering if I had a vocation. Worse yet, I might lose my soul.

Despite the heavy vocational trip she laid on me, I was able to put the idea of the priesthood on hold throughout my teens and early college days of dating and sexual activity, which included everything short of intercourse. Then, that visiting priest I mentioned in summer camp watered the vocational seed the nun had planted with the suggestion that the only way I could be sure God was calling or not calling me was to enter the seminary.

Return to Vietnam

We held hands as we walked along the water's edge, searching for words to match our feelings.

"Sharon, will you give me time to settle down and sort out my feelings? One thing is for sure. I must return to Vietnam. I can't say that I never want to see you again. I know I won't and can't forget you. But, I don't know if I can leave the priesthood, at least not right now. I've never been this close to trying. I've never been what I would call happy in the priesthood. It's like something I had to do. God was calling me and I couldn't say no. I struggled to enter and I struggled to stay, and now I may be struggling to leave. It's like I want something to happen, but I'm afraid to make it happen. Well, something, rather someone, *did* happen. *You!* Now what? You're right. This is certainly not the most ideal time to fall in love, if that's what's happening to me."

"Time and space is being forced upon us, Charlie. Let's wait and see what they tell us."

We did not make love with or without clothing on our last evening together. On and off we held hands, hugged, and kissed cautiously, restraining the passion we had so recklessly unleashed over the past twenty-four hours. Finally, we went to sleep in one another's arms, unable to separate until first light on the morning of my departure.

"Will you write, Charlie?"

"Of course. No problem. Our mail is not censored."

She drove me to the airport and dropped me at curbside as I requested. I did not want to prolong the agony of departure in a public place.

"Goodbye, Sharon. You'll be hearing from me soon."

"I'll be waiting."

There were no final ultimatums. Neither of us was ready for a final farewell. We had to wait and see what time and further reflection would bring.

Fall from Grace

Letters to and from Sharon began to flow regularly. Rare was the day that I did not write. A love affair had begun and I was in deep. I decided to leave the priesthood. To do so legally was important to me at the time. It would involve laicization, an ecclesiastical process impossible to begin before the completion of my tour of duty ten months away.

Among the most difficult tasks facing many Catholic priests giving up the priesthood is informing his parents, especially his mother, of his decision to leave. Mothers of priests share in the honor of a son's calling to serve God and do not easily let go of that honor. My mother was no exception. She was the proud mother of a priest. I thought my relationship with her was strong enough that I could tell her of my decision and allow her to share my happiness. I was not entirely right. Her initial reaction to a tape I mailed introducing Sharon is summed up in a remark she made to a mutual friend: "From hero to bum."

Somehow the tape ended up in the hands of my major religious superior in Washington, D.C. It's not clear to me who sent it and I'd just as soon not know. A week later I received a letter from the superior general of my religious order stating his concern and offering to help by sending a fellow priest to meet me in Japan to discuss the serious decision I had made. I did not need or want help. I responded, telling him I had no intention of doing anything until I returned to the States and it would not be necessary to send a priest to Japan. I learned later that the priest my superior intended to send was a good friend, who was disappointed to have missed a chance to see Japan.

"How could you do this to your mother?" a friend wrote. I knew Mother would be hurt, but I also knew that she loved me more than she loved the prestige of being the mother of a priest. When I learned of her dismay I asked her, "What is more important to you, my happiness or being the mother of a priest?"

Confronted with the question, she answered in a way that maternal love dictated, "Your happiness of course."

Another incident related to my newfound happiness and decision to leave the priesthood infuriated me at the time. My mother confided in an old friend of mine, no doubt seeking consolation and advice. (His name will remain known only to him.) He was a good friend and what he did was done on my behalf, which I failed to appreciate at the time. Being killed with kindness is one of the worst kinds of unkind wounds because the recipient is left with little room for redress. He did some investigating and discovered who Sharon was and where she lived. He wanted to make sure I had not been seduced by a loose woman. On borrowed time and money, he flew to San Diego. Their two-day visit must have been harmonious. Sharon never mentioned it and he never said a negative word about her. He shared this intrusion into my life while I was in Vietnam. I'm glad I was thirteen thousand miles away. Fury like I've seldom known welled up in me and moved me to write, "I can never trust you again." He responded sagely, "We cannot be friends without trust." I was not too angry to appreciate truth.

Emotionally, I was happily on the way to a new life, but mentally, I began to question whether my feelings for Sharon were those of love or lust, or a combination of both. I was thirty-eight and still a physical virgin. The curiosity of physical union with a woman was still with me. Fully clothed intercourse was as close as I had come to the mysterious pleasure I imagined flesh-to-flesh intercourse would hold. I did not mention my confusion to Sharon.

An Khe

After six months into my extended tour, I was entitled to some R&R, a week of rest and relaxation at one of a number of exotic places such Australia, Manila, Japan, or Hawaii, where most of the married met their wives and where many of the young single men sowed their wild oats. I suggested to Sharon that she meet me in Hawaii and she responded enthusiastically. Initially, I was excited over the prospect of being alone with Sharon for a whole week on a romantic island, but before many days passed, my past began to speak. I was able to slam the door on the intrusion; however, one question rose to puzzle me. Am I in love? Infatuated? Or simply responding to sexual needs long suppressed? I had never had sex in the strict physical, flesh-to-flesh manner. Premarital sex was a powerful Catholic taboo that kept me out of trouble in high school and college. Also, the possibility of having a child out of wedlock frightened me. I needed counsel, but from whom, where, and how?

The chance to share my confusion came with an invitation to participate in a day of recollection for Catholic chaplains sponsored by a nonmilitary Vincentian priest who ran an orphanage in Saigon. This was an opportunity to enjoy a sumptuous meal, swap stories, and share stateside news. I recognized one of the attending priests, Max, as a classmate from Chaplain School. He had just six months to serve on his second tour. He was assigned to the famous Eleventh Armored Cavalry, known as the Black Horse Regiment. Like the 199th, the Black Horse operated around Saigon. There was enough kinship between us for me to comfortably discuss my romantic story with him. Declining to laugh off my tale, Max reached into his wallet and pulled out a picture of the woman he said he was going home to marry. This time I was the one who laughed.

I began to think I had been living a terribly sheltered life. Neither the Franciscan nor Max expressed any guilt or apprehension over what they were planning to do. It was like the Church was wrong for demanding celibacy of its priests, and these men felt they had no obligation to continue participating in the error of the Church. Certainly, it was not my place to judge, and I was not inclined to discuss the matter further. Max was no help in helping me out of my predicament. I was on my own.

My chaplain duties required a lot of helicopter rides, which are not good for the ears. Too much exposure to the high-pitched whine of a chopper engine can destroy the fine-hair follicles that distinguish tonal sounds. I noticed myself frequently asking others to repeat themselves. An exam revealed a significant loss of hearing on lower-tone levels. The doctor recommended a less noisy environment. There was no such thing as a quiet place in Vietnam, but some duty stations were better than others, like hospitals.

A chaplain's slot opened up at a Mash (Mobile Army Surgical Hospital) unit in the central highlands, where wounded and dead soldiers were flown directly from the battlefield for stabilization or the morgue. My request was granted and expedited within a week. I think the general was happy to be rid of me. He gave me a glowing letter of recommendation, far in excess of what I deserved. I knew I had been a pain in his posterior.

The trip to An Khe, my new assignment, began at Tan Son Nhat Airport, Saigon. It was a four-hour helicopter ride due north along the coast to Quin Yon and another hour-long inland flight over mountains in which NVA (North Vietnamese Army) and VC military forces were roaming. I was scheduled for an early morning flight so I took a room in a small hotel close to the airport. The room was on the sixth floor beneath a roof-top bar and restaurant. Pungent scents of Asian cooking drew me to the balcony, where I heard the unfamiliar sound of Western songs sung in English by female Vietnamese vocalists. The singers spoke no English, but they had flawlessly memorized lyrics. The song sung over and over in Vietnamese bars and service men's clubs was "Detroit City": "Last night I went to sleep in Detroit City...." I doubt there is a Vietnam veteran anywhere who does not remember that song. I wonder if the Iraqi vets are singing the same song.

I entered the bar wearing a sport shirt and khaki pants, took a seat at a circular booth, and waited for someone to wait on me. No sooner was I seated than a lovely Vietnamese waitress took my order for Scotch on the rocks. Before she returned, four more young ladies appeared and seated themselves, without invitation, on each side of me. I was trapped in the middle of a scented Asian bouquet of beautiful women, each one gowned in a different color *ao dai* (the traditional woman's dress in Vietnam). I immediately felt uneasy, but did not protest.

When my Scotch arrived, I excused myself and walked out to the open-air roof-top terrace, relieved of the overwhelming presence of female pulchritude. Leaning against the waist-high wall, I looked out over the city dotted with multicolored lights and clouded with scents unmistakably Asian. I feared the sudden appearance of a U.S. officer who might recognize me. But before my second sip of Scotch, one of the girls nestled to my side, close enough for me to feel the pressure of her presence. All of a sudden I saw her as a means of satisfying my sexual curiosity. Slipping my arm around her slim waist, I drew her close, close enough for her to feel my excited interest. This was her cue. "Do you want me?" she asked.

Before I could answer, she took my hand and said, "We go to your room."

"I don't have a room. I'm staying with a friend," I lied.

I did not want to spend the night with her. For security reasons I did not want her to know where I was staying. In addition, I was leaving early in the morning. All I wanted was a "short time," the common term GIs used for a quickie.

"Just a short time," I said insistently.

"No short time!" she responded.

"Okay. Forget it," I said, releasing her and moving away. Separated, she looked at me pensively and said, "You wait here." Five minutes later she returned, held out her hand, and said, "You come with me."

She led me to a small, dimly lit room furnished with two wicker chairs and a futon single bed. All the comforts needed for a short time. There was no conversation. She went directly to the bed, stepped out of her slippers and dress, and dropped into a receptive position. Her body language spoke for her as my body responded. There was no foreplay. For different reasons, neither of us needed it. This was strictly business for her; for me, the end of curiosity. I'm sure she had no idea that it was my first time. Perhaps she thought so after it was over. I was at the peak of my excitement when we merged. It's a wonder I made it to her inner sanctum. Over in seconds, a short time for sure, perhaps the shortest time in her career. Before I could say thank you, she was on her feet and headed for the shower. I followed.

She laughed as she handed me the soap. It was stupid not to use protection; for her sake to prevent pregnancy, for mine to preclude disease. I'm sure she would not have objected, but I had to experience the real thing; otherwise, I would have blamed the absence of pleasure on the barrier of the condom, leaving curiosity unsatisfied.

This first-time sexual experience turned out to be the costliest thing I've ever paid for, but not in terms of the price of the short time. That was incredibly cheap, but the girl was not cheap. Her integrity, honesty, and good-heartedness surfaced when I opened my wallet. I had no idea of the going rate for a short time. A GI once gave me five dollars to give to the poor with the statement, "It's no big deal for me, Father. One less short time."

I had about twenty dollars.

I'm sure five dollars would have been sufficient, but I was in no mood to bargain. She counted the fist-full of money, looked at my empty wallet, and peeled off two dollars with the comment, "You need some money."

As I walked alone back to my hotel, I began to ask myself, "My God! Is this what everyone is so excited about? Is this what the soldiers literally risk their lives for?" (GIs would often sneak through the perimeter wire at night and go into a nearby village for short times.)

Alone on the rock-hard bed in my hotel room, looking at the ceiling through the whirling paddles of the overhead fan, the haunting voice of conscience began to worm its way into my reality and remind me of a sacred vow broken and the possibility of a disease contracted. "Suppose I've caught something? What am I going to do?"

The Morning After

I woke up the morning after, feeling the full import of the convoluted reasoning that led to my fall from grace. Curiosity satisfied, but at a price of everlasting regret. Reflecting on the merits of this particular act, the words of a popular Peggy Lee song came to mind: "Is That All There Is?" The feelings I had for Sharon were as mysterious as ever. The energizing chemistry of erotic love gave way to the enervating fear of having contracted a disease, the fear of public exposure, and the worry about sharing my situation with Sharon during my upcoming R&R in Hawaii. When fear and imagination unite to torment a person, the borders of the bizarre are unlimited. I had entered the forbidden territory of mortal sin and broken a vow as spiritually serious as breeching a marriage contract.

I believed God's forgiveness was limitless, but I knew nothing about Sharon's tolerance. We had no history of offending and forgiving one another. This comes after sharing imperfections, and this was one fault I was not ready to share. How could she possibly understand? Excitement over our planned rendezvous was waning. One problem at a time, I said to myself.

First, I had to be sure I was free from VD. Gonorrhea was not uncommon among the soldiers and occasionally a case of syphilis appeared. I was headed for a hospital, but not as a patient, at least not openly as a patient. I couldn't just walk in as the newly assigned, only living Medal of Honor chaplain, and say to the receiving nurse, "I'd like to be tested for VD." Such a revelation would rupture staff confidentiality. Some would find it funny, others would be scandalized. I was more afraid of social exposure than the disease itself. There were so many who would be embarrassed, my mother at the top of the list. I visualized my picture on the front page of the *Jacksonville Journal* receiving the Medal of Honor, captioned "Hometown Hero Disgraced." No doubt I would receive many requests for interviews.

At Tan Son Nhat Airport I boarded a C-130, used for in-country transport of military personnel. The sun was inching above the horizon as I strapped myself into a seat and continued to silently stew over a mistake I judged to be the worst I had made in my thirty-eight years. Two hours later the plane touched down in the coastal city of Qui Nhon, a forty-five-minute helicopter ride from An Khe.

The Seventeenth Field Hospital was a Mash unit not far advanced from the Korean War version depicted in the popular TV series, *M.A.S.H.* The chaplain in the sitcom series had problems, but never one like mine. Mine would not be suitable for public viewing. The Seventeenth was a small compound within the huge territory of the Fourth Division. Its mission was stabilization of wounded soldiers for helicopter transport to surgical hospitals in Qui Nhon and Saigon. The DOAs (dead on arrival) were sent to a makeshift morgue to be prepared for the flight home.

The jeep stopped on the lower end of a blacktopped road leading up to a rugged stone chapel, the first such example of church architecture I'd seen in Vietnam. I was told it was built by the First Division, commonly known as the "Big Red One." The chapel could have served as a community church in any small town in the United States.

My eyes went immediately to the smiling faces of men and women standing in front of four heavily bunkered reinforced-steel Quonset huts that served as wards, reception station, and emergency operation rooms. No doubt the entire staff had been ordered to greet the new hero/chaplain. I walked directly to the commanding officer, a full-bird colonel, saluted, and said, "Chaplain Liteky reporting for duty, sir." He smiled, shook my hand, and passed me down a line of white-clad doctors, nurses, technicians, and other enlisted personnel. One of the doctors said, "How do we rate such a highly decorated chaplain?" I forced a smile and moved on, thinking, "If these people only knew what was on the mind of this highly decorated chaplain."

I moved along the line of doctors, scanning each face for signs of compassion and listening to each voice as I tried to discern the virtue that would encourage me to share my problem, if it materialized. Confidentiality was paramount. Following this ritual, Dick, my newly assigned assistant, a short, stocky, farm boy from Gilmore City, Iowa, escorted me to my personal quarters across the road from the hospital. It was a wood-framed building surrounded by a double row of five-foot-high sandbags, except for the entrance. The tin roof was protection from rain only. A direct hit from a mortar shell would be a ticket to oblivion for the occupant. The place could have passed for a medical supply building but for the color, bright flamingo pink! "They call it the 'pink palace'," Dick said with an impish smile. I wondered why someone had painted the chaplain's quarters pink. Was it for me or my predecessor? Judiciously, I did not ask.

Duties at the Seventeenth were simple: meet the wounded and dying as they were flown in from the field, visit the injured during their short stay, and provide religious services for Catholics. I cannot recall a single person asking for a one-on-one confession. In a combat zone, general absolution given to those attending Mass was the rule, unless someone specifically asked for a personal confession. I would have loved to have been the recipient of general absolution. Direct support for the men in combat was over, yet I saw more of the sad results of war at the Seventeenth than I had witnessed in two years with an infantry unit. The arrival of the wounded and dead was daily fare: young bodies, severely mutilated, missing limbs, some losing life by the second. The emergency reception room was the first stage of bodily repair; one would think beyond repair, but the surgeons worked medical miracles. There could be as few as two or as many as forty casualties at once. It was blood-and-guts work. I marveled at the professionalism of the doctors and nurses who went calmly and efficiently about the work of stabilizing the injured and saving lives. They ran their own special body repair shop.

Occasionally, I administered the Catholic Church's Last Rites, euphemistically called the Sacrament of the Sick, to a seriously wounded soldier. Most of the time, the soldiers were semiconscious or unconscious. A young soldier realizing that he was receiving the Last Rites might panic.

I began comforting the wounded the day after my arrival, masking my venereal concern. No one asked me if I was worried about anything, as I harbored the fear of telltale symptoms appearing.

On the third day after my arrival, while walking along the breezeway in front of the wards, I could not help but notice a soldier walking awkwardly toward me as if he had been riding bareback on a broad-backed horse for days. He was wearing olive green crotch-less boxer shorts. With both hands he held his helmet filled with his gonads swollen to the size of small grapefruits, immersed in what I presumed was an analgesic fluid of some kind. He could not hide his pain. I had never seen anything like it. I thought, "What kind of VD is this?" The sight of this poor young venereal victim did not help my worries. I could see myself lying in a bed next to him, with IVs carrying penicillin to my swollen parts, smiling nurses passing by, and every doctor in the hospital stopping to look at Chaplain Liteky's chart.

A week passed before one possible symptom of gonorrhea appeared: a burning sensation during urination, but no pus. When the sensation continued unabated for three days, my fear escalated. I knew I had to consult one of the five doctors on station. I chose a lighthearted Irish Catholic from New York whom I had deliberately befriended in order to gauge his receptivity. Everyone liked Shawn, especially the nurses. Good-looking, unmarried, in his late twenties, and quick-witted, he buzzed around a bevy of admiring nurses and an occasional Donut Dolly, like a bee in a field of wild flowers. He did not attend my first Mass at the hospital chapel, which indicated that he did not take his Catholicism seriously. He was my man. I asked him to meet me in the chapel.

"I have something I'd like to discuss with you, Shawn."

He immediately became defensive.

"You missed me at Mass. Right, Father?"

"No. I don't count heads, Shawn. This is far more important."

"Happy to help, Padre. I'm free this evening."

I set up two chairs in the sanctuary, far enough away from

the front door to preclude unwanted ears from hearing my confession. Shawn arrived at 7:00 p.m. sharp.

"Right on time, Shawn."

"Catholic school, Padre."

I arranged the chairs at oblique angles so I wouldn't have to look directly at Shawn during the course of my confession. He did not know it, but he was my un-ordained priest. He could not give absolution, but he could possibly suggest a way I could soothe my anxieties.

"Shawn, what I'm about to tell you must be kept in the strictest of confidence, like the Seal of Confession. Okay?"

He gave me a look of puzzled wonder, and replied, "Of course, Father."

As many times as I had confessed sexual sins of desire, fantasy, or foreplay, I had never been so nervous. No sense in beating around the bush, I thought. I got right to the point: "Shawn, I'm afraid I might have VD."

Noticing his faint smile, I plodded on, relating my encounter with the bar girl in Saigon. I explained that it was my first time and I did not use protection. I did not mention Sharon or our upcoming R&R in Hawaii. In a tone devoid of surprise or incrimination, he benignly asked, "How long ago was this incident and what kind of symptoms are you having?"

I described the symptoms.

"It happened two weeks ago. Two days ago I began to experience a burning sensation while urinating."

"No pustular discharge?"

"No."

"I doubt that you have anything, Father, but just to make sure, I'll take a urine specimen and have it analyzed."

He must have seen me blanche when he said, "I'll take a specimen," for he quickly continued, "Don't worry! I'll submit the specimen as my own. No one will be surprised that I'm checking on myself. I'll give you the results tomorrow evening. In the meantime, relax. Give me ten minutes. I'll be back with an official urine specimen bottle."

Alone in the chapel, waiting for my sanguine Irish savior to return, I mused, "What a hell of a mess I've got myself into." And I prayed, "God help Shawn keep a confidence."

When he returned, I quickly filled the bottle, which he capped as he said, "Tomorrow, Father, around this time. Don't worry!"

"Don't worry." That was like telling me not to breathe.

The same time, the same place, the following evening I was sitting on the front steps of the chapel, looking down the empty road for the figure of a tall, thin man walking in my direction. Shawn was late. It was silhouette time. Finally, I saw the outline of the man I was expecting coming toward me. He was carrying a small package. When he drew close enough to speak softly, he said with a smile, "Good news, Padre. You're in the clear. No trace of anything out of the ordinary, but just to make sure, I want to give you these penicillin pills. Take one every four hours until the bottle is empty."

He should not have said "just to make sure." He was planting the seed of doubt in the mind of a patient given to psychosomatisizing under emotional stress. Other than a question of my reaction to penicillin, it did not occur to him to ask for my medical history. I had had a hives reaction to penicillin when I was sixteen, but I was willing to take a chance on hives for the cure. It did not occur to me that a reaction to penicillin could be serious. I said nothing about my earlier overwrought emotional reaction.

"If you have any problems, Padre, just let me know."

"Shawn, I am forever in your debt. I'll never forget you."

"It's no big deal, Padre. Don't be too hard on yourself. It goes along with being human."

As I watched the doctor walk back down the road to the hospital, I thought, "What a good man. He put himself on the line for me and I barely knew him." I was deeply touched, and I have never forgotten him. It is not far-fetched for me to say he saved my life. At the time, I doubt that I could have emotionally handled any public humiliation.

Sharon and Hawaii

The time to meet Sharon in Hawaii was rapidly approaching. What had formerly been an event to anticipate with excitement had now turned sour. I had new demons to fight. Even though I had medically assured health clearance, I was not emotionally free from the fear of a mistaken diagnosis. I did not want to take the risk of infecting or impregnating Sharon. Former feelings of erotic love were giving way to caution and dissolution. We had not yet made detailed plans, not even a specific date to meet in Hawaii. She needed at least two weeks' notice to purchase a ticket and apply for vacation time. I cooked up a plan. I knew she would be disappointed, but she would understand. How could she not understand?

The plan involved my mother, supposedly suddenly taken seriously ill. This was not true, but it was the best excuse I could think of at the time. This was the first in a series of lies I conjured up to protect Sharon, my mother, and myself.

I arrived in Hawaii on schedule, went immediately to a pay phone, and called Sharon. As I expected, she accepted the cancellation with resigned grace, ever so understanding. I told her I was headed home to Jacksonville to visit with Mother for three days before flying to San Diego for an overnight visit. This was the truth, but not the whole truth.

Mother was, of course, surprised to see me. "I didn't expect you home before December. I didn't know you could take short breaks." "You can't, Mom. This is my R&R. I'm supposed to be in Hawaii, but I'd rather have a few days at home with you." Another half-truth, but when I saw her failing health, I felt better about the lie. When I asked about her health, she did not hide the fact that she had been feeling weak. Her doctor had advised her to slow down, take an aspirin a day and an afternoon nap. For some time she had known about her fibrillating heart. She was sixty-two. I had had no idea that her health was failing. When I left for Vietnam nine months earlier, she was socially active and looking good for her age.

Our visit was over in a flash and I was once again on my way to Vietnam with a layover in San Diego. This was the same route I had traveled nine months earlier. Once again, Sharon was waiting in the reception area, but this time, she had a sullen look on her face. We embraced lightly, a brother/sister–like hug. She was slightly on the chilly side.

Her first words: "How's your Mom?" I tried to keep my lies to a minimum. "She's okay for now. Better than I supposed. She has a fibrillating heart. Do you know what that is?"

"No."

"I didn't either until Mom explained. It's a condition that causes irregular heartbeats. In her case, it's congenital."

Nine months had passed since we had been together, nine months of love letters flying east and west. Sharon sensed that something was amiss. I was beginning to learn firsthand about a woman's intuition.

"What is it, Charlie? What's troubling you? You're struggling. I can feel it."

We were sitting on opposite ends of the living room couch, I, sipping a martini, she, a glass of wine, neither of us making an effort to bridge the widening emotional chasm between us. "You're right, Sharon, I *am* troubled." I avoided her eyes as I readied the lie I was about to tell.

"Sharon, I can't leave the priesthood. I thought I could, but I can't. I hope you can forgive me." Moving closer, she fell into my arms, brimming over with compassion, and said, "Of course I can forgive you, Charlie. I know what it's like to break a commitment. I don't want to get between you and your God. From the beginning, I've felt that you might not be able to leave, but I had my hopes. You're a good person, and I hope you don't feel less a person for our experience."

After my performance and Sharon's generous reaction, I knew I had to retry living the celibate life required of Catholic priests. We slept in her bed that night and loved one another without making love. It was as if we both knew it would be the last time we would be close. We comforted one another until she fell asleep. I remained awake thinking about the mess I'd brought into her life and mine. One day I would tell her the truth, but not this day.

I've thought about telling her many times over the last thirty-five years, but I concluded that her need to know was not as great as my need to tell and ask for forgiveness. Best to leave the lie alone, I thought, and bear the burden of its dark presence in my soul. From what I've heard she is happily married with children she thought she might never have.

She does not need to know that she was the catalyst of my five-year struggle with God and myself to finally leave the priesthood or of my variegated efforts to find and marry the woman who is now my wife of twenty-eight years.

17

Save the Dogs

SHORTLY AFTER RETURNING to the Seventeenth Field Hospital, I met a new person, a young emergency room medic, Scott McNutt, who did not fit into the Army way of thinking or living. I'm sure he was a draftee. He would never have volunteered for a mind-numbing, authoritarian, rock-rigid organization like the Army. Scott was a college graduate, a political science major gifted with superior intelligence and clarity of speech.

As I recall, he was a private first class, having been demoted to that level because of a regulation infraction. I enjoyed listening to his stories of dealing with inhibiting regulations and demoralizing policies. He was a handsome young man about six feet tall. He wore a mustache, which was permitted as long as it met with specifications mandated by his first sergeant, meaning the hair beneath his nose could not extend over the top of his upper lip. Scott took sadistic pleasure in sculpturing the bottom edge of his mustache within a fly's leg of the fleshy part of his upper lip. I felt sorry for the man responsible for monitoring Scott's behavior.

He had a prestigious job as operating room medic, but his duties gave him little time to read and recreate. One day he sought me out to share some good news. He had volunteered and been assigned to the least desirable job on the hospital compound, hospital "shit burner." He was ecstatic, but I naturally wondered why such a bright young man would want to do such a disgusting chore. His explanation was in keeping with his intelligence.

There were a least three latrines (shit houses) on the hospital compound, one each for enlisted men, officers, and nurses. Each latrine had three or four toilet-size holes cut into wooden planks, set at a respectful distance from one another, but without partitions. Beneath each hole was the bottom half of a removable fifty-gallon drum positioned strategically to catch the daily deposits of hospital personnel.

Scott insisted that there was a distinct difference between the scent of officers and enlisted men's waste, the former being the foulest. Never having had the occasion to observe this particular disparity, I was disinclined to discuss the matter further.

Every other day, the drums had to be removed, emptied, and replaced. This was done with the help of a forklift. Each half-drum of human waste was taken to an out-of-the-way place, preferably downwind of the compound, where with the help of diesel oil, it was cremated, creating a scent sensation that every Vietnam veteran will remember.

Scott worked at his new job with the same dedication to excellence that he had exhibited in the operating room. Everyone on the hospital compound with working bowels had to endure the stench of the outhouse at least once a day. Scott, however, carried a nose full of foul-smelling waste matter for at least three hours each day. I shook my head in disbelief when he told me about his "good fortune."

"Why, Scott? Why in the world did you give up a prestigious position like operating room medic for a job most would regard as punishment?"

"Depends on your point of view, Padre. I'm sick and tired of all the BS an enlisted man has to take from officers. Yes, Sir! No, Sir! Right away, Sir! And the ever-tiresome saluting. The shit burner is his own man; no one bothers him. Even Sergeant Hammer leaves me alone. He no longer even scrutinizes my mustache. Maybe it's my odor. I work three hours a day – max. In two months, I'm out of here and on my way back to the world. This is a great way to spend my last days in Vietnam. I've always felt that this war is for the shits, more so than for the little people."

Even though I disagreed with Scott on most subjects, I liked his rebellious spirit and his sensitivity for the Vietnamese poor, the innocent victims of the war.

On Thanksgiving Day the chow line was a single-line pa-

rade along an all-you-can-eat smorgasbord of turkey and trim-
mings, a great morale booster and reminder of home. Scott chose
not to participate. Instead, he fasted in solidarity with the Vietnamese poor. I heard that a report of his Thanksgiving fast appeared in *Time* magazine. I'm ashamed to say that I did not share
his sensitivity at that time.

One day he appeared in my office in the back of the chapel
with a letter-sized printed leaflet on which he had typed an invitation to participate in a "Save the Dogs" demonstration. Scott
had composed and produced everything himself. The leaflet was
a scathing indictment of the Fourth Division general who had
promulgated an edict demanding that the population of the dogs
in the division base camp be reduced to one dog per unit.

This meant that numerous little pig-tailed canine pets GIs
had taken in would have to be euthanized. Scott saw this order as
a serious blow to division morale, not to mention animal rights. I
agreed. The dogs were a tactile distraction from the woes of war,
something to care for, hold, and play with during rear area
doldrums.

The general's concern was real. He feared the spread of rabies by some of the un-inoculated dogs running free in packs all
over the Fourth Division compound. To my knowledge there was
not a single case of GI rabies, although one eleven-year-old Vietnamese girl had been brought to the hospital, snarling and foaming at the mouth. Everyone who approached her, including me,
was ordered to take a series of anti-rabies shots. She was too far
gone to save.

I had no problems with the purpose of the general's edict; it
was his authoritative, autocratic manner of implementation that
troubled me. No consideration was given to the feelings of the pet
owners. The general had a severe case of "rankitis," an occupa-
tional disease of many officers; the higher the rank, the worse the
disease. It manifested itself in a grossly inflated opinion of one's
self.

Monitoring Morale

It was a chaplain's duty to monitor morale, a task I had never had
occasion to perform.

Scott's leaflet was an invitation to a demonstration to take
place at 5:00 p.m. in the PX parking lot, an area large enough to
accommodate hundreds of protesters. The demo was well adver-
tised. Scott had distributed his leaflet throughout the division

and I passed out a few around the hospital compound.

I walked a mile from the Seventeenth Field Hospital to the PX parking lot, arriving at a quarter to five. All was quiet on the western side of the parking lot as I awaited the arrival of the Save the Dogs demonstrators. At five o'clock sharp, I began to walk around the parking lot, a one-person protest, wondering as I walked, about the absence of Scott.

Five minutes later an open jeep slowly rolled around the northern end of the PX and headed directly toward me. The two passengers were not demonstrators. They were MPs (military police officers) sent to warn would-be protesters that there would be no demonstration. I was wearing the gold clustered major's insignia on my cap and fatigue collar. The driver of the jeep was a captain. Very slowly the jeep rolled up to my left side. The captain and I were eye to eye. He saluted and said respectfully, "Sir, may I inquire as to your purpose here?"

"I'm here to participate in the Save the Dogs demonstration."

"There will be no demonstration, Sir!"

"Are you telling me to leave, Captain?"

Bowing to my rank, he responded, "Sir, I'm not telling you to do anything."

About this time, three GIs, walking abreast and looking as if they were lost, joined our little group and commenced to ask if this was the demonstration site.

Before I could respond, the MP captain spoke with military gusto, "There is no demonstration. There is no such thing as a demonstration in a war zone. You men return to your unit *now*!!!"

Ignoring the captain's order, the three soldiers did not move. Knowing they could get in deep trouble for refusing to obey an MP, I encouraged them to leave. Obviously there would be no demonstration and this was not the time or place to employ the First Amendment.

Disgruntled, the GIs departed, while I continued my walking protest around the parking lot. I could hear the captain describing me to headquarters over his mobile radio unit.

"Sir! There is a major, a chaplain, walking around in circles on the west side of the PX. He says he is protesting against the order to eliminate the dogs."

I could not hear the response. The MPs drove away, leaving me in the fading light of a day in Vietnam I will never forget. Neither will I forget Scott McNutt. This was my first protest ever, but it would not be my last. I hesitate to call it political. You could say it was "canine-itarian."

I returned to the hospital looking for Scott. He had been apprehended by the MPs for questioning and was being held incommunicado. Rumor had it that he could be up for court martial. The following morning I requested and received an appointment to meet with the general of the Fourth Division.

He was the second general not to rise from the chair behind his desk when I entered his office. Nor did he salute or offer me the courtesy of a morning greeting. He knew I was the chaplain who the day before had walked around the PX parking lot protesting his edict to reduce the canine population.

"What's on your mind, Chaplain?" he said in the sterile, officious tone of a man possessed by power.

"Scott McNutt," I replied.

"McNutt is not a subject for discussion, Chaplain. He distributed leaflets throughout the division that could be interpreted as an effort to incite riot. His act was illegal and irresponsible and his indiscretion qualifies for a court martial."

"In all fairness, General, if you court martial Scott you should court martial me, because I too distributed the Save the Dogs leaflet."

"Chaplain, I'm surprised that you could be so derelict of duty."

"Sir, it is my duty to monitor morale and your edict is a serious blow to the morale of soldiers under your command."

With that, I turned and left the room, once again having experienced the arrogance of power. The last I heard of Specialist Four Scott McNutt was that he was home after receiving an early discharge without a court martial. I was pleased.

(*Note:* Throughout the telling of this story of my life, I refrain from revealing the true identities of some individuals whose reputation might be injured. Scott is an exception. He is one of the rare breed of men who stands firm on his ethics regardless of the cost. I'm judging that he would not mind the use of his real name.)

18

Back in the USA

Six WEEKS BEFORE THE END OF MY FINAL TOUR OF
DUTY, I noticed a small, olive-shaped protrusion on the left side of
my groin. It was not a strange new physical phenomenon. I had
had the same experience at the beginning of my freshman year at
the University of Florida. It was an easily diagnosable inguinal
hernia.

A hospital staff doctor confirmed my conclusion and suggested it be surgically repaired as soon as possible. Even though
hernia repair was a minor surgical procedure, he counseled me to
have the repair done immediately at the field hospital in Quin
Nhon to mitigate the possibility of infection. After the operation I
would be flown to Japan and on to Letterman General Hospital at
the Presidio in San Francisco. Agreeing to the operation meant
leaving Vietnam a month early, which appealed to my need to get
on with my life.

Two weeks after the discovery of the hernia, I was lying
prone on an operating table at Quin Nhon Surgical Hospital,
numbed by a spinal tap and clean shaved from the waist down,
waiting for the surgeon. A hernia operation was small-time stuff
for doctors accustomed to reconstructing bodies torn apart by
shrapnel and bullets. However, the repair resulted in an incision
five times the length of my right-side hernia. Three days later I
was loaded on to a stretcher, rolled into the belly of a huge jet ambulance, and flown to a military hospital in Japan for recovery.

The surgical wound was slow to close. It looked as if stitches had broken, creating a five-inch vertical gash rather than the nice neat, barely noticeable, razor-like incision on my right side. My bikini days were over before they began.

Within a few days I was on my feet, walking around hospital wards chatting with young men who had been severely injured, most by booby traps. A wounded soldier required more attention than a dead one. Needless to say, I was embarrassed to mention my noncombat laceration.

It was springtime in San Francisco when I arrived at Letterman Army Hospital, located on a beautiful piece of federal real estate known as The Presidio, with scenic overlooks to the Pacific and the Golden Gate Bridge. My surgical wound was healing nicely from the inside out, but was still an ugly looking creek of coagulated blood. Just three weeks remained between Army and civilian life. It looked as if my last Army post would be the Presidio.

After several days of walking around the hospital and the surrounding grounds, I was allowed freedom to explore the city; but I was not interested in sightseeing. I was preoccupied with thoughts about the future, which included plans for a leave of absence from the priesthood.

I took in a movie at the Post theater. Midway through the film, the screen began to blur like heat waves rising from asphalt on a hot summer's day. The experience lasted for about three minutes. This was a first-time episode for me. I immediately reported the event and underwent tests, which had negative results, but I reasoned it would be better to be in the Army should something more serious develop. So I extended my tour for six months and accepted an assignment to Fort Ord, California, two hours down the coast from San Francisco and three hundred miles up the coast from San Diego.

Discharge and New Life

After six months at Fort Ord, California, I was discharged from the Army – on New Year's Day, 1971. The war was winding down, but not fast enough for many Vietnam veterans, especially combat vets, some with lifetime wounds like the loss of limbs and organs; others with unseen wounds related to trauma and that no method of healing can touch.

At this time war veterans converged en masse on Washington, D.C., camped on government property, and refused to move under threat of arrest. They were angry and determined to make their voices heard by Congress and the president. The story of the Vietnam Veterans' Movement to End the War is well told in a book by Gerald Nicosia, *Home to War: A History of the Vietnam Veterans Movement* (Crown, 2001).

In or out of the Army, I did not protest the war. I lived in my head, rationalizing the suffering and loss of the war's victims. "War is war," I said to myself. "There is no clean way of fighting it. It's a necessary evil." In addition, I believed that dying for one's country was a breath below dying for one's faith. Further, I rationalized that communism was worse than war, worse than death itself. I had the "I'd rather be dead than red" syndrome.

Thus, despite two-and-a-half years of witnessing the carnage of war in Vietnam, including the death of innocents, noncombatant old men, women, and children, I did not protest. I remained adamant in my support of U.S. opposition to communism. I did not reflect on the damage inherent in capitalism, which places profit above people and greed above sharing. I was living on the assumptions of my capitalistic subculture.

While I did not protest the war itself, I was against the way we were fighting it. It was a war of attrition and the enemy was willing to do what we could not, namely, fight to the last person in order to win freedom from decades of foreign oppression. In my opinion, we could never have won the Vietnam War because we could never have won the "hearts and minds" of the Vietnamese people, just as we (the USA) cannot now win the hearts and minds of people in Iraq or Afghanistan.

How can we, when we are bombing innocent women and children into oblivion, poisoning their means of life support, and ignoring the sanctity of their culture? At best, we could have been South Vietnam's permanent security force, as we are now in South Korea and trying to be in Iraq and Afghanistan.

Mulling over these thoughts, I became aware that I had been adept at living as only half a human being, that is, on an intellectual level only. I had been disallowing feelings any entry into my worldview or decision-making process. At home and in the seminary, I had been educated to tolerate rather than act on feelings.

All this led me, while in San Francisco, to consult with a psychologist. After the visit, I took to heart his prognostic warning, paraphrased: "I fear you will have a nervous breakdown or commit suicide if you don't listen to your feelings."

So I began learning to attend to my feelings, and they were telling me not to return to the priesthood. They were saying,

"You are a lonely man, you need a companion; fall in love and get married." The possibility lifted my spirits. The challenge was attractive, but the way to achieve this goal was a journey fraught with difficulty and fear I could not have imagined.

Two weeks before discharge, I sold my only means of transportation, a 175cc Honda motorcycle, the smallest bike on offer – good for local transportation, but not suitable for cross-country travel. A cousin with a hobby of collecting antique cars made me an offer I could not refuse: a 1959 powder-blue Cadillac in mint condition for only two hundred dollars. It was the year of the unique, flying taillight fins. All of the luxurious Cadillac accessories worked: power windows and seats, automatic locks, air conditioning, etc. The four-door car was solid and armor-plated in contrast to the thin-skinned metal of later models and it cruised the highway at eighty miles per hour without a tremor.

The day after my Army life ended, I began what I considered the start of a new life free of the trappings of both the military and the religious life. I said goodbye to my friends at Fort Ord and took to the road. I drove from Monterey to Santa Monica, reflecting on the twists and turns my life had taken from the day I joined the Army to my discharge. In Santa Monica, I picked up Interstate 10, a straight shot across the southern United States to Jacksonville, where it intersected with I-95 South. I estimated a four- to five-day trip for the approximately twenty-five-hundred miles.

At the Interstate 10 on-ramp, two young men were trying to hitch a ride east to Miami. I picked them up and they were delighted to learn that I was going to Jacksonville. They offered to share the driving, and I agreed. Fifty hours later, I pulled into the driveway of my family home after dropping the boys off at Interstate 95 South. The cross-country trip was uneventful. We stopped for gas and snacks only, driving day and night, sleeping and making conversation I cannot remember. Toward the end of the trip I discovered that the boys had been smoking marijuana while I slept. The odor never woke me up. Perhaps that's why I slept so soundly. Had we been stopped, my new life could have taken a surprise turn into a southern county jail, with me protesting that I had never touched the stuff. I can just imagine the headlines of the *Jacksonville Journal*: "Ex-Army Chaplain Charles J. Liteky, Local Hero, Indicted for Possession of Marijuana on Interstate 10." Mother would have shaken her head in disbelief, but she would have never stopped loving me.

Mother no longer needed a four-bedroom house. She was slowing down at sixty-two, taking longer and longer afternoon naps, but still enthusiastically preparing meals for me. We decided to sell the house and rent a small pet-friendly apartment. There would be no going anywhere without our dog, Cris. I found the perfect place just two miles away from the old neighborhood, within walking distance of a shopping center. She would not have to depend on me and she could exercise Cris in a nearby park.

The three of us settled into a new life together: mother, son, and a perpetual-motion, white toy poodle. I was happy to be with Mother after spending so many years apart, and I felt like I could be of some service and comfort, especially after the shock I had given her. It was during this time that we talked family over breakfast at the kitchen table. Our friendship grew with her sharing.

Laicization Process

The laicization procedure involved writing a letter to the pope explaining why I wanted to leave. For me the issue was simple, celibacy. The pope at this time was Paul VI, an Italian of superior intelligence who had written a well-regarded encyclical on celibacy, honoring it with names like "a brilliant jewel" and "a gift of God." The pope's precious stone metaphor did not work for me.

It was important to me at the time to leave the priesthood legally by way of a process called laicization, meaning Vatican-approved reduction to the lay state. ("Reduction" is, of course, a poor choice of words, connoting as it does the superiority of the clerical state.) Many a priest leaving the priesthood did not bother about this formality; they just left. Some even continued to practice their ministry as married priests. Married or celibate, I had no desire to continue priestly practice.

The laicization process normally took around six months. This somewhat lengthy period of waiting for a response gave the petitioner time to reflect on the serious nature of his request. Ecclesiastical return of a priest to the lay state was a step down from an artificial, elevated plain termed clerical. At the time, I was under the impression that the street to laicization was one way, once the pope consented to the petition. Years later I learned that it was possible to be re-elevated, so to speak, to the clerical state. Marriage was the clincher. No turning back after marriage, as long as the Roman Catholic Church's celibacy requirement, which dates back to the twelfth century, was still in force.

Three months after I submitted my request to leave the priesthood, I began to feel uneasy, anxious about the salvation of my soul and guilt-ridden about breaking a sacred covenant with God. I had been warned early on by a well-intentioned, but misguided nun, "Charles, you will have a difficult time saving your soul outside of the vocation intended for you by God." Another warning, "If you end up in hell after frustrating a vocation, part of your punishment will be your hell-mates chastising you for not doing God's will, thereby failing to help them get to heaven." I was too young to ask the good Sister about the origin of such equine excrement.

As I sought to leave the priesthood, I had no appreciation of a God who could take No for an answer and still love me. Emotionally, the break was too much. I successfully hid my feelings from Mom, but not from Julie. She knew I was stewing over something. She was as good a person as I've ever known and would have been a good wife, but I would not have been a good husband at that time. I had too much emotional baggage to jettison.

The leave of absence from the priesthood left me without an income except for the Medal of Honor tax-free pension of one hundred dollars per month for the rest of my life. I was in no position to begin a new career. I needed a non-career job fast, something I could do without preparation, a job that would leave me free to explore the world and assist Mom.

Checking the help-wanted section of the *Jacksonville Journal*, I spotted an ad for a combination car wash and gas station attendant. The owner accepted me, despite my eleven years of post–high school education and my unimpressive job history. I told him about my leave of absence and my need to explore a different way of life. He could not have cared less.

He was a hardworking, middle-aged businessman. I think he felt sorry for someone his age just entering the job market. The job was simple: dispense gas into cars driving up to pumps that stood on a concrete island next to the car wash and the owner's office. Once filled, the cars were driven through a tunnel of whirling brushes and high-pressured showers into the waiting hands of four young boys who detailed the cars inside and out.

At the peak hours of six to eight in the morning and four to six in the afternoon, the boys and I were like ants on a sugar cube. For four busy hours a day, I hopped from tank to tank on either side of the island, pumping gas, processing credit cards, gathering signatures, and politely saying "thank you" to customers as uninterested in me as I was in them. This was before the phony "have a nice day" era. I was a human cog in a machine that exchanged gas for money. Drivers rarely left their cars.

Mother's Death

Meanwhile, Mother's heart condition was seriously deteriorating, forcing her to remain in bed most of the time. Our family doctor suggested she consider open heart surgery to replace the mitral valve, the valve between the left atrium and the left ventricle of the heart. An artificial valve would be inserted and hopefully bring rest to her fibrillating heart. The procedure had already been successfully performed, but its success rate was less than 100 percent.

Mother was advised that she had a fifty/fifty chance. If successful, the operation would afford her at least five years of ambulatory life, maybe more. She was then three-fourths of the way into her sixty-fourth year. There was no effort, medical or familial, to convince her to have or not have the operation. The decision was hers alone. She chose to take the chance for an improved life.

I elected to be optimistic about the success of the surgery and concluded that Mom would need financial aid for an indefinite period of time. Pumping gas wasn't going to fill the bill. I investigated the possibility of serving as a chaplain at a VA hospital. A position opened for a drug ward chaplain at a large VA hospital in Brecksville, Ohio. I was not a drug rehabilitation pro, but I *was* comfortable working with Vietnam vets.

While waiting for a reply to my application, Mother had her operation at the Medical Center in Gainesville, Florida, only fifty miles southwest of our Jacksonville home. My younger brother, Pat, left his teaching job in California to be with her. The operation was completed, but recovery presented irresolvable complications.

Eight hours after surgery, Mother had a severe heart attack that left her in a comatose state. She lingered on, dying little by little, for forty-three days. Occasionally, she opened her eyes, but I saw no signs of recognition. Her fingers and toes were turning blue and would have to be amputated even if the rest of her body recovered.

Deciding to terminate someone's life, especially that of a

loved one, is never easy. Pat and I agreed to tell the doctor that if recovery was out of the question it was time to "pull the plug." We buried Mother in a plot adjacent to our middle brother, Jim, the victim of a drowning accident four months after graduating from college and eleven years before Mother's death. She suffered three deaths: a son, her husband's, and her own.

Religious belief in an afterlife of endless happiness with God and reunion with friends helped us to accept our loss and imagine Mother in the company of the husband and son she had lost.

Since I was still a priest in good standing, I was permitted to say her funeral Mass. Sadly, I don't remember my public parting words. Though she was sixty-three at death, she looked younger than her years. From my perspective she was a person of great compassion, patience, prudence, and service to all, especially to her husband. She nursed him through eleven bedridden years of osteoporosis.

One of Mom's friends adopted Cris, the white toy poodle. By now Cris too has moved on. I like to think of Mom walking Cris around a park in heaven, where dogs, cats, and people all get along. Mother would no longer have to defend Cris with her umbrella against the neighborhood German shepherd.

Brother Pat returned to his cabin in the Redwoods of Boulder Creek, California, fifteen miles above Santa Cruz, by the sea. He had given up his teaching job in San Jose to be with Mom. Before looking for another, he was drawn into the political world by a longtime county supervisor incumbent who was suspected of unethical behavior. Pat was just a young man from nowhere – born, but not raised, in California. Long-haired as he was at the time, Pat was upset that long-haired men in Santa Cruz County were all dismissed as undesirable transient elements.

I did not know Pat very well. I was Big Brother, nine years older, an age span not easy to cross into the friendship of equals. I definitely was not superior, but our age difference made me paternal, which can prevent a deeper relationship.

19

Drug Rehab Work

MOM'S DEATH FREED ME from the need to work to support her, but I decided to take a hospital chaplain's job rather than return to mission work. (I had meanwhile resigned myself to celibacy, but my struggle to remain faithful to the vow was not over.) My new job was in a sophisticated drug rehabilitation program staffed by professionals with impressive educational credentials, each one dedicated to the task of helping young Vietnam veterans break the chains of drug addiction. The patient–staff ratio was nearly two to one: a psychiatrist, two doctors of psychology, a sociologist, a psychiatric nurse, a registered nurse, and a chaplain. An entire fourth floor wing of the mammoth VA hospital in Brecksville, Ohio, was reserved for Vietnam veterans.

It was a live-in, healing program. Everyone was well-intentioned, with the exception of several vets who were not ready to follow rules that prohibited drug use by those in the program. The program required the testing of a urine sample every day. A "dirty urine" (urine traced with any one of a number of drugs) resulted in expulsion from the program. Consequently, a few vets engaged in a "clean urine game" in which they invented ingenious methods of deceiving the staff nurse with a faked drug-free urine sample. Samples were generated in the privacy of a small lavatory close to the nurse's station. The nurse stood right outside the lavatory door waiting for the vet to emerge with his clear plastic jar of urine. Labeled with the time received and the vet's name, the sample was then whisked away to the lab for testing. Trickery in the confines of a guarded toilet room was impossible for anyone but an addict. One foolproof technique was using clean urine that had been given by a friend. Foolproof, provided the clean urine could somehow be smuggled into the testing room and poured into the official container before it was given to the nurse as if it were one's own. In a way, hiding their drug use was a game with the vets, but it was a serious, life-threatening game. The vets had survived Vietnam only to run the risk of losing their lives to chemical addiction.

Creating a Drug-free World

Despite their creative schemes of avoiding detection, a few were caught and discharged. Feeling the need to reach out to these discharged vets, I offered them a chance to live in a drug-free world of their own creation. Though I knew very little about clinical drug rehabilitation, I did know something about alcoholic addiction from a college course and from my association with alcoholics, which included attending Alcoholics Anonymous (AA) meetings.

The AA program is based upon the recognition of one's need for the help of a "higher power" to overcome the addictive and destructive power of alcohol excess. Another important component of the program is a willingness to help and be helped by other afflicted people. I reasoned that the AA program could be adapted to addiction per se – any kind of addiction. So, I approached the discharged vets and offered them a chance to help themselves and others break free from drug addiction. A desire to kick the habit and give up any game playing were prerequisites. They had to be honest with one another and me – no small task for addicts self-schooled in the arts of deception and manipulation. Five Vietnam vets, one with a small dog and a girlfriend, accepted my offer. (The girlfriend and the dog were not addicted, of course.)

By happenstance, a conversation with an elderly volunteer at the VA hospital resulted in an offer to use his unoccupied three-story home in East Cleveland. I jumped at the chance to start a no–BS drug rehab program based on the willingness of vets to help themselves and one another. From the start, I was up front with the participants about my lack of drug rehab experience. They could teach me about drug addiction, and in return I would share some basic psychological insights and my goodwill. I had nothing to lose and they had everything to gain.

The house – a one-time beautiful nineteenth-century Victorian now in need of repair – was located in a neighborhood that the home owner and other middle-class whites had fled and left to black newcomers. With a generosity often seen in the poor, none of our neighbors complained or inquired about six men (five whites and one black) and one young white woman moving into the neighborhood. I was glad we had at least one African American participant in the group. The house was spacious enough to provide a private room and semiprivate bath for everyone.

Furnishing began with my mother's household goods, accrued over her lifetime. My inheritance included a twenty-inch color TV and a unique and practically impregnable coin bank that my father had welded out of metal into an eight-inch-sized octagon. When I brought the bank from Jacksonville to Cleveland it was almost full. It contained eight years' worth of Mom and Dad's small change – savings intended to be used for my ordination expenses. For some reason the bank was never touched at home; perhaps Dad did not want to trouble any of his friends to open it, given the fact that he could no longer use a blowtorch or a sledge hammer. I gave no thought to the monetary value of the bank. For me it was a symbol of familial sacrifice.

Three days after we moved into our new home in the spring of 1972, the bank and the TV disappeared, along with Oscar, our only African American. The other vets were furious; they wanted Oscar's head. Each of them had a history of drug-related thievery, but this was their first taste of personal drug theft victimhood. I myself was not overly upset by the theft, having some understanding of the drug addict's need to satisfy his habit and having taken a religious vow of poverty that made me detached from material possessions. Morality, friendship, and even familial loyalty go out the window when faced with the gnawing, overpowering need to alleviate drug withdrawal pain. One of the vets related the story of his washer and dryer theft, a felony that could have sent him to prison had his parents elected to prosecute. It is difficult for parents, especially mothers, to do what needs to be done to their addicted children. When I asked vets how their parents could have helped their liberation process, they said, "They should have kicked us out." (This is sometimes called "tough love.")

The vets did not share my sympathy for Oscar. Had they found him the results could have been far more serious than Oscar's offense. Sensing a poetic justice in theft from former thieves, I made no attempt to assuage their anger. Fortunately, Oscar was never located, dead or alive. I later discovered a missing one hundred dollar check. Oscar did a fair job of forgery. He left well heeled, never to be seen again. I still wonder how he opened the bank.

I continued working at the VA drug program when we began our invented drug-free, live-in experiment. The job provided ample money to cover the cost of running and refurbishing the house. When news of our effort reached the director of the VA program, it was not well received. She called me to her office for some counseling. "You have no idea of the complexity of what you are undertaking," she said. "In addition, you could get yourself in serious trouble."

I did not argue with her. I simply listened, thanked her for her concern, and left. She had an authoritarian attitude that did not invite dialogue, evidenced by a tone of arrogance in her voice. I had no tolerance for authoritarian arrogance. She may have been right, the Oscar incident could have proved serious, but she was using the wrong approach for dialoguing with me. Religious life and the military had provided me with a surfeit of arrogant people in positions of power who moved me to retreat or recoil unless acquiescence mandated a greater good. Most of us are forced to eat crow (a euphemism for a more odiferous scent) at some time. If I could help liberate one addict, I thought, the project was worth the risk of trouble.

Two doctors of psychology on the hospital staff saw merit in our effort to address drug addiction and offered to help with once-a-week rap sessions conducted in the front room of our house. One or both doctors would drive into the city from their suburban homes and give up cherished Friday evenings to help us work through frustrations associated with drug-less group living. They were truly dedicated healers. They could have been sanctioned as I was for extracurricular activity judged to be counterproductive by the powers above.

Communal living is not easy, especially for North Americans raised in a culture that champions individualism. Add liberation from drugs to the equation and you have a challenge that calls forth the best from caregivers and addicted alike.

As self-appointed founder and director of the house, I an-

swered to no one except the vets and myself. In addition to providing the vets with food and shelter, I had the emotional
advantage of genuinely liking them. There was not a mean person in the group. I was old enough to be their father and once
again I felt the satisfying impact of the title "Father."

Initially, I was concerned about the lone female in the house,
Patty, companion of Jack. She was a lovely, lighthearted person
who gave us the benefits that only a female presence offers. Her
boyfriend Jack was a person of sturdy build and character, who
would take nothing negative from anyone. He was gentle with
Patty and obviously in love with her. Never did I see anyone in
the house make a move or "hit" on Patty. No doubt the energy required to resist the drug impulse helped moderate sexual desires.

The exterior of the house was in no immediate need of repair, but the interior screamed for attention. By good fortune, the
men were skilled in the trades necessary for remodeling, rewir-
ing, plumbing, and painting. The need for a complete internal
face-lifting provided us with ideal work therapy. Within two
months the interior of the house was restored to its former Victorian, high-ceilinged splendor, to the pride and pleasure of everyone. The most notable innovations were a new white-tiled
kitchen floor and the color schemes chosen by individuals for
their private space. Renovation of common areas, like the dining
and living rooms, was put to a democratic vote, which included
me. At first I found the dark purple ceiling and lavender walls a
little oppressive, but the color scheme grew on me.

About the time work therapy was running out, my superiors at the hospital and the VA administration in Washington,
D.C., counseled me to cease conducting a private rehab program
that they considered counterproductive to the VA program. Had
they come right out and said, "You're fired if you continue your
independent program" I would have asked for their decision in
writing. I was after all spending my money doing what I wanted
to do. From my point of view, it was that simple. At the same
time, I was tiring of the two-hour daily commute, eight-hour
workdays, and five-days-a-week grind that I endured in order to
supplement our income. In addition, my dislike for the clinical,
antiseptic, rule-heavy VA program was growing.

Consequently, I quit, thereby saving the government sixteen
hundred dollars a month, but laying a heavier financial burden
on myself and the vets. Money had to come from somewhere.
The vets were skilled in making money, a lot of money, to support

their drug habits. Unfortunately, we could not employ their sub-stance-related talents for making money to support our house and programs. But the entrepreneurial skills were still there. They just needed a new product, a legitimate product.

I was obligated by the vow of obedience to inform my reli-gious superior of my decision to stop working with the VA. He was not pleased. Strictly speaking, I should have asked him for permission to stop working at the VA and establish an independ-ent rehab facility, but my idea seemed so right that it did not oc-cur to me. With no discussion, he allowed me to continue the rehab effort, but he stressed that I could expect no financial sup-port from our Community. I did not ask for or expect any such support. All I wanted was permission to continue on my own, which he graciously granted, though reluctantly, I think. He was as good and kind as men go, fatherly, but not authoritarian. This would not be the last obedience request I would put to Father Stephen Quinn.

Reality House

We felt the need to give the rehab house in Cleveland a name. I do not recall how we arrived at "Reality House." I like to think it was the recognition that the drug world is not the real world. We were working together to live a reality free from the distorting, de-structive influence of drugs. I use the collective pronoun because I was part of the vets' liberation effort, I was lending them a help-ing hand in their incredible struggle, but at the time that I too needed liberation, freedom from years of suppressed feelings, freedom from a lifetime of unexamined cultural assumptions. Conflicts had to be resolved rather than ignored, and I was as much in conflict with my emotions as anyone in the house.

I continued to suppress feelings of anger and sexual desire, even though a psychologist had warned me to listen to my feel-ings or suffer the consequences: suicide or emotional breakdown. A decision to give up the priesthood meant surrendering to the flesh. I did not want to travel that laicization route again, fail again, and hurt another woman. However, I would discover that once broken, a vow (especially a vow of sexual abstinence) is more difficult to keep than when initially professed.

Rap sessions in the house were a forum for airing one's feel-ings, resolving disagreements, and discovering that everyone has problems of one kind or another. I had no idea that I too would benefit from these sessions. Despite the fact that I had failed more than once to keep the vow of chastity, I had the inflated self-image of a healer, a noble person dedicated to helping others, a man who had witnessed the horrors of war without cracking. Being called Father did not help. Everyone, other than other priests, referred to me as Father. People, especially Catholics, respected me and expected me to have an answer to their questions and a solution to their problems.

The vets in Reality House respected me, but they told me frankly that I needed help. They counseled me in the rap sessions to express anger when it was first felt, rather than allow one disturbing episode to build upon another until it filled my internal volcano and the suppressed anger gave way to an eruption disproportionate to the problem. From their point of view, my challenge was anger expression and management. The vets never inquired into my struggle with celibacy, nor did I refer to it in rap sessions. The feelings related thereto went unattended, smoldering like coals buried deep in my bottled-up feelings. It certainly helped that there were no attractive females looking for a male companion in my immediate environment.

Following my resignation from the VA chaplain's position, the big problem facing Reality House was paying bills. I took weekend assignments in suburban parishes to bring in extra money, and I had enough in savings to cover a month's worth of expenses, but this was a far cry from my VA chaplain's salary.

I don't recall how we decided to try the candle-making business. None of us had ever made a candle before, but it seemed simple enough: a wick, some wax, and a market was all we needed. We soon discovered that making saleable candles was no simple matter. We needed a place to work, a stove to melt the wax, a means of cutting slabs of wax, perfume to scent the candles, vats for a water bath, dyes for color, metal shaping molds, plus patience and a determination to ward off discouragement. Even though we were guided by easy-to-understand "how to" books, a full month of trial and error was necessary to create a marketable candle.

We dug out the basement of the old Victorian, laid down a cement slab, and went to work. By pure coincidence, Terry, a friend from my Army days, owned and operated a plastics factory in the city. He volunteered to make plastic vats for bathing the candles and plastic windows for the work room. When the room was complete, we scrounged up an abandoned, four-burner electric stove for melting two-inch squares of wax, which we cut on a radial arm saw purchased from Sears at a discounted price.

Fumes from the boiling wax rose to the rafters beneath the kitchen floor, gassing longtime-resident termites by the hundreds. They fell like rain on the workshop floor. It is a wonder the kitchen floor never collapsed. Within a month we were in daily production of twenty-five colored, scented candles of marketable quality. Substandard candles, at least one out of five, found homes throughout the house, filling it with soft light and blended perfumed scents. All we needed to be in business now was a market. The place that came immediately to mind was the parish hall of local Catholic churches. All I had to do was convince pastors of the value of Reality House, which was easy because the city of Cleveland was awash with drugs and rehab programs. Good people, aware of the need for drug rehabilitation, responded generously.

The candle-making business and the meager stipend from my weekend work brought in enough money to meet expenses, but it fell short of critically needed funds to pay household bills. From a friend, I heard about the "Soldiers and Sailors Relief Program," which provided two hundred dollars a month to help indigent veterans. An advocacy trip to City Hall in downtown Cleveland resulted in a monthly grant of one thousand dollars to help liberate five vets. The money was entrusted to me. I gave each vet fifty dollars and used the remainder to pay bills.

* * *

With financial problems solved, candle-making therapy working, and no foreboding signs of serious problems, I was feeling pleased with Reality House and myself. In the first three months of operation, we had lost only one vet to drugs, not a bad record when compared to the VA program as a whole. Johnny left of his own volition and even bade us farewell. I was sad to see him go. He was such a beautiful, gentle person. Shortly after his departure, another vet arrived asking for admission. The resident vets admitted him without dissent. Eddie was not a VA dropout. He had heard about the Reality House program from someone else in the house. Eddie was a lighthearted small man (5'6" at the most) who looked younger than his twenty-two years; he was a charmer with an engaging smile, a threat to no one.

A month after joining us, I noticed him tilling the soil just inside the chain-link fence in front of the house. How great, I thought, a good example. When I praised Eddie's initiative to the other residents, they laughed and told me the reason for his horticultural enthusiasm: he was planting marijuana. Eddie had not broken the cardinal rule of the house (no drugs in the house), but indirectly he was threatening the existence of the program. If a passing police officer had spotted marijuana growing in our front yard, it could have spelled the end of Reality House. While I appreciated his moxie, I could not tolerate the loss of the house to cannabis. The problem called for a house meeting, which resulted in a unanimous decision to expel Eddie for a month. I hated to see him return to a life on the streets, sleeping in abandoned cars, scrounging food, and possibly selling drugs, but I was elated over the group decision. It signified that they valued their sanctuary. Eddie returned on schedule in a month, looking worse for his street-life experience.

* * *

I never inquired about the military experience of the vets; it was none of my business. However, one vet in particular shared part of his Vietnam tour with me when I asked about his damaged right forearm and hand. A bullet from an AK-47 had torn away tendons and muscle, leaving him with limited use of his right hand. Despite this limitation, Howard qualified to become a member in the electricians' union.

In Vietnam, Howard had been a member of an elite group of six highly trained soldiers known as LRPS (pronounced LERPS). They were flown by helicopter deep into enemy territory at night, dropped into heavy jungle terrain, and missioned to gather intelligence on troop movements and locations. They could call in air strikes on a field radio and set up ambushes whenever appropriate. Their aim was to harass the enemy and let them know they were not safe in their own backyard. LRPS were feared and hated by the enemy, but respected. Howard never spoke of his experiences. He possessed the calm composure of a person who had made friends with danger. Only recently have I learned of a Vietnam memory that haunted him throughout his post–Army life: seeing his friend and teammate blown up in front of him on Christmas Eve. Like so many Vietnam combat veterans, Howard looked to drugs for relief from pain.

I was often privately critical of vets who could not put the wounds of war behind them and move on with their lives. I had seen as much carnage as many – in jungles and rice paddies, in hospitals and makeshift morgues – and I was able to bury images of dead and wounded young American and Vietnamese soldiers in the graveyard of my subconscious. Why couldn't they?

The answer, I have concluded, is twofold. My seminary training had taught me to how to compartmentalize mind from emotions and thereby shield myself from the basic human feeling of compassion. Even when writing to the mother of a young soldier who had bled to death in my arms, I did not allow myself to feel her pain. Deaths and wounds of soldiers on both sides of the conflict and deaths and wounds of noncombatant women and children were the daily fare of war. Furthermore, I had never lost a close friend to a bullet, mortar shell, or booby trap or suffered the loss of a friend who I would never hear of or from again.

Howard wanted a motorcycle, but without collateral or sufficient monthly income, he could not qualify for a loan or make payments. My financial assets were no better than Howard's, but I had the Roman collar, a symbol of trust in 1973. The bank required no collateral whatsoever of me. When I applied for a bank loan, my word that I could make the monthly payments was sufficient surety. Consequently, I offered Howard the option of joint ownership of a motorcycle and shared payments on the loan. The bike was a Honda 500, large enough to ride the freeways, but light enough to handle if it fell over. I wanted a motorcycle too.

I had no worries about the longevity of our relationship. There was something about Howard that inspired trust.

* * *

Out of the blue, our landlord informed us that he wanted to sell the house. His decision came shortly after we had completed the interior renovations. He wanted only sixteen thousand dollars for the house, a reasonable price, but far more than I wanted to borrow. It was time to move on.

I was a firm believer at the time that adversity could be a blessing in disguise. I'd seen the hypothesis work many times. None of the current residents was upset; they were all ready to give reality a try. The blessing came in the form of an offer from a friend to open another Reality House in Gainesville, Florida, a college town beleaguered by drug traffic. He would provide a rent-free, three-bedroom house with two acres of land on the edge of town.

The offer was especially attractive to me. It would mean returning to my home state, and the hometown of the University of

Florida, where I began my collegiate studies, or more truthfully, started my football career. Two Reality House residents, Howard and Michael, plus the son of a friend, wanted to be a part of Reality House South.

Moving to Gainesville, Florida

We left Cleveland in mid summer, 1973, in a caravan of three vehicles: the old 1959 powder-blue Cadillac, an oil-chugging Ford minivan (always seconds away from collapse), and a U-Hall truck loaded with household furniture and a 500cc Honda motorcycle. Howard, Michael and Eric were looking for a new life in Florida. I was drifting along after yet another brief romantic experience, this one terminated by what I thought I was bound to do: namely, live the celibate life of an avowed Catholic priest, regardless of the cost.

The Gainesville house sat fifty feet up a gentle incline from a dirt road that ran through a forest of muscular oaks and tall pines. There was ample room for a twenty-square-foot garden next to the house. The bungalow was located about eight miles north of downtown Gainesville; not a neighbor in sight.

Once again we faced an immediate income problem. The solution came unexpectedly in an offer to all of us to work in a door-assembly factory owned by the same friend who had provided our living quarters. It was minimum wage work, but it paid for groceries, utilities, and other living expenses.

In addition, I picked up a few extra dollars saying Sunday Masses at a parish adjacent to the University of Florida. It was a mixed congregation of students, faculty, and parishioners living in the immediate area. The pastor was a professor of religion who taught at the university and ran a weekly, radical radio program. His assistant, a young Irish priest, appropriately named Pat, was studying for a doctorate in psychology. It was my first time in a long time to enjoy the occasional company of fellow Catholic clerics over meals in a rectory. As far as I knew, they were both straight arrows free of any difficulties with clerical celibacy.

* * *

In the end, Reality House South never materialized. We attracted no new members and the old, rehabilitated former members wanted to go their separate ways: two to sweethearts and later marriage and one back to Ohio.

20

Reentry Struggles

I DID NOT EXPECT MY REENTRY into religious community life to be easy after eight years of independent living, with full freedom to pick and choose my ministries. But it wasn't long before the restraining yoke of obedience and the sting of celibacy began having their effects on me – taking the form of depression. I felt like I was between the proverbial rock and a hard place: the rock, leaving; staying, the hard place. Experience had taught me that I could not handle the anxiety overload of leaving, but I thought I could live with the hard place: remaining faithful to a commitment made twenty-four years earlier.

I was wrong. The warning of the psychologist I had consulted in San Francisco echoed off the walls of my memory, "If you don't listen to your feelings, you will have a nervous breakdown or commit suicide." Listening to feelings related to loneliness and recognizing my attraction to women and the felt need for one woman in my life had led me to involvements with several other women, broken vows, and two unsuccessful attempts to request a formal release from the priesthood.

Each of these women had suffered because I could not follow through with a commitment to marriage. Each would have suffered more had we married – in the fervor of romantic love or, better said, erotic love or just plain lust – before I was ready. I felt like a prisoner with a lifetime no-parole sentence. It was time for me to seek counsel.

Help came from an unexpected quarter in the person of a Jesuit priest whose advice I had sought while participating in a week-long spiritual retreat. Responding to my predicament, he surprised me with a simple question: "Do you think God wants you to be happy?" After a short reflective pause, I answered, "Yes." He agreed, then directed me to a psychologist in New York City, an hour's drive north of the Shrine.

Once a week, for eight weeks, traveling to and from New York City on a motorcycle that Howard, a Reality House vet, had turned over to me, I openly shared my life and feelings with a male, middle-aged Jewish psychologist. I was not impressed with the man, however. He came across as cold and clinical. He listened more than he spoke. After six sessions, he surprised me with a question: "What do you think is going on here?" Happy to hear his voice for once rather than my own, but puzzled by the question, I answered (without saying it's about time you said something), "I'm pouring my guts out and you're doing nothing." "Time's up," he said. "See you next Thursday."

Why had he waited till the end of our session to ask me such a perplexing question? I left in a huff, feeling as though I was wasting my time and thinking that the doctor was not earning the hourly wage of forty dollars my religious community was paying him. For a week, I pondered his question. Finally, I realized that as he listened to me talk, he was patiently waiting for me to listen to myself. In effect, I was talking myself into leaving. When I told the doctor I was calling it quits, he advised against the decision, saying, "You're not ready. You're going to need more help." He was right, but I did not have the patience to endure more of his indirect counseling. I knew the decision to leave had to be mine, and I wanted to get on with the pursuit of happiness. Having failed twice earlier to live peacefully with my exit, I again felt some apprehension, but this time was different. I had the help of two people interested in my well-being and distance from any emotional involvement with a woman who would be affected by my decision.

For the third time I petitioned the Vatican to let me go. I doubt if my two earlier requests had ever reached the pope's desk, given the large number of laicization petitions that were being submitted in the seventies, but I knew that Pope Paul VI — in spite of his recognized high regard for celibacy — was granting dispensations liberally. I attribute his willingness to release those of us asking for dispensation to his exceptional intelligence. Ordinarily, release from religious vows and the obligation of celibacy took at least six months. My third petition was granted in three. I'm of the opinion that the powers-that-were at that time did not want to give me a chance to change my mind again.

Too well known as a priest in my hometown of Jacksonville, I decided to try California, where my brother, Pat, had settled. I failed, however, to take Pat's high profile into account – he was then one of six county supervisors in Santa Cruz – and I thought it better to look elsewhere. I did not want to be known as Supervisor Liteky's brother. I decided to go south to San Diego, a city with fond childhood memories.

As the summer sun was setting, I boarded a Greyhound bus for San Diego. Seated in darkness, by a right-side window, I easily slipped into slumber, listening to the music of the motor humming and tires parting air, feeling mildly excited over the new adventure before me, feeling free to explore a life that included the possibility of a guilt-free romance.

A half hour into the trip, I woke to the groan of an engine gearing down. When the bus rolled to a stop beneath a street light, at an intersection in the city of Watsonville, I could see a crossroads sign right out my window. Bright white letters painted on a green background reflected the names of intersecting highways: Freedom Blvd. and Green Valley Rd. I smiled and contentedly drifted back to sleep as the bus moved on, thinking this was God's way of telling me I was on the right track. Over the years I've passed through this intersection many times and each time I do, I smile, with no regrets. Writing this reminds me of the time I ran away from home on a bus from Florida to Virginia when I was twelve. This time I felt like I was running *toward* rather than *away from* something.

Settling down in San Diego was no burden financially, at least at the start. The U.S. government was sending me two hundred dollars a month: one hundred for the Medal of Honor pension and one hundred for a 30 percent disability, related to stress-induced blurred vision and a temporary loss of speech. In 1975, two hundred dollars was enough for me to rent a studio apartment, pay utilities, and eat.

Shortly after moving into the studio apartment at the end of a cul-de-sac, a tiny, gray, tiger-striped kitten started hanging around my front door, obviously looking for room and board. I reasoned she could earn her keep mousing around.

One day into life with this little creature resulted in divorce. She was a mobile home for a family of fleas that now found a new comfortable place in which to settle down and populate. Overnight, the fleas traveled to the four corners of my studio and took up residence in rugs, chairs, and clothing. When I dressed in the morning, fleas by the thousands blackened the first eight inches of my beige trousers. Kitty, oblivious to the residents she carried, seemed comfortable enough sleeping on a throw rug. Out the front door and over to a hardware store I hustled, leaving kitty and her companions to the comfort of the studio. I returned with two aerosol bombs, activated the pair, and took kitty to the local animal shelter.

I spent the rest of the day exploring downtown San Diego and nearby Balboa Park, a piece of urban real estate adorned with royal palms, select shrubbery, exotic flowers, and young, carefree lovers strolling about, hand in hand, or hip to hip, lost in the wonder of one another, stopping on biological cues, for an impulsive embrace. I would be envious until I found a love of my own, but where to look for the woman of my dreams outside of my dreams?

"Rich Uncle"

My earlier relationships with women had come about by way of happenstance. I never had to initiate an involvement. At forty-three going on twenty (the age I entered the seminary), I felt like a teenager: shy, yet excited about the search for the woman I fantasized was looking for me. However, there was the problem of employment. I was not naïve enough to believe that my financial insecurity would not have been an issue when the right woman came along, so I decided to use my GI benefits and return to college to study psychology, learn more about myself in the process, and make a decent living.

A trip to the San Diego Veterans Administration resulted in a change in my college plans. When a benefits counselor reviewed my Army discharge certificate, he noticed the Medal of Honor listed in the awards section. He informed me that I was entitled to a job like his at the VA.

"How come?" I asked.

"By way of an executive order of President Truman, who thought so highly of the Medal of Honor that he never wanted a recipient to be without a job."

"What does the job pay?" I said in a tone of peaked interest.

"To start, sixteen thousand a year."

I felt as though I had received an inheritance from an un-known rich uncle, named Harry Truman: a lifetime job with a middle-class salary – more than enough courtship and marriage money. I was on my way to a new goal and a new life with no idea of how I was going to find someone to share it.

Women at work were all either too young, too old, or too married. I felt that God might help with a happenstance, as he had done in the case of women I had dated earlier. He knew the woman I needed who needed me. All I had to do was be patient and wait. Such was my faith in those early days after my exit from religious community life.

While President Truman's gift of a job at the VA satisfied my financial needs, I knew it was not what I wanted to do for the rest of my already half-lived life. In addition, my emotional needs re-mained unsatisfied. Consequently, after eight months on the job, I quit and reverted to my original plan of using my GI benefits for job education. This meant returning to a survival-income exis-tence and fewer chances to meet Ms. Right. But my gut instinct was to move on.

Molly

No sooner had I resumed my formal education than providence gifted me with an opportunity that called for personal initiative and courage. She was alone, seated in a coffee bar located in the basement of the cathedral where I attended Sunday Mass. With three empty stools on either side of her she must have sensed some invasion of her space as I nonchalantly slipped on to a stool to her left. She paid no attention to me as I sat and ordered a cof-fee, but I swiveled to the right and risked engagement with a friendly "good morning."

She responded with an invitational smile and a sonorous "hello," seasoned with a rich Irish brogue. I was immediately in-trigued. Molly was a classic blue-eyed blonde with flawless fair skin, rosy cheeks, attractive facial features, and an inviting smile. I judged her to be about thirty-five. Casual, introductory conver-sation flowed smoothly, until we entered the political arena. It was 1976, the year of presidential campaigning. When I men-tioned my preference, Jimmy Carter, she passionately dismissed my choice in a tone of Catholic moral rectitude that caught me completely by surprise.

This woman was definitely not playing around the fringes

of politically correct conversation, nor did she feel she needed to impress me. She was who she was, and she was letting me know it. With the infallible authority of a pope, she informed me that Jimmy Carter was not pro-life and therefore a poor presidential choice. I responded with a plea for tolerance and respect for differences of opinion.

No way! No room for differences in a matter as morally clear as abortion. She countered with "That's the trouble with people like you: fuzzy thinking." At this juncture I should have bid this Irish hellcat a fond-less farewell and saved myself from future verbal abuse, but lust is not easily tethered.

She was too attractive to dismiss on the grounds of an untimely remark. She was also the first attractive woman I had encountered in my renewed search for Ms. Right. I could not let her slip away without another attempt to engage. I simply ignored her verbal thrust, skipped over an invitation for coffee, and invited her out. Without hesitation, she accepted as if she knew I was hooked.

For a few months, we enjoyed the energizing, magical chemistry of romantic love. Neither of us mentioned Jimmy Carter again. Due to our respective Catholic beliefs on the relegation of sex to marriage, we never made it to bed, an experience I regret to this writing. Foreplay was also forbidden, but near impossible to avoid, requiring confession before receiving communion. For the most part, we endured the emotional torment of tactile restraint. Our romantic relationship hummed along nicely until a subject of great moral import surfaced in the form of a single word: homosexuality.

On a cool spring evening, while lying on a soft, white, flokati rug in front of an open fireplace, she asked me to look over an essay she had written for a civics class. I cannot remember the subject of her work, nor how we drifted into the subject of our respective siblings. However, I will never forget her reaction when I revealed that my brother Pat was gay.

With the heated passion of an overzealous fundamentalist preacher, she morphed from a lovely Irish lassie into a Joan of Arc regaled in shining armor, astride a white stallion, verbally charging at me with lethal intent, blurting out an admonition of moral rectitude that lifted me to my feet, sending the civics paper flying across the room, and setting me on an escape route to the door. She was too busy gathering in her essay to react to my departure.

It was a five-mile walk back to my apartment. In the cool of that late evening, I decided to cut my losses and move on, but breaking up was easier said than done. We did not talk for two weeks. When we did meet again, I was for reconciliation, but she could no longer tolerate my moral liberality.

She told me I had "too many coo-ca-ra-chas" – I had never heard the term used in this context, but immediately understood its meaning: fuzzy thinking, wishy-washy moral positions – to continue a romantic relationship. She then did what I could not: she terminated our relationship.

Since we were parting, I had nothing to lose by sharing an observation I would have never brought up during our romantic interlude. I told her it was she who had, in her colorful metaphor, coo-ca-ra-chas, Catholic coo-ca-ra-chas that were too rigid for me. Furthermore, she was more Catholic than the pope.

We walked out of one another's lives, but not forever.

Back into low-budget living, I needed a low-rent place to live in so I could follow my desire to write about what I knew, namely, my life and my ongoing search for a woman to share what remained of the journey. As luck or Providence would have it, a perfect place to write popped up in the form of a rent-free beach-front cabin on kidney-shaped Pine Island, thirty yards off the west coast of Florida, connected to the mainland by a rickety old bridge.

When I told Molly of my good fortune, she wished me well and encouraged me to stay in touch.

Vietnam

Photographs of Chaplain (Capt.) Charles J. Liteky during his three tours of active-duty service in Vietnam.

Medal of Honor

Medal of Honor awardees at the White House with President Lyndon B. Johnson, November 19, 1968. (l-r) Gary Wetzel, Dwight H. Johnson, Sammy L. Davis, James Allen Taylor, and Charles (Angelo) Liteky.

Fr. Charles (Angelo) Liteky (center) shares his Medal of Honor citation and medal with his mother, Gertrude, and his brother, Patrick, 1968.

Veterans Fast for Life

Senator Ted Kennedy addresses a news conference during the Veterans Fast for Life. Liteky is seated far left, with Mizo, Murphy, and Willson. (Credit: Terry Ashe/The LIFE Images Collection/ Getty Images)

Veterans Fast for Life participants (l-r) on the steps of the U.S. Capitol in Washington, D.C.: George Mizo, Duncan Murphy, Charlie Liteky, and Brian Willson.

Actor/peace activist Martin Sheen (left) walks in solidarity with Veterans Fast for Life fasters Charlie Liteky (pictured here), George Mizo, Duncan Murphy, and Brian Willson (not shown), September 22, 1986. (Credit: Michael Norcia/ New York Post Archives / © NYP Holdings, Inc. via Getty Images)

Thirty-five-day water-only fast in 1990 at the main gate of Ft. Benning, Georgia, calling for the closing of the School of Americas. Charlie Liteky is pictured second from the right. (All photo credits: SOA Watch)

School of the Americas Actions

Blood-pouring action at the headquarters of the School of the Americas, Fort Benning, Georgia. (l-r) Patrick Liteky, Charlie Liteky, and (in the foreground) Roy Bourgeois.

Charlie Liteky is arrested after the blood-pouring action at the School of the Americas, Nov. 16, 1990, to honor the murdered Jesuits and two women in El Salvador.

Charlie Liteky (above right) in the November SOA Watch vigil, Fort Benning, 1995.

Iraq

Charlie Liteky is pictured here (upper right-hand corner) with an Iraqi mother and her child during his solidarity service in Iraq in 2003. (Credit: Voices for Peace, 2003)

Home in San Francisco

Back home in San Francisco, Charlie Liteky
enjoys life with his wife, Judy, and their pet dog,
Scarlett (above), and a day together by San Francisco Bay (below).

21

Pine Island & Judy Balch

THE PINE ISLAND CABIN WAS AN ART PIECE, a potpourri of cast-off lumber, glass, wire, and pipes that the now deceased eccentric father of a friend had built. It sat precariously ten feet above the low-tide mark, bolted to rough wooden pilings driven deep into the sand. The builder was neither a carpenter, plumber, nor electrician, but he was a bundle of whimsical, senior-citizen energy, unafraid to make mistakes and willing to live with the consequences. I venture to surmise that he did not own a level or a square. With vision and determination to build his own place, he succeeded in creating a seaside shack that he called home.

After installing a large recycled window in the front wall of the cabin, I was able to enjoy an unobstructed view of the Gulf of Mexico, usually a sleepy, wave-less body of water, but on occasion subject to stormy weather. The sunsets were an artist's delight. When storms arrived, lightning bolts zigzagged across the horizon in an awesome display of Mother Nature's power and creative beauty. Storms also sent waves breaking against the pilings, rocking and shaking the cabin like a ship in choppy water.

Faithful to the advice of my creative writing instructor, I wrote for five hours a day for two years, allowing for time out to swim to a raft anchored a hundred yards off shore, bathe in the sun, and scan the beach for a woman to share my idyllic environment. I often thought of Pine Island as a paradise, waiting for the arrival of Eve.

Several women did appear at different times during my stay in the Pine Island cabin. One of them was Molly, my old flame, who called one day and proposed a visit. I was excited to think that she might now be open to a renewed relationship despite my "cucarachas."

No such luck. She just wanted to use me. She had inherited a 1976 Lincoln Continental from a relative in Atlanta and needed a companion to help her drive back to California.

It was the end of my second year on Pine Island. The writing was not going well. I chose fiction based on fact and the third-person narrative technique. The result read like a dull novel, contrived, insipid. I recognized my impoverished writing style and the dearth of real-life experience so essential to good writing. Furthermore, I needed dental work, which meant money I did not have. So I decided to help Molly drive to California, return to the VA, tend to my teeth, and resume searching for the woman of my dreams. The older I became, the more distant the dream.

The cross-country drive in the confines of a luxury car, with shared meals and motel rooms, was a mix of pleasure and frustration due to the mutual physical attraction that separation had not dimmed. In the fog of passion, we forgot our differences and came dangerously close to sexual intimacy, but we were too Catholic to cohabit without marital commitment.

Renewal of my attraction or more honestly stated, lust, moved me to suggest marriage, despite knowing that close-quarter living with Molly would drive me to the brink. I reasoned that pleasure would outweigh pain. Molly did not see it as I did, and reminded me of my cucarachas. She was undoubtedly right, but I still regret missing the fun of trying. Expressing gratitude for my cross-country assistance, she let me down gracefully. I was neither surprised nor crushed by her stance. I left her at a friend's house in Palo Alto, never expecting to see her again.

By way of Greyhound I continued north, having chosen San Francisco over San Diego as a place to resettle. Strange as it may sound, I did not like the constant clement weather of San Diego. Limited income led me to lodge at the YMCA on the banks of the bay, two blocks away from the VA building, President Harry Truman's guaranteed employment site for Medal of Honor recipients. I began again at the VA in January of 1980.

After two-and-a-half years away from the job, I needed some brushing up on the rules and regulations governing veterans' benefits. Unsolicited help came from a tall U.S. marine, a

Vietnam veteran, a man I came to regard as the best benefits counselor in the system and a good friend. George was devoted to the veteran, but not to the VA management's mandated time-limited interview schedule. Consequently, he was forever being chided by supervisors for giving too much attention to veterans' personal problems. I tried to follow his example.

Though threatened with dismissal, George continued his human approach. He had a special strength that made him immune to threats of separation. He was the in-house, irate veteran appeaser. Because of his size, humor, boxing talents, and common sense he was able to calm brewing storms. There was no need to hire security. George was it.

With my first paycheck, I moved into a low-rent hotel room in downtown San Francisco, in a neighborhood called the Tenderloin, a pocket of poverty in the midst of luxury hotels, restaurants, and upper-class department stores. Tourists were advised to avoid the area, but I wanted to experience the life of the poor in one of the most beautiful and wealthiest cities in the world, a city named after a universally recognized servant of the poor, St. Francis of Assisi. It was incongruous to me that a city named after a charitable person like Francis would tolerate poverty.

Judy Balch

A year passed and I was still single and still looking for the right woman. I had not dated for a year, but I remained vigilant. One day, George asked me how it was going. I responded, "Okay, but for the absence of a woman in my life. What ever happened to the one your wife thought would be good for me, the woman she met in Arnie's Bar, the ex-nun?"

Slightly embarrassed, George confessed that it had slipped his mind. He then excused himself to break for lunch. I later learned that he spent his lunch break feverishly fingering through the Yellow Pages looking for the cash register company that employed a woman named Judy. After many calls a woman with a lighthearted voice answered the phone.

George introduced himself as the husband of Kathy, whom Judy had met at Arnie's Bar. At the time Judy was dating Kathy's friend Mike. She remembered Kathy and allowed George to make a pitch for me. Blind dates are risky, like night parachute jumping into dense fog on a moonless night. You never know where or how you are going to land. In addition, there is the fear of rejection and the fear of losing respect for a friend's judgment.

Moreover, the chance that two perfect strangers might meet and meld is not high on the probability chart. But, as a man approaching fifty, wandering in the dateless desert of romantic aridity, I was desperate enough to take another chance on the mysterious thing called love.

George told Judy that I was an ex-priest, a qualification an ex-nun might consider appealing. But not this ex-nun. My clerical background was not a plus. As a nun, she had met too many priests negatively affected by the adulation given them, but she was willing to take a chance on a possible exception. On the fourth of February 1981, ex-priest met ex-nun in Arnie's Bar, a middle-class, after-work watering hole in downtown San Francisco. He had been looking for a wife for six years. She did not have marriage on her mind. She was not looking, just exploring.

On the short walk from the VA to Arnie's, George confessed that he had never met the woman I was about to meet. He accepted his wife's description of Judy and concluded that she and I would be good with one another. I shook my head, chuckled and assured George of my willingness to risk rejection based on the chemistry of mutual attraction.

Seated at a table with a view to the door, George, Kathy, and I ordered drinks and awaited the arrival of the mystery woman who had agreed to meet a mystery man. She appeared shortly, walking sprightly through the open door directly to our table. Before she sat down, I noted her height, figure, and hair color: approximately 5'10" tall, symmetrical, with brunette-colored hair, darkly shaded. She was totally at ease in a situation that would cause anxiety in a person less at home with herself. So, I relaxed. After ten minutes of introductory conversation, George and Kathy left us on our own, feeling that the introduction had been made. The rest was up to us.

After finishing our cocktails, Judy agreed to dine with me at a Chinese restaurant. At the time, I did not own a car, so she drove us to the edge of Chinatown, where we began our walking search for a suitable restaurant, preferably one frequented by Chinese patrons. On the way, we passed a poor, middle-aged Chinese man lying on the sidewalk, obviously suffering the debilitating effects of excessive alcohol. He groaned as we approached and she moaned as we passed. Living in the Tenderloin, the sight of inebriants was commonplace for me. I could say "too bad" without feeling bad. Judy, however, was moved to react with a compassionate moan that said more than words about the kind of person she is.

The meal was vintage Chinese, good and plenty. Conversation begged for more. We shared our personal histories. Both of us had come from religious community life. Both of us had taken vows of poverty, chastity, and obedience. However, I sensed that my exodus from religious life was more traumatic than hers. I left because I did not want to live my life exclusively with men and with the ever-burdensome tension of clerical celibacy, which in my case had led to experimentation and defeat. Judy left religious life along with six hundred other nuns in opposition to the male domination of an ecclesiastical prelate who had arrogantly interfered in the internal affairs of her religious order.

Shared values and preferences held the promise of future dates and the possibility that I had been gifted with the woman I'd been seeking. She insisted on paying her share of the bill and offered to drive me home even though she knew my hotel was in the heart of a neighborhood known to be unfriendly after dark.

I suggested she drop me off a block from the Tenderloin. Before I could politely say "good night, hope to see you again," she leaned across the bench seat of her Mercury Comet, kissed me on the cheek, smiled, and said, "Good night, Charlie."

Surprised but not dismayed by this forward, first-date move by an ex-nun who clearly had no inhibitions, I asked, "May I call you?"

"Yes," she said, as if she were expecting me to ask. As she pulled away, I stood frozen in amazement, watching the taillights of her Mercury Comet disappear around the corner.

Courtship began. Within a month, Judy had narrowed her dating partners to me. We frequently played San Francisco tourists, riding cable cars, strolling hand in hand along Fisherman's Wharf, hiking through Golden Gate Park, and rowboating on Stow Lake, where we had our first lover's full-blown kiss.

We were falling in love, but not free falling. The chemistry of love was not new to either of us. Sexual excitement was monitored and controlled. Catholic moral limits for me, and fear of pregnancy for her, barred the door to complete sexual intimacy.

Early on, I cautioned her to consider the implications of our age difference. She was eleven years younger than me. In just fifteen years I would be eligible for Social Security and she would be married to an old man. She replied, "That's okay, Charlie. I've been around old people a good portion of my life."

Throughout our courtship, we shared the cost of everything,

placing our money in a common wallet she suggested I carry, since checks are usually presented to the man.

After three months of weekend dating, I concluded that she was the woman I'd been seeking. She had it all: looks, values, sense of humor, and a luminescent smile to balance my serious bent. We discussed marriage and she made it clear that she was not ready. I understood her caution. I had been looking for a wife for six years. She was still in a male experimental mode. In fact, she had dated two Charlies prior to me.

When I woke up to the fact that Judy and I were not on the same marriage track, it made no sense to continue working for the sake of making money. Compliments of Harry Truman, I could come and go, to and from the VA as necessity dictated, so I quit and returned to writing.

Termination of employment to pursue a questionable goal like writing did not sit well with economically conservative Judy. Dating grew less frequent and romance began to cool, but the coals had not turned to ashes. One morning I woke up to a thought bubbling up from my subconscious, "Scratch her and you'll find gold." I decided to let her know in an unobtrusive way that I was still thinking about marriage.

She lived with another former nun, Marcia, near the top of a small mountain within the city called Mt. Davidson. Marcia was also exploring the new world of men, but less cautiously than Judy. Two years older than Judy and more worldly wise, she advised Judy to sleep with her man before marrying him. (Not bad advice, given the fact that personality traits, selfish and unselfish, surface in pleasurable events like eating and making love.) Here, I'm not encouraging anyone to do anything. My homespun aphorisms are just that, homespun and therefore, subjective.

From a large bay window, Judy had a grand view of South San Francisco and on clear days, you could see to the ocean. Below and a mile distant, you could see the north side of a huge hundred-square-foot empty cement reservoir, stretching laterally for a quarter mile. As the reservoir was empty its walls were an ideal canvas for graffiti artists, used liberally by students from the community college across the street. Taking a cue from the students, I conceived the idea of sending Judy a graphic reminder.

In the still of a cold, mid-December morning, I climbed over the six-foot-high chain-link fence around the reservoir. I was lugging a tan duffle bag containing three gallons of paint (one red and two white), plus two three-inch brushes. Aided by rubber-soled sneakers, I descended twenty-five feet down the thirty degree angled side of the reservoir, planted my feet, looked around for security guards, and started creating a primitive romantic symbol that would bring marriage back to the front of her mind.

Finished before daylight, I proceeded to the legal side of the fence, feeling relieved that I had not been arrested for trespassing and defacing public property. Reflecting on this romantic caper now, I wish I had been arrested and had my police mug shot plastered on the front page of the *San Francisco Chronicle*, with the caption, "Love is not only for the young," or "They try to tell us we're too old."

The symbol I painted was of a white arrow piercing a large red heart over the name ALICE and the question WHEN? Signed L.E.L., an acronym for Lancelot. I had dubbed Judy "Alice" after the Wonderland girl because of her lighthearted, other-worldly spirit. For myself, I immodestly chose Lance, short for Lancelot, fearless, romantic knight of King Arthur's Round Table in the mythical kingdom of Camelot.

I was, and am, a hopeless romantic, still enjoying it. Discussing this incident with Judy twenty-six years after the fact, she informed me that the symbol used by her religious order, Sisters of the Immaculate Heart of Mary, was a silver heart pierced with a sword to symbolize the sorrows of the Mother of Jesus, the principal sorrow being a witness to the barbaric crucifixion of her son. Unwittingly I had used the pierced heart to symbolize our romance. As I sit and write, I cannot help but reflect on the series of sorrows Judy has endured throughout our twenty-seven years of marriage. I will recount some of these events as these words roll on, but for me, they pale in color alongside the moments of love we've shared.

My artistic endeavor went unnoticed for weeks. Frustration led me to buy a pair of high-powered binoculars and point Judy in the direction of my hand-painted symbol. Intellectually, she appreciated my whimsical effort to move her along, so to speak, but she remained cautious; she was not about to be rushed or even nudged into marriage.

Once again, I understood her hesitancy and stopped mentioning marriage. At this juncture, I think she saw me as an idealistic dreamer, and worse yet, unemployed – hardly a good marriage risk. So when I asked her for an answer to the question painted on the side of the reservoir, she expressed her caution and her doubts about our compatibility.

Financially, I was then struggling along on three hundred dollars a month. But, once again, providence smiled on me when I was most in need.

Colorado Retreat

A friend who knew I wanted to write offered an ideal place, a small cabin in the Rocky Mountains of Colorado, five thousand feet above Boulder and fifteen hundred miles from San Francisco. When I told Judy I intended to leave San Francisco, she listened with no signs of sadness or protestation. On the contrary, she encouraged me to do what I felt I had to do.

This woman was and is the most rational person I've ever known. I never say to her what I've said to other women, "You're not being logical." It follows that she is a math major with a master's degree in statistics. We agreed to write, and write we did – strangely, enough, love letters, greater in volume than pages of the forever-in-progress book I'm still trying to finish. Hopefully, I will conclude this story of my life before going to whatever lies beyond the millisecond of my last breath.

The separation was just what we needed to realize how much we meant to one another. The Colorado mountain cabin was even more isolated than the one on the Gulf of Mexico. Sitting two hundred yards back from the paved highway leading to Boulder, one could easily pass it unnoticed. The owner of the cabin offered me a twenty-two-caliber pistol to discourage unwanted guests or animals. I could not see the house of my nearest neighbor, the mother of the friend who directed and delivered me to Colorado. The cabin was a pine-slab creation, inside and out, appealingly rustic, but ill-suited for winter residence. I offered to insulate the place in exchange for free rent. The landlord agreed and I was off to a fresh writing start, in another rent-free writing space, in an idyllic environment.

Again I wrote four to five hours a day, drawing from my experiences as an Army chaplain in Vietnam with the same passionless results. In addition to book writing, I wrote three or four letters a week to Judy and received as many from her. The footpath to the mailbox on the side of road in front of the cabin was worn to dust in the summer and never covered by the snows of a Colorado winter. After six months of letter writing and lonely living, I invited Judy to come for a visit.

Via the written word we had ascended to another level of love, referring to former marital reservations as "rocks in our garden," that could be either removed or circumvented. We spent five days together, enjoying the awe-inspiring colors of fall: brilliant reds and yellows and shades of both and the golden leaves of white-barked aspens.

It was a time for me to reveal more of who I thought I was. I'd been searching for identity since the day when I was no longer called Father. Judy listened intently, but refrained from revealing anything about herself unless specifically asked. I was not into the labor of intimate interrogation. I wanted free-flowing personal revelation based on trust from the woman in my life.

After leaving religious life, I became a student of the fascinating subject of female perspective. I wanted to see life through the eyes of a woman, especially the woman in my life. In Judy's reticence to reveal her thoughts and feelings, I had run into a rock, I dare say, a boulder I had not noticed before, and I could not see a way around it. Now it was I who began to grow cool on the idea of marriage, just when she was approaching the threshold. I later learned that she had come to Colorado ready to accept a proposal if offered. My newfound reticence was not easy to explain to Judy without hurting her. I told her I had to do some more thinking before taking the big step, but I did not mention the real problem.

San Francisco

Returning to San Francisco without the proposal she had been finally ready to accept was deflating, but not discouraging. It was her turn to wait, if she was willing, and my time to reflect, which I did for two months, reaching the conclusion that she needed time to grow in love and trust of me before giving me the gift of herself, her hopes, fears, likes and dislikes, and feelings about anything and everything.

The time she needed did not preclude marriage. I reasoned that if she trusted me enough to begin an unknown lifetime journey with me, that trust would grow and free her to reveal the person I wanted to know. I was maneuvering around the rock.

Shortly into January of 1983, I proposed via a long-distance telephone call. "Judy, I think we should get married." I did not say, "Will you marry me?" I was protecting myself against the pain of rejection, by simply rendering an opinion, "I think we should get married."

I was surprised and elated with a rapid response that did not require further discussion. That she took it to be a proposal is indicated by her answer: "I cannot accept a telephone proposal." An implied Yes was enough for me to catch the next flight to San Francisco and give her the direct proposal she wanted, deserved, and accepted.

22

El Salvador

SOCIAL LIFE IN SAN FRANCISCO FOR MY NEW WIFE, Judy, and me revolved around the church of our marriage, St. John of God. The pastor, Father Mickey McCormick, the same priest who married us, was a kind, avuncular man possessed of a wonderful sense of humor and the good sense to lead by leading least. He directed indirectly, encouraging us to think for ourselves and respond to Christ's command to love all humanity, inclusive of enemies, as we felt called.

But early in 1985 church networks also faced a significant challenge: refugees from El Salvador, fleeing from a civil war, began to arrive in San Francisco in large numbers, and local church people began to support them. Churches, Protestant and Catholic, encouraged parishioners to host house meetings and listen to people who had risked their lives to flee their oppressed homeland. Their tales of murder, rape, torture, and disappearance of loved ones were unbelievable.

The two sides of the conflict in El Salvador were the oppressive rich, supported by the Salvadoran Army, which had been trained and equipped by the United States, and the oppressed peasants, who were self-trained, self-supported, and deeply motivated by a desire for freedom and justice. Many of the refugees from the U.S.–supported oppressors had left spouses, children, parents, and grandparents buried or missing in El Salvador. Many mothers carried children with them, in and out of the womb.

While I found it ironic that poor people persecuted by agents of my government should flee to the United States for sanctuary and freedom, I was also deeply touched by the plight of these poor people. Still I found it difficult to believe that my government was funding and training Salvadoran soldiers who were guilty of the horror stories I was hearing. Despite my experience in Vietnam, I still believed that the leaders of my country's government – itself the proud child of a historically acclaimed revolution and, as such, a champion of the oppressed – could be guilty of such blatant, inhuman complicity.

The rationale offered by the White House under President Ronald Reagan for supporting the war against the poor in El Salvador was fear of communism, which was seen as a socioeconomic cancer metastasizing its way north and threatening to enter the United States. In the Reagan administration's view, if communism was not stopped in Central America, we would be fighting communists on the Texas–Mexican border. The absurdity of this rhetoric was evident.

I needed more proof, however, to dispel Reagan's warnings that the communists were coming. Before and after marriage, I, like most Americans, was too occupied with making a living and maintaining a middle-class lifestyle to be any more than casually interested in what was happening beyond one's locality.

In March of 1980 while I was busy at work, Archbishop Óscar Romero was assassinated while celebrating Mass in San Salvador, the capital of El Salvador. This news had passed me by like many other tragic accounts of death anywhere outside the perimeter of my life. Then eight months later in El Salvador, on December 2, three Catholic nuns and a woman layworker were raped, murdered, and buried in a shallow grave by five Salvadoran soldiers. Sad, but what could I do about it? The tragedy had happened hundreds of miles from San Francisco in a foreign country.

The Salvadoran refugees seeking sanctuary in San Francisco, however, were in my face – demanding attention just by being in the city, inviting me into their reality without demanding such, moving me to address my ignorance without calling me ignorant. Little by little the stories of these humble people commanded my attention and pressed me toward a decision to travel south and see for myself.

I was not the only one in need of on-site evidence to be convinced of my country's participation in the misery of the poor of

El Salvador. Nine Vietnam veterans from around the country were planning a fact-finding trip. The organizer was an Air Force veteran who had awakened to the carnage he had been part of in Vietnam. He gave up a promising military career, embraced pacifism, became a medical doctor, and dedicated himself to alleviating suffering. His name was Charlie Clements.

While tending to the ills of Salvadoran laborers in the lettuce fields of Salinas, he noticed unmistakable signs of torture: cigarette burns, cuts, bullet wounds, and broken bones. Reluctantly, his patients told their stories of the brutality inflicted upon them. Mindful of his own participation in a war that had killed and maimed millions, Charlie Clements, former-warrior-become-pacifist and doctor, decided to go to the aid of the most vulnerable victims of the civil war in El Salvador.

To do this he had to travel secretly to the war zones. Once again, he was risking his life for his beliefs, this time as a healer rather than a warrior. What he did to reach the victims of a U.S.–supported war and what he did when he found them constituted enough stories to create the book he eventually wrote, *Witness to War: An American Doctor in El Salvador* (Bantam Books, 1984). I recommend it to anyone who wants an informative, inspirational read. But be careful, it may change you.

He spent a year living with, walking with, and nearly dying with Salvadoran guerrillas and their families. Flying C-130 supply missions in Vietnam placed him above the blood and gore of that war. But, in the mountains of El Salvador, he was in the middle of the sights, sounds, and scents of war, and ironically on the receiving end of bullets and bombs manufactured in and supplied by his own country.

Dr. Clements did not go to El Salvador to support the revolutionary cause of an oppressed people. He went as a healer, a saver of life, to heal civilian casualties, casualties inflicted by the Salvadoran Army trained and supported by the United States.

He reported that he saw no evidence to support a U.S. president's fear-monger's claims of Russian or Cuban military aid to the rebels of El Salvador. He further reported that the vast majority of the revolutionaries were simple peasants, farmers with wives and children, who lived off the land before and during the revolution.

So, in addition to listening to refugee horror stories, I read Dr. Clements's book. I was left in a state of wonder.

Charlie Clements is a man of extraordinary integrity and

one of the bravest men I know, a nonviolent hero who will always be remembered by the Salvadorans whom he risked his life to serve. When he invited me to join a veteran's educational trip to Central America, without hesitation I accepted. The education changed my life.

Journey to El Salvador

We boarded a plane in Miami at three in the afternoon, mid September, 1985: eight Vietnam veterans, including Dr. Clements and Maria, a woman in her twenties who would be our translator. Fluent in Spanish, Maria regularly accompanied groups traveling to Central America.

Two hours' airtime landed us in the middle of a country at war with itself over issues that had plagued Central America since the days of the European invaders: land, power, wealth, and poverty. Ninety-five percent of the wealth of this country was enjoyed by two percent of its inhabitants. The landed gentry in El Salvador – the so-called fourteen families – traced their origins back to Spain and the conquistadors. (Actually there were more than fourteen families, but this label covered the lot of them.)

Dr. Clements briefed us on the danger level in the city and counseled against walking about alone. For the most part, the war was being fought in the countryside and mountains, but the city was not without episodes of violence directed against meddlesome foreigners seeking truth or good people dedicated to helping the poor. For "safety's sake" we were lodged at the Sheraton Hotel in downtown San Salvador, El Salvador's capital. Two years prior to our arrival, two North American land reform experts had been murdered in the dining room of our hotel.

Civilian-clothed death squads, three to four armed men, traveled around the city in tinted-windowed Cherokee jeeps, abducting anyone suspected of subversion. Once forced into the dark interior of the jeep, a man or woman might never be seen again. The government and the army denied any complicity with the death squads, but no effort was made to stop them. And it was generally known that these terrorists, in the strict sense of the word, were military, paramilitary, or hired guns of the rich.

After settling in, another veteran and I decided to check out the neighborhood looking for a snack. It was just before dark when the streetlights popped on, casting pale shadows over the sidewalks and onto storefront windows. The air was hot, humid, and seasoned with scents of charcoal-barbecued meat. Traffic was nil and we were among the few evening strollers.

Following our noses, we walked into a huge canvas-covered, open-air market bordered with food stands alive with families seated around picnic tables eating a variety of local dishes, especially rice, beans, chicken, and tortillas. We seated ourselves at an empty wooden picnic table, ordered local fare, and commented on the orderly, subdued behavior of small children seated around us.

No sooner were we seated than a young man, woman, and child of four, asked to join us. My Spanish was restricted to bare essentials like "hello, goodbye, and where is the bathroom?" But my companion Dave was fluent in the language and immediately began engaging the couple, who were happy to find a Spanish-speaking gringo.

After several rounds of convivial conversation, I asked Dave to question the young man about his opinion of the war. The man stood up immediately, answered with a polite statement, and a friendly smile, "I hope you enjoy your visit to El Salvador. It's a beautiful country and the people are friendly," and left.

We walked briskly back to the hotel. I began to understand why the children were so well-behaved and the streets of San Salvador so empty.

The following morning, we began our quest for truth at the American Embassy, with a country briefing session given by a State Department official assigned the unhappy task of defending U.S. support for a military accused and guilty of human rights abuses calculated to induce fear and submission.

He denied U.S. complicity in, or approval of, atrocities and reiterated the tired argument of the need to defeat communism, but he offered no proof of Russian, Cuban, or Nicaraguan military support.

We listened attentively and patiently to the State Department man as he droned on – figuring we would learn more by nonconfrontation than by argument. He seemed to incorrectly assume that, as veterans of war, we were in sync with military thinking and understood situations that demanded heavy-handed measures. I left the briefing feeling that I'd just met a future used car salesman.

From this propagandistic session with the State Department salesman, we visited the office of aggrieved Salvadoran women known as the Mothers of the Disappeared. Dr. Clements had arranged the meeting. After his year of traveling with and doctoring to Salvadoran peasants in revolt, he was well connected. The room was gloomy, like an empty union meeting hall. We sat on straight-backed wooden chairs arranged in a semicircle.

The mothers wore identical long black dresses that covered their bodies from neck to ankles. Despite the heat and humidity, each Mother draped a bright white scarf gracefully over her head and onto her shoulders. No camera was needed to fix these women in our memory. Short in stature, they immediately, yet unintentionally, drew attention to themselves by their quiet, dignified presence.

The atmosphere was somber and serious. No nervous smiles. No humble deference. They knew what we wanted and they were ready to share their truth despite the personal pain of recollection. One by one they told their stories. A few choked up, a few eyes watered, but not a one lost control. They were hardened to suffering, fearless of death, and determined to find their loved ones, dead or alive. I was in an emotionally frozen state of awe.

Their stories of missing loved ones were much the same: a spouse, a teenager, or a child left home one morning for work, school, or play, and never returned. They just disappeared.

When the women went to the local police station or military post to report a missing person, they were given large black-and-white photos of male and female bodies that had been discarded on the streets of San Salvador or left atop a garbage heap at the city dump. Many of the bodies, some without clothing and mutilated beyond recognition, showed signs of torture that were calculated to strike fear in the heart of the viewer. The Mothers of the Disappeared were not afraid.

When reviewing the pictures offered to the mothers as identification aids, memory whisked me back seventeen years to the blood and gore of Vietnam, blood on the bodies of young men, and their blood on my body. Buried memories never wanting to be unearthed, memories of events I thought I had experienced without emotional injury.

Thus began my epiphany, my wake-up call to the horrors of war, horrors I'd seen before in Vietnam, but had suppressed and filed away in a folder labeled for my eyes only. Words of a professor at Manhattan College referring to a lecture given in defense of the Vietnam War came echoing back: "You need to rise above the assumptions of your subculture."

After leaving the mothers, we traveled by bus to a small, bombed-out village halfway up a rugged mountain named Guazapa, overlooking the capital, a stronghold of the rebels, the same mountain Charlie Clements had crisscrossed on foot while doctoring to guerrillas and their families.

A quarter mile up the rocky road, a uniformed Salvadoran soldier stopped us – a small fellow with a big gun, the U.S. Army M-16 of Vietnam infamy. (Why infamous? Because the bullet of an M-16 tumbles and tears and zigzags through its victim on a destructive path of unknown direction.) He stood boldly alone in the middle of the road, twenty feet from the front of the bus. Three additional soldiers were resting in the shade on the side of the road, with weapons ready.

This was the moment for beauty to meet beast. As if it had been rehearsed, our translator, Maria, stepped from the bus carrying safe conduct papers that a colonel in San Salvador had signed. Approaching the soldier from his left, so as not to block his view of us or our view of him, she offered him the papers along with a friendly smile.

I've always appreciated the seductive power of a beautiful woman, but I'd never seen it so effectively employed. In an instant, the soldier's body language changed from stiff resistance to compliant receptivity. After a studied perusal of the papers, he returned them to Maria and waved us on with a smile.

I don't know if Dr. Clements intended to use Maria as our point person, but she assumed the position without hesitation as if she knew exactly what she was doing. I had no idea when we met in Miami that her good looks and talents would be employed to smooth our way through potentially dangerous territory.

Another mile ahead, the road became a scramble of rocks and potholes that made it impossible to drive. We piled out, left the bus to the driver, and walked a rugged inclined mile to a one-time thriving village that the army had burned and bombed in an effort to deprive guerrillas of support. Typical of Salvadoran villages, the town square was proportionate to the size of the village. In this case the perimeter was roughly four hundred yards around.

One of our group was an Oglala Sioux Indian with peace pipe privileges, meaning he was authorized to conduct peace prayer sessions and pass the pipe. He invited us to participate in a prayer for peace, Indian style. On rocks in a circle at the edge of a square, we were about to begin the peace ceremony when men began to appear on the edge of the woods around twenty meters from our circle. There were six in all. We neither heard nor saw them coming. It was as if they had been beamed down from a spaceship.

Clad in ragged peasant clothing, with bandoliers of bullets draped about their shoulders, the six stood quietly, cradling their weapons like sleeping infants, curiously observing our group of nine men and one woman.

Obviously, they meant no harm and responded to Dr. Clements's welcome and invitation to join in the ceremony for peace. They knew him, either by sight or reputation, the friendly gringo doctor who lived and traveled with resistance guerrillas. Apparently, he had arranged for a meeting with the opposition force. The gringo doctor had returned with more gringos, including a woman who spoke their language. But we would not stay and neither would they.

After passing the pipe, we said *adios* and returned to San Salvador with another vivid impression of people affected by a war our country supported. The peasant warriors melted into the woods as mysteriously as they had appeared.

The courage and simplicity of our visitors impressed me. I found it impossible to believe that any one of them could even define communism. The revolution was homemade, a struggle for a way out of poverty and unbearable oppression by upper-class wealth protected by a brutal army, supported and trained by my country.

Another day was scheduled for El Salvador. We were all emotionally beat and I credit the choice of our next activity to the attentive sensitivity of Dr. Clements. We drove to one of El Salvador's beautiful lakes with a volcano in the background – formerly a tourist attraction, now abandoned, one more casualty of war. I relaxed and tried to decompress, feeling like I'd been pummeled by a herd of stampeding cattle, struck again and again by accounts of atrocities and unwelcome memories of Vietnam.

23

Nicaragua

HEAVY OF HEART, I next decided to travel with a group to Nicaragua, a country like El Salvador, once ruled by a wealthy class protected by a military dictator. The poor, led by a few intellectuals, had successfully defeated the National Guard (NG), bodyguard of a family dynasty of Somoza dictators.

For more than forty years, the Somoza family dictated the lives of millions – maintaining a dictatorship supported by the United States of America. The Somoza National Guard of Nicaragua, like the Salvadoran military, protected the dictatorship and the wealthy from the revolution of the poor before the popular Sandinista revolution toppled the government on July 19, 1979.

The final Somoza dictator, Anastasio Somoza Debayle, had amassed a fortune by way of imperial decree and theft (e.g., pocketing millions of dollars from international earthquake relief aid in 1972). After being overthrown, he took his ill-gotten fortune and raced to Paraguay, where he was later assassinated.

The government of my beloved country – self-acclaimed champion of freedom, democracy, and human rights – had supported dictators in Nicaragua for forty years before the successful Sandinista revolution in July of 1979. Very little impartial news about the overthrow of the Somoza dictatorship ever found its way into U.S. media.

In comparison to El Salvador, Nicaragua was a breath of fresh air. Even though a U.S.– supported counterrevolution was draining the country economically and terrorizing the people in the countryside, Managua, the capital, was relatively calm. People were going about the business of living, enjoying the fruits of the revolution, namely, free health care, education, the right to vote, and above all, an internationally applauded land reform policy.

Again, we lodged in a five-star hotel, reduced by the deprivations of war to three stars. You would not have known that the country was fighting for its life. Able-bodied men were conspicuously absent, however. They would have been an integral part of the work force necessary to create a new Nicaragua, had they not been needed to fight the U.S.–backed Counterrevolutionary Army (Contras). When I first went to Nicaragua with Dr. Charlie Clements's delegation of veterans, I knew little about the history of this country of a mere 3 million people, half of whom were below the age of sixteen.

After El Salvador, it came as no surprise to learn that my country had supported the dictatorship of the Somoza family from its inception. Of course, support of dictators is often no exception to U.S. foreign policy. Historically, U.S. government support for dictators the world over depends not on the way they treat their people but on the way they enhance U.S. economic or strategic interests.

Despite the fact that a revolution to overthrow a dictator in Nicaragua had been going on since the early 1970s, and finally succeeded in 1979, when we landed there in September of 1985, I knew next to nothing about the history of Nicaragua.

Nicaraguan peasants were not pouring into San Francisco as were Salvadorans, telling stories of torture and death at the hands of the new revolutionary government. The poor of Nicaragua were the beneficiaries rather than the victims of a revolution.

However, some Nicaraguan refugees were unhappy with the new Sandinista government, many of them wealthy landowners and businessmen who, along with the dictator Somoza, had lived luxurious lives in a lopsided economy that relegated the poor to a submarginal existence. After the revolution, many of the malcontents fled to Miami, where some continue to enjoy lives of luxury in the country that had supported their privileged lives in Nicaragua.

Also fleeing Nicaragua were members of Somoza's National Guard. Many of the defeated NG forces fled to neighboring Honduras and Costa Rica, where they became part of President Reagan's beloved Contras under the tutelage of the CIA.

The Contras

U.S. military strategy taught to the Contras was called "low- intensity warfare" (low-profile killing and destruction) and was aimed at destroying Nicaragua's infrastructure, especially aid stations, schools, farms, and electrical grids. Most effective was the use of terror to intimidate and discourage the peasants from participating in the reconstructive goals of the revolution.

All such terror tactics were, of course, against the rules of war laid down by the Geneva Convention. Protocol II of the Convention states explicitly: "It is prohibited to attack, destroy, remove or render useless, objects indispensable to the survival of the civilian population, such as foodstuffs, agricultural areas for the production of foodstuffs, crops, livestock, drinking water installations and supplies."

International law protecting the lives and life supports of noncombatants means nothing to many political leaders in the United States. This was clearly demonstrated in Nicaragua and in the U.S. invasions of Panama and Iraq. The political leaders of my country have become a law unto themselves, shaming every citizen who values human life and justice. Small wonder many in the world hate the U.S. government, especially in the so-called Third World countries we exploit. (Pardon the aside.)

Thanks to President Reagan's vilification of the Nicaraguan government, I had known about the counterrevolution. But I had not known the extent to which Reagan and the U.S. Congress had initiated and supported the counterrevolution.

I would soon learn via personal conversations with Nicaraguan politicians and members of the army and through visits to the countryside, how much damage Ronald Reagan's Contras were doing to the country. Reagan called them "freedom fighters, moral equivalents of our founding fathers." But they were anything but freedom fighters. They were mercenary cutthroats who preyed upon defenseless peasant farmers in the countryside – destroying crops, schools, health clinics, and infrastructural life-support services. They never took and held territory for any significant length of time. Rather, they attacked from across the borders of neighboring Honduras and Costa Rica, thus violating international law. But Honduras was a U.S. lackey (still is) and Costa Rica had no army to prevent Contra intrusion.

As a victim of childhood indoctrination and high school–expurgated American history, I had believed that my country, child of a revolution, should have been on the side of revolutionaries fighting as our forefathers fought for freedom from tyranny and for a better way of life.

But so many leaders of my country betrayed the ideals of our founding fathers and chose instead to defend the wealthy few over the impoverished majority by way of military dictatorships guilty of unspeakable cruelty and total disregard for human life. For me the cries of the poor of El Salvador and the terror caused by the Contras in Nicaragua began to erase at long last the mistaken patriotic cultural assumptions that I had never before questioned.

So I encourage you, dear reader, to follow the advice given to me earlier by a professor at Manhattan College at a time when I was defending U.S. aggression in Vietnam in the name of "freedom and democracy." Again, that advice was: "Rise above the assumptions of your subculture."

Return from Central America

After my intense experiences in Central America, I returned wrung out, weighed down with emotional baggage, and angry over the revelation of my country's political leaders' complicity in the suffering of the poor in El Salvador and Nicaragua.

In addition, I had begun to recall my own participation in the similar misery of which I had been an integral part in Vietnam – an integral part because there I had been a chaplain, a symbol of moral rectitude. The very presence of a chaplain lent support to the morality of the war – morality, that neither I nor any other chaplain, to my knowledge, publicly questioned.

Two weeks after the trip, I received a phone call from a congressional aide who invited me to share my Central American experience with selected members of the U.S. Congress. The opportunity to share insights from our trip with members of Congress did not come as a surprise. The two congressional aides who had accompanied us on our trip told us they might be able to arrange appointments with representatives open to hearing about our firsthand experiences. Aid to the Salvadoran Army and to the Nicaraguan Contras was a hotly contested issue in the 1980s.

Even though I was born and partly raised in Washington, D.C., I had never seen the inside of the white marble buildings where representatives from around the nation made laws and created policies that affect millions of U.S. citizens, as well as people the world over. I would have been in awe of the place had I not been so angry.

I was there to tell elected officials about the inhuman results of their laws and policies in El Salvador and Nicaragua. Surely, they would listen to a Vietnam veteran who had put his life on the line for his country. (My God, was I naïve!) It was clear to me that our policies of support for the military in El Salvador and the Contras in Nicaragua were tantamount to complicity in human rights abuses too grisly to describe.

Most of the assembled congressmen and congresswomen listened to our testimonies with courteous attention, but some were clearly following the president blindly down the anticommunist road, regardless of human rights abuses. One congressman angrily called me a communist. Then I began to realize what I was up against – even feeling sorry for people who had to work with his ilk. I refrain from mentioning his name because, sadly, he is still in Congress.

I'll never forget being called a communist in the hallowed chambers of Congress, but this was not my worst congressional experience. The legal aide of one highly respected senator responded to my moral indignation over U.S. policy with a remark that revealed to me a putrid cesspool of political life: "A moral argument will not wash here on the Hill."

The aide was not being arrogant. He was being honest and I was being educated. "What does wash on the Hill?" I asked him. "Threats," he said, "loss of votes if one does not support a specific bill or policy."

I was not about to play politics with peoples' lives. So I left the senator's office disillusioned with politicians who were more concerned about being reelected than with the morality of what they supported or refrained from supporting. Primacy of conscience seemed to have no place in the store of values of such politicians. The Central American and congressional experience awakened me to the reality of my ignorance of U.S. foreign policy and of how to effect change.

Returning to San Francisco, I began reading everything I could find on Central America and on Vietnam. Personal experience and a plethora of books confirmed my conclusion that my government, once trusted by me without reservation, was complicit in three illegal and immoral interventions: one in Southeast Asia and two in Central America.

In particular, one book on Central America helped me to understand why I and many Americans had failed to grasp the machinations of certain leaders of our government. The book, which South End Press published in 1999, is titled *Turning the Tide: U.S Intervention in Central America and the Struggle for Peace,* by Noam Chomsky, a professor of linguistics at M.I.T. He introduces the book with the following:

> We live entangled in webs of endless deceit, often self-deceit, but with a little honest effort, it is possible to extricate ourselves from them. If we do, we will see a world that is rather different from the one presented to us by a remarkably effective ideological system, a world that is much uglier, often horrifying.

This quote spoke clearly to me, but I had difficulty admitting self-deceit. Why would I do such a thing? Why would anyone? Professor Chomsky was shaking me awake to what it means to be a responsible citizen in a democratic society, to be a part of the whole of a body politic. I felt like Rip Van Winkle waking up from a lifetime of sleep, looking around and wondering, "Where have I been all these years?"

James Madison, fourth president of the United States, was big on the essential relationship of knowledge to democracy: "Knowledge will forever govern ignorance; and a people who mean to be their own governors must arm themselves with the power which knowledge gives." For me, this meant adding my voice to a growing protest movement against U.S. involvement in El Salvador and Nicaragua. Thus began my life as a civilian peace activist.

I woke up too late to protest the war in Vietnam, as thousands of citizens and veterans had done in the late sixties and seventies. Why had I remained silent in the midst of so much carnage, some of which I had witnessed personally? Over the years I have asked myself this question many times. It is only recently that the answer has come.

I did not lose close friends in Vietnam. I saw many men die, some directly in front of me, another in my arms. I administered Last Rites to some, helped load dead and wounded soldiers on helicopters, and visited many soldiers who had lost limbs. But the emotional trauma of losing a friend in arms never touched me. Consequently, the barbarity of the war did not descend on me, as it had done on those who lost friends.

I accepted the war with its horrific results philosophically, a necessary evil when confronting a greater evil, communism.

Now I deeply regret having done nothing to stop the war in Vietnam, and I admire everyone, especially veterans, who did try. They left the war in Vietnam to join the war at home, the war to end the war.

Two months of sequestered study back in San Francisco passed and I still did not feel comfortable about speaking publicly about U.S. foreign policy in Central America. There was so much to read, and I'm a slow reader.

Then Charlie Clements telephoned and asked me to cover a speaking engagement that he was too busy to meet; that call moved me to respond, ready or not. To my surprise, I spoke non-stop for forty-five minutes, paused to gauge audience fatigue, and, when no one objected, continued for another forty-five.

I thought I was ready to take the show on the road, but requests to speak were not building up. Perhaps Charlie had received some negative feedback and refrained from telling me for fear of hurting my feelings. Consequently, I continued to study and to attend lectures by knowledgeable people like John Stockwell, a former CIA agent who became conscience-driven to go public. He was not the first, nor the last, CIA agent to abandon an agency that operates in the shadows of secrecy where morality is a foreign word.

When Stockwell left the CIA and began revealing the immoral activities of the CIA and other governmental agencies, I was just beginning to lift the lid on our foreign and domestic Pandora's box. Like Noam Chomsky, Stockwell encourages us to read, reflect, and act.

I urge everyone to read. Television gives us capsules of news that someone else puts together. In newspapers we are fed what the editors select to publish. If we want to know about the world and understand, to educate ourselves, we have to get out and dig and find books and articles for ourselves.

Chomsky and Stockwell were traveling on the same road, the road to truth. That truth may or may not move the seeker to action, for action requires sacrifice of some kind and sacrifice requires courage. No one is completely at ease living in a denial of truth – especially truth covered over with layers of lies that impact upon people's lives, especially the lives of vulnerable people. So much of the good we enjoy today is the result of people who lived and died yesterday for truths that led to freedom.

24

Renunciation

MISERY LOVES COMPANY, SO THEY SAY. My "company" came in the person of a Vietnam Air Force veteran, Brian Willson. Every bit as upset over our government's intervention in Central America as I was, Brian came into my life by way of the telephone – while I was ruminating over what to do about my experience in El Salvador and Nicaragua.

From another veteran, Brian had heard that I had gone to Nicaragua on a fact-finding tour and returned convinced that the United States was definitely on the wrong side of justice. He too had been to Nicaragua, but on a more extensive and viscerally wrenching trip than mine. He had lived in a small Nicaraguan town with a peasant family for two months – learning Spanish and observing firsthand the effects of Contra activity like hit-and-run attacks on noncombatants and their meager life supports.

Neither of us needed further proof of the injustice or immorality of our government's complicity in the oppression of the Nicaraguan poor, an oppression labeled a "fight against communism" by President Reagan. In reality, Nicaragua's revolution was a fight for independence and for nonalignment with the United States or any other foreign power.

After sharing our concerns, we agreed that it was time to do something to stop our country's support for Reagan's so-called freedom fighters. But, what were we to do?

I explained that I had already been to Congress and left disgusted, without hope for a change in policy. Brian mentioned Mahatma Gandhi and nonviolent action. I knew nothing about either. I had never been a pacifist and at that time had no intention of becoming one. However, for reasons I could not explain, I felt complimented for being thought a pacifist and subsequently began to study the life of Gandhi. Reaching no conclusions on the phone, we promised to keep in touch, said our goodbyes, and let the question of what to do simmer.

Witness for Peace

Shortly after our first conversation, an opportunity arose to revisit Nicaragua, this time with a group sponsored by Witness for Peace (WfP), an organization dedicated to hands-on experience with oppressed people by living with and among them, sometimes acting as human shields. WfP members were ordinary citizens, young and old, men and women, courageous enough to risk their lives for peace and justice. Even though I'd been to Nicaragua once, Brian's stories about life in conflicted areas there told me I needed more personal experience.

My first visit had been short and sanitary in comparison to his. He witnessed what I had only heard about. Mine now would be a two-week trip around the country, seeing firsthand the damage to schools and hospitals, interviewing victims of Contra terror, and documenting the lie of Reagan's propaganda efforts to elicit U.S. citizen support for his Counterrevolutionary Army.

A month passed before I was able to join a delegation of twelve people from around the nation en route to Nicaragua. This second people-to-people trip deepened my appreciation for the peasants of Nicaragua and confirmed my conviction that they were not communists either in theory or in practice.

For the first time in their lives, they were now working for themselves at labor formerly done for wealthy landowners or for the dictator Somoza. They were former economic slaves who had been freed by the revolution to work their own land or to work cooperatively with others to better their lives. The main obstacle to their quest for peace and prosperity turned out to be the same government that had supported the Somoza family dictators, the government of my country.

In a small village near the top of a mountain in central Nicaragua, we visited a recently formed community of peasants, around four hundred men, women, and children, who had fled from the Contras to the relative safety of a larger community. The government had given them an abandoned coffee plantation and land enough to farm and to raise pigs, cows, and chickens. We stayed for a night and a day, helped with the coffee harvest, and listened to incredibly sad stories of death, torture, and destruction. The story of one person in particular touched us deeply.

Her name is Francesca, a widow from a small village who joined the cooperative after her husband was abducted by the Contras at three in the morning. His mutilated body was found nearby, missing his heart and his tongue. Our delegation of ten people accompanied Francesca back to her home for the first time since her husband's murder months earlier.

Other women who had taken refuge in the village of Venecia spoke of the loss of children kidnapped by the Contras and never seen again.

But there were also stories of hope, joy, and determination to begin life anew. The coffee cooperative was doing well; its members had created their own protective militia, independent of the overburdened government army. With their homegrown protection they had a chance of holding off any attack until the army arrived.

We were invited to help harvest the coffee crop. Most of us had never seen a coffee bush, much less picked the beans. It was tedious, boring, fatiguing work that forever elevated my appreciation of a cup of coffee. If you pick the beans, you will never again take the black liquid for granted.

The evening before leaving, we were honored with a meal reserved for VIPs: chicken, rice and beans, fried plantains, and, as always, heavily sugared black coffee. Just before climbing aboard our truck to leave the following morning, a middle-aged reed of a woman clad in a threadbare, faded dress (I'm sure, the best and perhaps only dress she owned) approached me, looked directly into my eyes, placed her thin, brown, work-worn hand on my chest, and said, "Go home and tell your president to stop killing us."

I do not know why she chose me to scold the president, but I assured her I would try. The people knew we were North Americans, yet they did not blame us for the behavior of our country's political leaders. This was very generous of a people who had lost their homes and life supports because of U.S. mercenaries.

The name Reagan may evoke esteem in the memory of many North Americans. They have even named the international airport in the heart of our nation's capital after him. However, the name Ronald Reagan will forever be spoken in anger by Nicaraguan peasants.

Alzheimer's disease is a terrible tragedy, erasing the past and relegating the victim to life in a permanent present. Bad as well as good memories cease to exist. But, in Reagan's case, it had to be a blessing – erasing memories that, if ever recalled, could have haunted him like memories of war that drive surviving soldiers to their death.

There is little justice for the poor in this world, which makes me want to believe in life hereafter: heaven for those who knew nothing of peace and justice in this life. As for hell, I wish no one the sort of pain depicted in the Bible. An eternity of serving the oppressed will be enough for oppressors, murders, and rapists.

My respect for the WfP activists grew with each encounter that they arranged for us with the beneficiaries of the Sandinista revolution. Likewise, my respect grew for the Nicaraguan government, which was trying to do for its citizens what our government had often failed to do after our revolution, namely, be a government for the people, for *all* the people.

Returning the Medal of Honor

The day before leaving Managua I met the person behind the voice on the telephone who had motivated me to return to Nicaragua, the Vietnam Air Force veteran Brian Willson. He too had returned to Nicaragua to visit his adopted peasant family. He said he needed to renew his visceral connection with them and the country.

He was ready to act and so was I. We discussed a protest fast, Gandhian-style, water-only, open-ended, until we discerned a significant response from U.S. citizens determined to work for Nicaraguan policy change.

Neither of us had ever undertaken an open-ended fast that could result in death. We were flying blind, so to speak, preparing for a moonless-night parachute jump into unknown territory.

Reflecting on my participation in the Vietnam War and reading Gandhi on the renunciation of medals, I decided to renounce the Medal of Honor, just as thousands of other Vietnam veterans had done when they tossed their medals over the fence around the White House. This was a dramatic act of opposition to the Vietnam War by men who had fought the war at great price to themselves and their families.

There was no official procedure for returning medals. All sorts of mementos have been left at the Vietnam Veterans Memorial wall (hereafter Vietnam Memorial Wall) in Washington, D.C., each one expressing the sentiment of the donor. My sentiment was sadness over the needless loss of life, mainly young lives that had never had a chance to mature. I wanted to make a symbolic public statement about the immoral nature of U.S. foreign policy. The Vietnam Memorial Wall seemed to be an appropriate place to leave the medal, along with a written statement.

I began to see the names of over fifty-eight thousand soldiers, etched into panels of shiny black marble, as the names of victims of propagandized patriotism. The highly polished stone acted as a mirror, blending the image of the viewer with the names of the soldiers killed in action. The reflected image of one's self, blended with names of dead soldiers, speaks to the complicity of every American who failed to protest that war.

Before going to the Wall, I called a press conference in the meeting hall of a Methodist church in Washington, D.C. The press release read:

Renunciation of the Congressional Medal of Honor

July 29, 1986

The Capitol, Washington, D.C.

> *It is with great sadness that I renounce the Congressional Medal of Honor, but compassion for the victims of U.S. intervention in Central America says I must. I received the Medal of Honor in November of 1968 from President Lyndon Johnson in the East Wing of the White House. The award was given for saving lives under hostile fire in Vietnam.*
>
> *At the outset of this statement, I want to say that my renunciation of the Medal of Honor in no way represents disrespect for the medal itself or for the recipients of medals of valor throughout our history. My action is directed toward the inhumane foreign policies of my government, policies that cast shadows of shame over the heritage of this country and place the United States outside of the company of civilized nations that respect international law and universally accepted norms of morality.*
>
> *I find it ironic that conscience calls me to renounce*

the Congressional Medal of Honor for the same basic reason I received it – trying to save lives. This time the lives are not young Americans, at least not yet. The lives are those of Central Americans of all ages: men, women, children, and vulnerable innocents of the conflict.

I first became aware of atrocities funded by the American tax dollar from the victims of these atrocities: refugees from El Salvador and poor peasants in Nicaragua.

Their stories of incredible cruelty started me on a search for truth that has led me through book after book and report after report on the conditions of poverty and oppression in Central America and my government's response to these conditions.

The U.S. government has responded to the needs of oppressed people in El Salvador by supporting their oppressors, wealthy elites who control the lives of the poor through brutal military force.

In Nicaragua, the U.S. government response to the oppressed is the creation, direction, and support of a counterrevolutionary guerrilla army known as the Contras. Winds of controversy whirl around the Contras over the question of human rights abuse.

In one of his speeches to the American people, President Reagan referred to Contra atrocities as "much ado about nothing." In his most recent speech on aid to the Contras, the president acknowledged the atrocities of the Contras and assured us that Contra human rights abuses would be corrected under U.S. direction, much the same as we have helped the Salvadoran Army become respectful of human rights. This does not speak well for the future of the Nicaraguan poor. This makes me wonder if the president has read the human rights abuse record of the Salvadoran army for the year 1985.

In a word, the policy of our government in Central America is primarily militaristic. It is devoid of the creative nonviolent conflict resolution known as peaceful negotiation. The art of diplomacy has given way to the artless use of brute force, exercised insanely on the weak and dependent.

While the Latin American neighbors of Nicaragua patiently struggle in protracted nonviolent dialogue in a process known as Contadora, the United States pursues a gunboat policy of military aid to the Contras.

    In my opinion, America has become a nation that arrogates to itself the right to impose its way of life on any country too weak to defend its independence. Nicaragua's fault is trying to break the pattern of Central American dependence on the United States. She no longer wants to be a patch of grass in the mythical North American "backyard."

    Lest anyone conclude that I have been duped by a slick Sandinista propaganda program, I want to say that I am not unaware of the human rights abuses of the Sandinista government. They exist. But they pale in comparison with the atrocities committed by the Contras or the U.S.–backed military in El Salvador.

    Let's take one of the State Department's favorite complaints against the Sandinistas: persecution of the Church. In Nicaragua, the Catholic Church radio has been silenced; also fifteen priests and a bishop have been expelled. Evangelical pastors have been harassed and a cardinal of the Catholic Church has been censured.

    In El Salvador, however, an archbishop has been murdered, his assassin still at large. Four American churchwomen have been brutally raped and murdered. Hundreds of priests, nuns, and lay catechists have been killed or disappeared.

    Now why is our State Department so silent about persecution of the Church in El Salvador and so vocal about persecution of the Church in Nicaragua?

    I am not a devotee of the Nicaraguan government. I don't have to be. I don't pay taxes in Nicaragua.

    I am, however, an advocate of the U.S. government. I am responsible for what it does in the name of America. If I am to be a true patriot, that is, a person who loves this country even when it's wrong, I must monitor and criticize its policies. It is my duty and my right.

    On the basis of eighteen months of intense study of the history and nature of the problems in Central America, which includes two trips in the last year, I conclude that U.S. policy toward Nicaragua and El Salvador is grossly immoral, legally questionable, and highly irrational.

    At the conclusion of this press conference my Medal of Honor will be placed in an envelope along with a letter to President Reagan and laid before the Vietnam Memorial

Wall. The label on the envelope reads:

> *This Envelope Contains the Congressional Medal of Honor of the United States of America, Awarded November 19, 1968, to Charles J. Liteky for Valor in Vietnam. The Medal Was Renounced on July 29, 1986, in Protest of United States Intervention in Central America.*

My God!!!
In Spite of the Names Etched
On This Wall, We Are Doing It
Again.
"When Will We Ever Learn?"
God Forgive Us.
Again.

Following the press conference I proceeded to the Congressional Gardens and laid a letter-sized manila envelope at the junction of the east and west walls. The envelope contained the Medal of Honor and a typewritten letter to President Ronald Reagan signed with my name. The letter reads as follows:

July 29, 1986

President Ronald Reagan
The White House
Washington, D.C.

Dear President Reagan,

> *The enclosed statement of my renunciation of the Congressional Medal of Honor and its associated benefits represents my strongest public expression of opposition to U.S. military policies in Central America. You have been the champion of these brutal policies. I hold you most responsible for their origin and implementation.*
> *You publicly stated your identification with some of the most ruthless cutthroats in Central American history when you said, "I'm a Contra too." You insulted every American patriot when you referred to these killers of children, old men, and women as "freedom fighters" comparable to the founding fathers of our country.*

In the name of freedom, national security, national interest, and anticommunism, you have tried to justify crimes against humanity of the most heinous sort. You have made a global bully of the United States. You would not dare do to countries capable of defending themselves what you have done to tiny nations like El Salvador, Nicaragua, and Honduras.

Mr. President, you are clearly set on a course of U.S. domination of Central America. There are a lot of us Americans who do not care to be counted among the oppressors of this world, and we intend to let the government you lead know it by way of a series of nonviolent protests that will end when you stop the killing, the raping, the torturing, and the kidnapping of poor people in Central America.

You are not without company, Mr. President. There are other Americans who justify the murder of innocents in the same vigorous way that you do. You are polarizing this nation. One day you may have to repress your fellow Americans with the same kind of terror tactics you sanction in Central America.

I pray for your conversion, Mr. President. Some morning I hope you wake up and hear the cry of the poor riding on a southwest wind from Guatemala, Nicaragua, and El Salvador. They are crying Stop Killing Us.

I never met a Central American peasant who did not know your name.

Regretfully,

Charles J. Liteky
Former holder of the Congressional Medal of Honor

25

Veterans Fast for Life

AFTER MY PUBLIC RENUNCIATION of the Medal of Honor, Brian Willson and I began to prepare for the fast. Neither of us had ever undertaken a fast that could end in death – death by starvation, a slow, increasingly painful death distinct from the rapid-fire death of immolation.

We were aware of two American men who had engaged in both types of sacrifice: Norman Morrison, a Quaker from Maryland, and Mitch Snyder, an ex-convict converted to nonviolence in prison by Daniel and Phil Berrigan, two radical Catholic priests who protested the U.S. invasion of Vietnam by pouring homemade napalm on the draft files of potential soldiers.

Norman Morrison's immolation was also a protest against napalming Vietnamese women and children. He immolated himself beneath the Pentagon office window of Secretary of Defense Robert McNamara, November 2, 1965.

Mitch Snyder fasted as an advocate for the homeless living on the streets of Washington, D.C. He fasted on water only for fifty-one days in Washington, D.C., shaming the government into providing shelter for the homeless.

Norman's death did not stop the Vietnam War, but the ghastly sight of his body aflame did break through the wall of Secretary of Defense Robert McNamara's single-minded fixation on the ways and means of winning a war.

Mitch Snyder's numerous fasts had moved the federal government to help with the homeless problem in the nation's capital by providing a renovated, block-long, three-story building suitable for lodging hundreds of people.

Norman Morrison and Mitch Snyder evoked controversy among moralists, people of faith, and even politicians. Some labeled them suicidal; others, martyrs who were willing to sacrifice their lives for the oppressed.

I had no moral problem with either man or either method of protesting the killing of innocents in Vietnam and the injustice of relegating the homeless in Washington, D.C., to the merciless life of the street.

Mitch Snyder – experienced in long-term, water-only fasting and himself living in the Washington, D.C., shelter for the homeless that he had helped create – responded positively to my request for his counsel on the nature and wisdom of fasting. He escorted me to the third floor of the huge D.C. shelter, still under renovation, seated me at a bare folding table, and proceeded to educate me about the pain and perils of fasting.

Hunger pains are one thing, starvation pains another. "After thirty days," he said, "you can spot a single crumb of white bread on a white table cloth the second you walk into a room." At some point of starvation, hunger becomes a carnivorous animal insatiably devouring flesh until there is no more.

Mitch offered no encouragement to fast. On the contrary, he painted a grim picture of bodily deterioration toward slow, excruciating death. When I asked him if our fast would make a difference, he replied without hesitation, "If you die you might make a difference."

In the course of our conversation, a hefty fly flew through a screen-less, open window and landed on the upper side of my left forearm. Having no affection for flies, I waved it away, with no thought of impropriety. Mitch disapproved. He stopped the interview and chastised me: "That fly was not hurting you, Charlie."

Shades of Albert Schweitzer, the famed nineteenth-century doctor whose reverence for life extended to all creatures, even mosquitoes. I had too much respect for Mitch to argue the merits of swatting flies. Happily, none of the fly's brothers or sisters joined us.

Inspired by Mitch, Norman, and Gandhi, Brian and I decided to publicly fast for peace in Central America on the East steps of the Capitol – calling the fast "Veterans Fast for Life."

I had previously discussed the matter of fasting with my

wife, Judy. I needed her permission to proceed. Thoughtfully, she cautioned me, "as long as what you do is motivated by love."

Looking back, I think I was not entirely honest with her. I knew I was angry, but I felt there was enough love to answer. "Well, I think I'm coming primarily out of love." She did not argue – saving me from an emotional impasse I did not need.

It was Judy who initially had directed my attention to the plight of the poor in Central America by inviting me to join her in a protest at a public park in San Francisco. This was before we were married, when we were in the first stage of falling in love. I would have followed her anywhere.

Metaphorically, I see her as a beautiful young woman holding the reins of a great white Arabian stallion, her rich black hair against his white mane, leading the horse to me. As she hands me the reins she says, "This is a gift for you, Charlie. His name is Justice. Mount up and get going."

Justice and I have become close companions, but I must say, at times he takes me where I'd rather not go.

The Fast Begins

On a mild mid morning, September 1, 1986, standing on the marble-hard east-side steps of the U.S. Capitol, its bright white dome aglitter in the early morning sun, Brian and I began a water-only fast. We called it an open-ended fast, implying that it could end whenever we felt that the fast had accomplished its purpose.

If the goal of the fast was not met, however, we were willing to die in order to make the strongest case possible for the immorality of U.S. support for a brutal military in El Salvador and Reagan's Contras in Nicaragua. The possibility of our death landed hard on the hearts of friends and loved ones and splattered against a wall of arrogant absurdity erected by people unaware of or without care for victims of U.S. policy.

Initially, we intended to go for broke, that is, calling for the cessation of U.S. complicity in Central American carnage in the hypocritical name of freedom and democracy. But the collective wisdom of our supporters convinced us that the goal of any fast should be attainable. This is distinct from the goal of self-immolation, which is the witness of death for a cause.

We were asking for the impossible, given the insensitivity and power-driven nature of the majority of our elected representatives in Congress and of the White House. A government willing to collude in the death of thousands of poor people could not be expected to be deterred by a few people starving to death, veterans or not.

Consequently, we changed the goal of the fast from the cessation of U.S. government support to a "significant" response from the American people, potentially the true power of our democracy. The operative word in our statement was "significant."

Initially, there were two of us – both Vietnam veterans recently returned from trips to Central America. But two weeks before beginning the fast, we were joined by two more veterans, a senior citizen from World War II, Duncan Murphy, and another Vietnam vet, George Mizo.

Each of us knew the horror and cost of war. Each of us had answered the patriotic call to risk his life for his country. Simply stated, the fast was another way of risking one's life for peace.

Even though we were four strong, we began with two water-only fasters, reasoning that if the other two drank juice they might last at least two additional weeks in the likely event that the water-only fasters died. I cannot remember why George and I were the first to dine on water only.

And perhaps, just perhaps, our deaths might inspire other veterans who had risked their lives in wars to step up and nonviolently do the same for peace. I envisioned funeral services on the East Capitol steps, followed by processions to Arlington.

The first week passed with little notice by anyone but a few friends living in the city who joined us on the Capitol steps at the end of each day to pray for courage, guidance, and the conversion of hard-hearted political leaders who expressed no concern for the Central American poor on the lethal end of our military aid.

Hard-heartedness and arrogance were not true of all members of Congress. There were many who acknowledged the barbarity of the military brutes in Central America and refused to vote them aid. Some, like Senators Ted Kennedy (of happy memory) and Richard Durbin even visited us on the steps.

The second week passed and the first signs of weight loss began to appear; Brian Willson and Duncan Murphy then switched from fasting on juice to water only. We were losing around three-quarters of a pound a day.

George Mizo was a gentle, likable, soft-spoken, slow-talking man enveloped by an aura of sadness resulting from his Vietnam combat experience. Like so many combat veterans, he never spoke of what he had seen or done. Until long after the fast was over, I never knew that he was the sole survivor of an enemy engagement in the jungles of Vietnam.

Brian Willson was a U.S. Air Force Vietnam veteran who had an experience in Vietnam that he calls his "Epiphany." Cradling the dead body of a victim of a U.S. bombing raid on a Vietnamese village, Brian unashamedly dropped to his knees and burst into tears. The victim was a girl of nine or ten who could have been his child. His behavior was incomprehensible to his Vietnamese army officer counterpart.

Reaction to this incident cemented Brian's resistance to the war and galvanized his determination to resist violence, especially the violence of his government when used to defend oppressors and exploit the poor. A full account of Brian's epiphany can be found in his own memoir, *Blood on the Tracks: The Life and Times of S. Brian Willson* (PM Press, 2011). Two more weeks passed and the drastic loss of weight began to change our facial features; our gaunt looks showed that we were serious, that we might go the distance. George and I were entering the voracious hunger phase that Mitch Snyder had described so graphically: "the crumb of white bread on the white table cloth."

Supporters increased daily, arriving from all points of the compass. Logistical and emotional support was amazing. As the word of the fast spread from coast to coast, letters poured in by the hundreds, as did money to help with expenses. Senators and representatives committed to vote down military aid to the Salvadoran army and the Nicaraguan Contras frequently dropped by the Capitol steps to lend support and make brief speeches. My wife, Judy, was granted a leave of absence from her job in San Francisco and joined the support team.

Every day at sunset, supporters and fasters circled and prayed for the end of hostilities. Despite the fact that George and I had begun the starvation phase of fasting, a spirit of joy (incomprehensible to tourists) prevailed. None of our supporters tried to dissuade us from fasting. They understood the gravity of U.S. military involvement in Central America and its resultant loss of innocent lives. Our lives were of no more value than theirs.

At the conclusion of each day we retired to a five-bedroom house donated specifically for lodging the fasters; it was located in a District of Columbia middle-class neighborhood.

On the thirty-ninth day of the fast, I sent the following letter to Members of Congress:

October 9, 1986

An Open Letter to the Congress of the United States

Dear Members of Congress,

   *My name is Charles Liteky. I served as a Roman Catho-
lic chaplain in Vietnam from 1967 to 1970. Along with three
other war veterans, I am currently undertaking a fast in protest of U.S. policy in Central America. Today I enter the
thirty-ninth day of my fast. Each afternoon, the other veterans and I hold a vigil on the East steps of the Capitol.*
   *I am writing to you regarding the issue of U.S. support
for the Nicaraguan rebels known as "Contras."*
   *To those of you who voted against aid to the Contras,
thank you for your long arduous struggle to uphold the
moral and legal principles of the Constitution of the United
States, the Bill of Rights, and the Declaration of Independence.*
   *In both the Senate and the House of Representatives,
the vote on aid to the Contras was decided by a slim margin.
This was painful to all of us who want to live in a country
that purports to respect national and international law and
to live according to the tenets of our Judeo-Christian heri-
tage.*
   *Still, despite the setback, we applaud you. You have
brought honor to our country. History will show that yours
was the morally correct and prudent stand.*
   *To those of you who voted in favor of Contra aid, I want
to remind you of Santayana's adage, "Those who fail to learn
from history are condemned to repeat it." It is appropriate,
for I have yet to hear of a justification for support for the
Contras that does not stem from fear which borders on para-
noia. Such fear flourished during the McCarthy era and poisoned public debate about the great issues facing the Nation.*
   *Your statements today echo the President's, who says if
we don't stop them in Nicaragua, we will have to fight them
in Harlingen, Texas. Such absurd claims are reminiscent of
the verbal terror tactics used by the Johnson administration
to seduce Congress and build popular support for the war in*

Vietnam.

Yet, in the name of national security, you are willing to sentence thousands of peasants to death at the hands of disaffected Nicaraguan youth who are led by remnants of Anastasio Somoza's infamous National Guard and who are directed by the Central Intelligence Agency.

Tragically, CIA–sponsored destabilization is nothing new. The agency helped undermine the governments of Iran in 1953, Guatemala in 1954, and Chile in 1973. The consequences were disastrous. The short-term stability bought by intervention in Iran later brought political convulsions, American hostages, and the deaths of thousands.

The coup that we engineered to oust Jacobo Arbenz in Guatemala was followed by three decades of murderous military government which produced over one hundred thousand dead. Chile now is unraveling, following thirteen years of the tight-fisted rule of General Augusto Pinochet.

The ugliest stain on our nation's soul is intervention in Vietnam. We never allowed the free elections in Vietnam scheduled in 1956. Again we used subversion, installed a brutal dictator, called the government democratic, and lied to the American people. Between 1961 and 1973, there were over 5.7 million casualties – living and wounded – in Southeast Asia. Over fifty-six thousand Americans died and over two hundred thousand were wounded. Since the end of the war, some seventy-five thousand Vietnam veterans have taken their lives.

History is repeating itself. Just as it did in Southeast Asia, our government lies about its involvement in Central America.

Thus, the four of us have been forced to become students of U.S. post–World War II history and to reflect again upon what we did in Vietnam. The sins of our past are being repeated, sins which we have yet to acknowledge, much less repent for. And we say: not again, not in our names.

If we cannot prevail upon your sense of reason and moral responsibility, then this war on Nicaragua will happen over our dead bodies. Indeed, we are willing to die for the truth, rather than live on in the darkness of lies and distortions while our government shames our nation by complicity in crimes against humanity in Central America.

Your vote for aid to the Contras is tantamount to an un-

declared war on a country eighty times smaller than the United States. For me, this is unconscionable. While visiting the office of a senator, a veteran aide told me a moral argument would not wash on the Hill. However, I will never accept that the moral dimensions of an issue are irrelevant.

By supporting the Contras, you have identified yourselves with a band of killers who employ terror to force vulnerable people into submission. Accordingly, you might be called North American Contras. And, although their acts of torture and brutality against Nicaragua's civilian population are well documented, you persist in referring to them as "freedom fighters."

We deplore the equation of freedom fighters with the Contras. We believe legislators who subscribe to this view are unqualified for making policy. How can they discern the common good of people here at home, as well as abroad, when they defend a policy that has rendered the United States an outlaw among civilized nations?

As you who favor Contra aid return to your respective districts and states, please reflect on the biblical and constitutional precepts upon which this country was founded, and ask whether your support is consistent with those precepts. We will continue to pray and fast for your change of heart.

In Peace and Justice,

Charles J. Liteky

26

A New Beginning

On the forty-second day of the fast, while resting with Judy on the grass in the shade of historic oak trees in front of the Capitol, a good friend dropped by, but not to say hello or lend support to the cause of the fast. I had not seen him since the day I officiated at his wedding. He was a successful businessman in the business of making helicopters for the military.

Possessed of the singular purpose of stopping me from continuing the fast, he stood between me and the Capitol steps, declared that I had no right to take my life, and threatened to stop me if I insisted on continuing. He assured me that he had the power to do this. He was politically connected. There was no discussion of the matter. It was to be as he dictated.

I cannot recall exactly what I said to my friend, but I do remember the wave of anger that swept over me. Extended fasting had made me short-tempered. I excoriated him for his arrogance and did not wish him well on his way. It was inconceivable to me that anyone, much less a friend, would address me so arrogantly, as if I were a subordinate in his charge. He was a good example of how money and perceived power can change a person. That breach of tact on the part of a man with an inflated opinion of himself resulted in a fraternal divorce bitterly remembered to this day.

By mid October, 1986, the summer heat of Washington, D.C., was history. The chilly winds of winter were blowing south, and we were bundling up beyond normal winter wear in an effort to retain maximum caloric warmth.

I had lost thirty pounds, but was buoyed up emotionally by the support of friends and like-minded protesters of U.S. policies and actions in Central America. I felt good enough to accept speaking engagements in Los Angeles and Boston.

In addition, the four of us were invited to appear on the Phil Donahue TV show. It was the first time any of us had been on national TV. The exposure brought in more letters, more than our voluntary staff could possibly answer.

By the forty-sixth day of the fast, George Mizo, the youngest faster, was in trouble. Our doctor gave him less than a week to live. This news forced us to assess the results of the fast in terms of national response. We voted three to one in favor of the response being significant enough to discontinue the fast. I initially held out but relented the following day – feeling that my reticence to stop would be interpreted as misguided heroism.

On October 17 we officially ended the fast with a celebration meal prepared by a friend of George Mizo, a former professional chef.

With the fast behind us and hostilities in Nicaragua and El Salvador continuing unabated, we faced the question of what to do next. To this day I retain a lingering doubt and an occasional twinge of conscience about terminating the fast. I do not know if it accomplished anything but trouble for a lot of good people who were already protesting U.S. policies. The oft-repeated metaphor "preaching to the choir" may apply here.

Thousands of people were concerned enough to write letters and offer financial support. To my knowledge most of these letters were never answered. Consequently, in the event that an unacknowledged supporter may be reading this, I need to express my appreciation and gratitude.

In recognition of our efforts to stop the war, the president of Nicaragua, Daniel Ortega, invited us to visit his country to celebrate the fifth anniversary of the revolution and enjoy the hospitality and appreciation of his people. It was a gracious gesture on the part of Nicaragua's president, but I felt the need to continue protesting U.S. militaristic policies in the nation's capital.

Judy not only agreed with my desire, but she also consented to pack up and leave San Francisco and friends to join in an effort to maintain an expression of public dissent in the center of U.S. power. Leaving San Francisco to relocate in Washington, D.C., is one of the many sacrifices Judy made with me and for the people of Central America.

The East Capitol steps became our living room, where we sat, stood, and paced for four hours a day – holding signs and conversing with tourists from around the country. Brian, George, and Duncan flew to Nicaragua and toured the country for six weeks and personally viewed the disastrous results of our country's financial and military support of the Contras.

Peace Walks

Brian's observation of the destruction of the country's infrastructure – which incidentally, is against the Geneva Convention – and of the suffering of the poor, moved him to conceive the idea of peace walks around the country's conflicted areas to witness and report atrocities committed by Reagan's Contras. What better group of people to participate in this humanitarian effort than veterans? He would call the group Veterans Peace Action Teams (VPAT).

While traveling around Nicaragua, Brian met a woman from California with a concern for the poor that matched his own, especially for mothers and pregnant women. Her name is Holly Rauen, a practitioner of midwifery. She was working with a health care delegation.

Big hearts and common purpose led them to marriage and future joint efforts to help the Nicaraguan people. When they returned to the United States, they joined efforts to create the first VPAT, headquartered in Santa Cruz, California.

By February of 1987, a team of ten veterans was walking the mountain roads of Nicaragua, unarmed and undeterred by the possibility of death or injury. Several other VPATs followed throughout the year, in a nonviolent demonstration of courage and compassion. There were numerous close calls. Fortunately, no one was killed or seriously injured. The number of lives they saved by their presence will never be known.

Duncan Murphy resumed doing what he had done since the end of World War II, protesting and speaking against war whenever and wherever an opportunity arose. He traveled all over the country in an old bread truck converted to a camper and supported himself by trimming trees, large and small. He is a kind of Johnny Appleseed character, planting seeds of peace wherever his bread wagon home rolled. Occasionally, the aged truck needed repair or replacement of parts. Tree-trimming came to the rescue, giving him enough money to fix the problem.

George Mizo returned to Vietnam to offer to Vietnamese government officials a gesture of peace, the creation of a peace pagoda to be built by U.S. veterans. The idea was graciously received, but the Vietnamese countered with a needier project. They suggested a village with homes for orphaned children, complete with a hospital and medical staff to treat the wounds of war and the ongoing ailments of the aged. This was no small request, but George could not refuse. The government would provide the land if he would raise the money. George accepted the proposal and the Vietnam Friendship Village was conceived, born, and still exists today.

Concord Naval Weapons Station

After organizing several VPATs, Brian, Holly, and Holly's twelve-year-old son, Gabriel, settled in San Francisco. When Brian learned that trains carrying weapons for the army in El Salvador were being loaded at the Concord Naval Weapons Station, Concord, California, he, Holly, and several like-minded activists decided to protest.

The protest was potentially dangerous insofar as it involved standing on tracks in front of an oncoming train. The presumption was that the train would stop, allowing blocking participants to be removed and arrested. The protest was at best symbolic, but despite calculated assumptions, it did involve risks.

To insure safety, the speed of the munitions train set at five miles per hour. Upon leaving the legal limits of the military base, the trains moved on to public property and across a two-lane highway running parallel to the Naval Weapons Station. Once over the highway, the trains traversed another small stretch of public property before entering a fenced-in section of tracks presumed to be an extension of the base.

Blocking protests were named "Nuremberg Actions," calling forth the principles of justice generated by the celebrated war trials held in Nuremberg, Germany, following World War II. The Nuremberg Action of vigiling and blocking trains and trucks loaded with military ordinance began on June 10, 1987.

The action was totally nonviolent, public, and transparent, after the example of Martin Luther King Jr. and Mahatma Gandhi. Once begun, this nonviolent presence on the environs of the base continued throughout the summer of 1987. Many people were arrested, but no one was seriously hurt. When one lone protester stood in the middle of the train tracks, the munitions train stopped long enough for local authorities to arrest and transport him to jail.

With the first anniversary of the Veterans Fast for Life approaching, Brian Willson, Duncan Murphy, and two local peace activists decided to fast again, right smack in the middle of the train tracks running from the naval base. Holding gallon jugs of water, the foursome positioned themselves on the tracks and waited for the train to do the expected: start moving, stop at a safe distance away, and allow the police to escort them to a squad car.

In solidarity, I decided to fast with a small group of local activists on the East steps of the Capitol, as we had done a year earlier. However, we chose to do a mitigated fast using the food eaten by the poor in Central America, rice and beans. We never went hungry, but eating the same food every day for forty days gave us an appreciation for people who do not have the luxury of food selection.

Both East and West Coast fasts began at 9:00 a.m. local time, which placed us three hours ahead of the Nuremberg Action fast. Around twenty people gathered on the Capitol steps, holding signs, singing songs, and speaking on an open microphone.

Around mid afternoon, a friend approached the Capitol steps bearing a message from supporters of the fast in California. The Concord Naval Weapons Station train did not stop for the fasters on the tracks. In fact, it sped up and ploughed through the foursome, leaving two injured in its wake.

Two of the fasters jumped clear. Duncan Murphy leapt onto the engine's cowcatcher, but Brian Willson was caught as he tried to rise from a seated position between the tracks and tossed about beneath the train until both legs straddled the track in front of mammoth wheels that completely severed one leg and left the other dangling by too little flesh to save it. He was also struck in his head by metal parts beneath the engine – removing flesh and bone from his left temple and leaving an ear nearly severed.

Medical attention could have been immediate had Navy authorities responded, but a half hour passed before an ambulance arrived from the county hospital. Fortunately, Brian's wife, Holly, was there to apply first aid, using her skirt to stop the bleeding from legs severed just below his knees.

I was not surprised to learn that the weapons train carrying weapons to implement U.S. policy in Central America did not stop for the protesters, but I was amazed over Brian's survival and continue to be inspired by the quest for peace and justice he has pursued since the loss of his legs. With the aid of prosthetics, he stands and walks as tall as ever, a living example of how strong the human spirit can be.

One can read about the life of Brian Willson on the Internet by entering his name, unusually spelled Willson, son of Will.

Protesting Continues

After visiting Brian in the hospital, I returned to Washington, D.C., to resume protesting on the East steps of the Capitol, as a reminder to congressmen and congresswomen passing by that citizens were still protesting support for the wars in Nicaragua and El Salvador.

With the help of inheritance money, Judy made a down payment on a row house in the city within walking distance of the Capitol. The location was perfect for purposes of vigiling, visiting Congress, and offering hospitality to peace workers from everywhere.

It was here that I met Daniel Ellsberg. To me, he is the civilian hero of the Vietnam conflict. He risked prison, career, and life with family to expose "The Pentagon Papers." His book *Secrets: A Memoir of Vietnam and the Pentagon Papers* (Viking, 2002) is a great aid to understanding the machinations of a government ever hypocritically echoing "freedom and democracy" as the motivation behind foreign policies of intervention in countries failing to cooperate with U.S. economic goals.

When our personal savings were near exhaustion, Judy went to work for a nonprofit organization dedicated to lobbying Congress on issues of peace and justice. Along with friends, I continued vigiling on the Capitol steps – taking occasional breaks to encourage Congress members to vote for the closure of the School of the Americas.

I found that I lacked the patience needed to talk with politicians about life and death justice issues. I found the majority of the men and women representing us to be without concern for people suffering from policies they had created. They struck me as being more concerned about remaining in office than in exercising the powers of office to stop injustice. The legal congressional aide's words, "Moral arguments do not wash on the Hill," remain imbedded in my memory, surfacing whenever I consider lobbying Congress. Frequently, while walking the halls of Congress and the streets of Washington, D.C., I found myself involuntarily muttering, "I walk among the living dead."

There were notable exceptions to the living dead, but too few to effect change. Some congressmen and congresswomen on their way to their Capitol chambers stopped by the steps to chat and offer words of encouragement. Representative Joe Moakley and Senator Ted Kennedy from Massachusetts, Senator Richard Durbin from Illinois, and Senator Tom Harkin from Iowa were exceptions to the caricature of plastic politicians.

While we four vets were engaged in our citizen efforts to change U.S. foreign policy related to supporting oppressive dictators in Central America, a foreigner, a man of diminutive stature but great largess of heart stepped into the breach of Central American hostilities. He spoke a message of peace and understanding via dialogue – insisting that peace through violence cannot long endure. With the help of Ronald Reagan's propaganda, he had seen one peace effort fail, namely, the Contadora peace process, which Mexico, Venezuela, Colombia, and Panama had initiated. Reagan wanted "peace and freedom" U.S. style, which amounts to rule by the rich for the rich, with the best government money can buy.

This newcomer with the heart of a lion was Óscar Arias Sánchez, the president of Costa Rica, a country that abolished its military in 1948 after a brief civil war that took two thousand lives. This bold military abolition resulted in channeling the nation's resources into improving infrastructural necessities like education and health care, elevating the country to the highest standard of living in Central America.

Do these national needs of a Third World country sound familiar? Hopefully, one day we North Americans will have the wisdom and courage to follow the example of Costa Rica. However, for the foreseeable future we are too rooted in individualistic, narcissistic capitalism.

Thirty-eight years after the disarmament of his country, Arias was elected president of Costa Rica, the same year we four veterans were fasting for peace. Despite pressure from Washington to rearm, Arias steadfastly honored the nonmilitaristic legacy of his predecessors. Defending disarmament, he said,

> The abolition of the army helped us avoid the quagmire that in the following decades would engulf our neighbors: deepening poverty, military oppression, guerrilla movements and foreign intervention. If Costa Rica had an army in the eighties, we almost certainly

would have become like Honduras, a militarized out-post of the United States in its campaign against Nica-ragua.

By way of the Arias peace plan, and a willingness to negotiate, the Central American leaders chose dialogue over force of arms and signed peace agreements. For his enduring efforts, Arias received the Nobel Peace Prize. He used the money to establish the Arias Foundation for Peace and Human Progress (one component of which is the Area for Peace and Human Security) in Costa Rica.

Peace imposed by military might does not meet the criteria necessary for true peace, namely, freedom and tranquility of order. Order forcefully imposed will forever suffer the threat of revolution. The history of our country tells us as much.

The Declaration of Independence sanctions our right to revolt if our government is not serving all of us equally, but God help those elsewhere who try to revolt against dictatorial oppression without our approval. We North Americans are a people born of a revolution. We proudly celebrate our freedom and independence on the Fourth of July. You would think our government would appreciate and even champion revolutions of oppressed people anywhere. You would think our government would feel some affinity with the oppressed. Not so.

Not only does our government fail to condemn dictatorial oppression the world over, it also supports dictators as long as they cooperate with our efforts to exploit their people (slave labor) and their natural resources (oil, minerals, and a variety of marketable goods).

With Arias's peace plan in the offing, I no longer felt the need to vigil or remain in the seat of misused power. However, Judy enjoyed a different perspective. Here I am reminded of the words of the nineteenth-century writer Oscar Wilde, "Two men looked through prison bars. One saw mud, the other, stars." Judy can live through tragedy with a calm approaching detachment. She can see stars where I see mud.

Judy expressed no interest in leaving D.C. She was enjoying the opportunity to learn about grassroots congressional lobbying for new domestic and international policies. Yet, once again, she acceded to my needs.

But, where to go? I was not inclined to return to San Francisco. I felt the need for a different environment, a fresh start in a new place, free of the putrid scent of Capitol Hill hypocrisy. The bright white marble legislative and executive buildings made me think of Christ's description of the Scribes and Pharisees, "Woe to you, Scribes and Pharisees, hypocrites, for ye are like unto whited sepulchers, which indeed appear beautiful outward, but are within full of dead men's bones and all uncleanness" (Matt. 23:27).

Of course Christ was comparing people to buildings; I'm equating buildings with his description of people.

Do I feel the same today, twenty years later? Sadly, yes. U.S. barbarity has not improved since Vietnam. We go on thinking that peace is the product of military domination; so we continue killing and misspending our tax dollars on bombs and bullets that effect destruction and misery, a negative return for the investment of our tax money. The sparkling white buildings housing the offices of legislators who legalize crimes against humanity should correctly be stained with bright red dye symbolizing the blood of innocents seeping from wounds inflicted by bombs dropped from B-52s and bullets shot from M-16s.

We have erected a sobering black granite memorial, etched with the names of young Americans pressed into military service by the laws of misguided legislators and power-driven presidents shouting and touting "freedom and democracy." The Vietnam Wall stands partially submerged in the soil, a mile west of the Capitol, invisible until you walk the path at the base of the wall and stand close enough to see the names of our nation's youth, neatly etched into the wall, one after another, numbering fifty-eight thousand. You also see a reflection of yourself in the polished black granite, a stark reminder of citizen complicity and irresponsibility.

It bothered me that there were no graffiti on the white marble buildings, calling attention to the illegal and immoral depravity created within, but I was not yet willing to risk prison in an attempt to scribe in red the names of peasants killed in Vietnam by the U.S. military or the names of noncombatants killed and tortured in Nicaragua by CIA–trained Contras, or the names of innocents murdered, raped, and kidnapped in El Salvador by an Army trained and equipped by U.S. soldiers. But the day was nearing when bloodstained government walls would lead me to prison.

As I pondered possible places for our next move, dream material floating near the surface of my subconscious offered imaginary scenes of a pastoral countryside, flowering meadows, corn-studded fields, and a brook running with crystal clear water. I consciously added a rustic cabin and a dog or two. The dream also included the pursuit of self-sufficiency, living off the land.

Guatemala

Before I had a chance to explore agrarian possibilities, a friend invited me to join a team of twenty activists, fly to Central America, and do a protest action against atrocities supported by U.S. tax dollars. Even though peace agreements had been signed, hostilities continued to take the lives of vulnerable people. We targeted three countries for protest actions: Guatemala, Honduras, and El Salvador.

I had never been to Guatemala, but I had read Stephen Kinzer and Stephen Schlesinger's book *Bitter Fruit: The Story of the American Coup in Guatemala* (Harvard, 2005) and was immediately interested. My government's collaboration in Guatemalan human rights abuses, approaching genocide, began in 1954 under the direction of a president I once voted for and admired, Dwight D. Eisenhower. In one of many CIA clandestine operations, a democratically elected president was forced from office and replaced by a military dictator. The ousted president was Jacobo Arbenz. The new man, "our man," was a Guatemalan army general, Carlos Castillo Armas. He lasted two years before his assassination.

Thirty years of civil war followed the CIA replacement of Arbenz – leaving over one hundred and fifty thousand Guatemalans dead or disappeared. Tens of thousands were forced to flee to Mexico, one million displaced inside the country, and hundreds of Indian villages destroyed. To the shame of my country, the U.S. government has consistently supported the Guatemalan military with supplies and training, inclusive of the dark art of torture.

To his credit, President Bill Clinton apologized for U.S. complicity in the war in Guatemala that followed the U.S. installation of a dictator. He offered condolences to the descendants of Guatemalan victims, but conveniently omitted a pledge of restitution.

It is easy to say "I'm sorry for someone's loss," but not as simple is restitution for damages done, a moral obligation foreign to the U.S. concept of justice. For example, the U.S. government left the people and the land of Vietnam poisoned for as long as it takes the defoliant dioxin to lose its toxic power (an unknown period of time). In the meantime, contact with dioxin can produce cancer and birth defects. Vietnam veterans and their families can attest to this.

We arrived in Guatemala City, twenty activists strong, men and women, young and old, all with a history of protesting that included multiple arrests and prison time. After a night's rest in a guesthouse, we convened for a strategy meeting, separated into three groups, and decided what action to take and where.

I chose to join a small group of women and men in an attempt to chain shut the iron entrance and exit gate of the U.S. Embassy, guarded by uniformed Guatemalan soldiers armed with M-16s. The two remaining groups traveled on to El Salvador and Honduras.

We had no idea how armed military men would respond to a nonviolent blocking action carried out by citizens of the country that supported them. We hoped they would recognize us as North American gringos by our looks and language and at least be cautious.

Five of us, girded with heavy chains concealed under coats or sweaters and cautioned by experience to avoid quick movements, slowly approached the gated embassy fence, while two women in support engaged a soldier in a small guardhouse a few feet from the fence. The women were young and attractive, ever a distraction when approaching men, especially armed men.

I had the best opportunity to chain the gate, but the guard on the inside of the compound responded before my shaking hands could wrap and lock the chain around the gate and fence post. Rather than lose the chain, I withdrew. I chose a spot along the fence beside the others who had successfully chained and locked themselves to the enclosure.

Chained to the fence and seated on concrete ten feet back from the public walkway, we waited an official embassy reaction. The Guatemalan guards did not panic or threaten us. They were surprised, but not alarmed. No doubt the sight of lovely gringo women amused them.

Ten minutes into the chaining, a balding, middle-aged, officious white man emerged from the embassy, looked us over, sized us up, and, without a word, hastened back to what I presume was his phone line to the State Department. He made no effort whatsoever to converse with us, not even a bland bureaucratic hello or phony Mona Lisa smile.

When the sun began to cast afternoon shadows over our

protest, it was obvious that the powers within the embassy were going to ignore us. There is nothing more dampening to a nonviolent political protest than the absence of recognition.

This placed the ball in our court, so we did the political thing. Seated as comfortably as possible on the cement next to the fence, we stretched our chains to the max and wiggled our way into a semicircle. A half hour later we reached a unanimous decision to remain the night – the weather being favorable and streetlights along the boulevard fifteen feet to our front being bright enough to provide public security.

Passersby gave us curious glances, but no one stopped to ask questions or make comments. We were a sideshow of a sort. A code of prudential silence prevailed. To my knowledge it was the first time a group of Americans had staged a protest in the capital city in front of a symbol of foreign presence. We reasoned that we were doing what a Guatemalan could not do without risking his life.

After a period of intermittent sleep on concrete that had cooled during the night, we woke with heads full of suggestions. We were not ready to pack up and leave. We had too much time, money, and passion invested, and so far we had accomplished nothing resembling a serious protest. Leaving was out of the question. A fast in place was suggested, followed by another of a water-only fast, a seven-day fast – each day dedicated to specific human rights violations linked to U.S. support. We easily reached consensual agreement.

For seven days and nights we sat chained to the heavy iron fence, ignored by officials and curiously observed by Guatemalan city folk. I should mention that we unchained ourselves for bathroom breaks at a fast food eatery, a Latin version of McDonald's, directly across the boulevard. Each day we fastened a new poster to the fence, depicting a social justice crime. The posters were large enough to be seen by pedestrian and vehicular traffic. A smiling, U.S. Peace Corps group stopped to question our motivation and left unimpressed.

Local people avoided contact with us, but midway through the fast a gringo I recognized stopped to say hello. He was a retired Lutheran minister who had moved to Guatemala to work with the poor. His wife studied nursing in her fifties for the specific purpose of opening a clinic to serve the poor in a barrio outside the city. I had previously met this dedicated couple on the U.S. Capitol steps during the Veterans Fast for Life.

Familiar with my protest activities, the minister asked what I would do next. When I shared plans to move from Washington, he suggested I consider moving close to his home in Maryland, a house on five acres of land occupied by a Mennonite woman and her two teenage sons. He assured me that the woman, born to farming, would welcome help and happily share her considerable agrarian skills. The opportunity sounded providential. All I had to do was convince Judy.

Our protest fast ended without interruption from the Guatemalan or U.S. military. Ironically, we were victims of government nonviolence. The other two protest teams were expelled from El Salvador to Honduras, where they were jailed and held incommunicado for three days before deportation to the United States. We knew nothing of their fate until we returned to Washington, D.C.

My trip to Guatemala was not entirely fruitless. It gave me an appreciation of the level of fear still pervading the country thirty-three years after President Eisenhower ordered the CIA overthrow of the democratically elected president. The military was still in control, violating human rights at will, even after peace accords were signed and a new president elected. The military was not about to transfer real power to civilian leadership.

Eden Valley

When I returned to Washington, I told Judy the story of meeting the minister from Maryland in Guatemala. She agreed to visit his home. The place was everything he described and brimming with subsistence possibilities: five acres, sufficient arable land, and a human-made pond fed by an adjacent stream. The minister had euphemistically named his little farm Eden Valley. Equidistant from Washington and Baltimore, the property was ideal for our new venture into the unfamiliar and our need to maintain contact with social justice friends in Washington.

After selling our row house in Washington, we found and purchased a three-bedroom split-level home five miles from Eden Valley in a sparsely populated Maryland town called Glenelg.

Under the guidance of Betty, an experienced Mennonite farmer, we planted corn, beans, spaghetti squash, and watermelon. Years earlier Betty had introduced grapes, blackberries, and asparagus – this last being a marvelous vegetable that comes and goes on its own bi-annually. She also raised sheep for wool and meat and chickens for fresh eggs.

Judy and I arrived in the spring of 1988, just in time to join Betty in the farming chores of tilling soil, planting seeds, watering, and then waiting on the miracle happening an inch beneath the soil to show itself. We even planted popcorn for the fun of it. Everything we seeded grew to fruition, as if Mother Nature were rewarding our first agrarian baby steps.

It was a marvelous way to live, but no way to make a living. Once again Judy employed her marketable teaching talent, providing enough income to pay the mortgage and living expenses. She never complained about her utilitarian role, and I never stopped to think about how she may have felt being the nontraditional bread winner.

Murders in San Salvador

Withdrawn from political activity for nearly a year, I was shocked back into the reality of Salvadoran military brutality and my country's complicity – via training, weapons supply, and on-site advice.

On November 16, 1989, before the light of day, eight people were murdered on the grounds of the Catholic University in San Salvador. The murderers were Salvadoran soldiers; the murdered included six Jesuit priest-professors targeted because of their outspoken opposition to oppression and for preaching a gospel message of liberation from oppression, aptly titled liberation theology.

The priests were dragged from their beds, forced to lie face down on the grass outside their bedroom windows and one by one, shot in the head, splattering blood and brains onto the soil around them. In a mini-second, six of El Salvador's brightest intellectual lights were snuffed out. Thus six Catholic priest-professors became martyrs for their faith and international heroes to proponents of peace and justice.

Also murdered with the priests were the priests' housekeeper and her sixteen-year-old daughter, who had taken up residence at the university to escape the violence in the city. Ironically, when they were assassinated along with the Jesuits, the fate they had feared in the city became the reality they suffered in the perceived safety of the university campus. (The soldiers had been instructed to take no prisoners and to leave no witnesses.)

The news was sickening. I had to do something to satisfy my

outrage. I could not go on living the peaceful life of a gentleman farmer and allow my government to hide its involvement in propagandistic platitudes of "freedom and democracy." But, once again, the question of what to do challenged my imagination, a question that arises as frequently as the revelation of my country's complicity in injustice of one sort or another.

I needed to make a public statement strong enough to equal my disaffection with the U.S. government. Actually, disaffection is too weak a word. I was fed up and alienated to the point of considering renouncing my citizenship and looking for another country; but where to go to escape a country that has become a giant military octopus with tentacles reaching out the world over, feeding off of the natural resources of small countries too weak to defend themselves or their possessions?

The notion of universal and unlimited U.S. expansion began in the nineteenth century, and the United States has been about expansion at any cost ever since. "Manifest Destiny," masquerading as democracy, has led us to the creation of an economic empire ruled by a plutocracy of the super-wealthy.

I cannot remember the origin of the idea of a Citizen's Declaration of Independence. It occurred to me that the Fourth of July and the Capitol steps would be the ideal time and place to publicly disavow a government complicit in crimes against humanity. As an incensed and disenchanted U.S. citizen, I could think of no better way to convey what I had to say about U.S. government policies, than to say it in the words of our forefathers via the simple change of the plural to the singular plus the addition of thoughts of my own.

In addition to reading an individualized Declaration of Independence, I envisioned using a 4x5–foot American flag, bordered in black and stained with the blood of Vietnam veterans. The red stripes would symbolize the blood of innocents and the white would be initialed with the names of countries and people killed or oppressed by agents of the U.S. government. (At the time, hypocritically patriotic congressmen were bellowing patriotic platitudes from the floors of Congress, clamoring for a constitutional amendment to exempt flag desecration from the protection of the First Amendment.)

Over the years legislators have tried many times to criminalize flag desecration, but the majority has always supported the free speech guarantees enshrined in the First Amendment. Consequently, there was no fear of being arrested for breaking the law; however, there was apprehension over the very real possibility of physical abuse from so-called patriotic citizens who were ignorant, as I once was, of the misery their country was inflicting on the poor in Central America.

With the help of veterans and friends, we prepared for a different kind of Independence Day commemoration. On the Fourth of July 1990, we stood on the lower East Capitol steps holding an American flag, stained with the blood of Vietnam veterans. Over the bloodstains we printed the names of groups of people oppressed by the U.S. government from Native Americans to Central Americans. We also included women who had suffered gender discrimination under the rule of men until they began to free themselves, inspired by the example of Susan B. Anthony.

Hundreds of tourists passed by our little demonstration, but only one lone young man stopped to see the flag of his country so disrespectfully displayed. At first he was upset, but when he saw that Vietnam was included on one of the red stripes, he relaxed, nodded in ascent and quietly moved on.

The desecration of the flag and my personal Declaration of Independence mollified my anger, but it accomplished nothing politically. But, as a result of the murder of the Jesuits, U.S. aid to El Salvador was halted temporarily, as if to imply intolerance for such gross barbarity. Within a month, however, aid to the Salvadoran military was renewed under the guise of humanitarian assistance.

Even so, one good thing did come about as a result of the assassination of the Jesuits along with a mother and her teenage daughter. A month after the murders, Speaker of the House of Representatives Tom Foley appointed Representative Joe Moakley, a congressman from South Boston to investigate.

Representative Moakley was a good man for the task, a pugilist by choice, a lawyer by education, and an effective advocate for the working class of his constituency. Literally, he was a fighter, having attended the University of Miami on a boxing scholarship. In addition, he was a Jesuit-educated Catholic.

He headed up the investigation and, with little help from his own government or from the Salvadoran military, doggedly pursued those directly and indirectly responsible for the heinous crimes clothed in the secrecy of a dark November 16, 1989, night. Finally in 1992, peace accords were signed and some, but not everyone involved was tried, convicted, and imprisoned. The Salvadoran military was purged of soldiers known for their brutality and members of the revolutionary party were granted representation in a new government.

27

School of the Americas

AFTER READING MY DECLARATION OF INDEPENDENCE from the East steps of the U.S. Capitol, I was ready to return to Eden Valley and the life of a farmer. But before I could even work up a blister, the phone rang with an invitation from a noted peace activist and advocate for the oppressed worldwide. His name is Roy Bourgeois, a Catholic priest, who was then a member of the Maryknoll Society (the Catholic Foreign Mission Society of America).

Maryknoll (broadly defined) sends priests, Brothers, nuns, and laypeople all over the world to work with the poor. By doing so, members not only endure the lot of the poor, they also subject themselves to the fate of the poor, which too often involves torture, death, disappearance, and, in the case of women, rape. This happened to Maryknoll nuns and a layworker in El Salvador when the United States was supporting the Salvadoran military.

Roy's first missionary assignment was serving the poor in Bolivia, where he narrowly escaped death but failed to avoid torture. He tried to help poor tin miners whose labor was being exploited by a dictatorial government. He and other priests were expelled from the country and barred from returning. From Bolivia, he went to El Salvador to witness the plight of the poor there. Peasant farmers were revolting against an oppressive government supported by the United States.

I did not know Roy well, but I knew enough about his passion for justice to listen to any proposal he made regarding opposition to injustice. His phone call was the beginning of a lifelong relationship resulting in new and memorable experiences, inclusive of federal imprisonment. He was calling from his newly rented apartment in Columbus, Georgia – a stone's throw from the entrance to Fort Benning, the U.S. Army post where I had begun my chaplaincy.

Roy invited me to join him and others in a forty-day water-only fast in front of the entrance sign to Fort Benning. I had no idea then why he had chosen Fort Benning as a place in need of protesting.

He informed me that he had recently learned from an Associated Press article that a school for training Latin American soldiers had been moved from Panama to Fort Benning. I had never heard of the school, but it was well known throughout Latin America as the School of Dictators, or School of Assassins, or Nursery of Death Squads. Some of Latin America's most infamous dictators and murderers had attended the School of the Americas in Panama. Roy knew about one dictator from personal experience in Bolivia: General Hugo Banzer.

When Roy explained that nineteen of the twenty-five soldiers involved in the murders of the Jesuits in El Salvador were SOA graduates, it was enough for me to decide to participate in the fast. Everyone invited to join the fast had activist credentials. Some had done prison time for illegal protesting. I felt privileged to be included. My brother, Pat, decided to join the group – assuming the essential role of the support person who enables each faster to concentrate on fasting rather than waste energy on logistics.

Close the SOA!

On the morning of September 1, 1990, ten months after the massacre of the Jesuits and women in El Salvador, ten of us – nine men and one woman – gathered at the entrance to Fort Benning, with each person carrying a jug of water. For forty days and forty nights, we were to maintain a presence there, with signs reading "Close the SOA." The men were a mixture of priests, teachers, a carpenter, and a former Salvadoran soldier. The lone woman was a young school teacher from Chicago, Kathy Kelly.

From seven in the morning to six o'clock at night, traffic in and out of the post passed within shouting distance. Most of the passersby ignored us, but occasionally a soldier who lived off post or a civilian employee would flip us the finger and shout "go home!" Understandably, people associated with Fort Benning did not appreciate our protest, but we finished the fast without a serious incident.

Our meanest adversary was the Georgia weather: hot, humid, and merciless, elements I had failed to consider. Consequently, we did not finish our intended forty days of fasting. With the exception of one person, Father Roy, we stopped at thirty-five days after a medical consult. I was disappointed that I could not reach the forty-day goal, but my kidneys felt as if they were about to explode. I was feeling worse after thirty-five days of ingesting water only than I had felt after a forty-seven-day fast on the steps of the Capitol in Washington, D.C.

But for his lost weight, Roy was as enthusiastic as ever. I think the man was born to fast.

Following the fast, all but two of us went home. Father Roy, however, *was* home. It was mid morning, October 6, in Columbus. My brother, Pat, Father Roy, and I gathered in a public park, a mile away from the entrance to the post. Seated at a picnic table, we discussed the fast, satisfied to discover more local support than we had imagined: a few soldiers, some locals, and even the wife of one of the instructors at the School of the Americas. We also shared feelings about the rigors of the fast.

But for the loss of weight, Roy was feeling fine. After an hour of animated discussion, we agreed on a plan that would symbolically demonstrate the results of SOA training to the administrators, instructors, and Latin American students in attendance.

As far as we knew, none of the instructors had followed up on the activities of their students. We wanted them to see vivid poster pictures of the six slain Jesuit priests, shot through the head execution style, lying face down on the ground in the courtyard outside their bedroom windows. There would also be a poster-sized photo of the middle-aged housekeeper and her teenage daughter lying side by side on the floor of their bedroom in pools of blood flowing from their execution wounds.

Along with the pictures, we would splash human blood throughout the interior of the SOA headquarters. The walls, the rug, showcases, and portraits of distinguished graduates would be doused with blood dispensed from baby bottles to represent children slaughtered by SOA graduates. One of the portrait pictures was of Hugo Banzer, the Bolivian dictator of ill repute, regaled in a military uniform bedecked with medals, gold braids, and insignia indicating his rank of general.

To even more realistically depict the barbarity of the murder of the six priests, professors all, we would purchase pig brains at the local market and spread them around us as we lay on the ground outside the headquarters of the SOA. If carried out, the plan would be a grisly depiction of a heinous crime: human blood and pig brains to symbolize the shattered brains blown from the heads of the Jesuits and the women. The blood would be donated by a plethora of activists.

The aim of the action was to shock the military instructors at the SOA and to move them to reflect on the results of their training. Intentionally blowing out the brains of the Jesuit professors and murdering the two women were indicative of the military's fear of liberation theology, which the priests were teaching.

We did not expect the SOA to close as a result of our action. At best, the action would be a start, a beginning of what we hoped would grow into a movement of dissent by a chorus of U.S. citizens outraged over the misuse of our tax money.

We chose to carry out this action on the first anniversary of the SOA atrocity; we had a little over a month to prepare.

On November 16, 1990, my brother, Pat, Father Roy, and I conducted a brief memorial service in front of the Fort Benning entrance sign. Representatives of the local press were invited to cover the event. Two reporters and a TV anchorwoman showed up. The TV woman, miffed over the lackluster memorial event, sarcastically remarked, "Is this it?"

We had wasted her valuable time on a simple memorial service. A massacre in a faraway foreign country was not noteworthy enough for the evening news in Columbus, Georgia. She was expecting a big story event. I responded to her dismay, "Please follow us. You won't be disappointed."

A freelance reporter volunteered to drive us onto the post. We gave no thought to the fact that he might be tagged as an accomplice to our bloody protest. Followed by several media vehicles, we were driven to the front door of the headquarters of the School of the Americas, a small two-story, nondescript, brick building about thirty feet from the road. A four-foot-square sign (white letters on brown background) mounted between two wooden posts, positioned left of the entrance door, read, "SCHOOL OF THE AMERICAS." No attempt had been made to conceal the control center of a military institution. Dressed in our formal best, coat and tie for Pat and me, black clerics and Roman

collar for Roy, we walked briskly along the narrow sidewalk leading to the front door. Pat took point, I the middle, and Roy the
rear. When Pat opened the front door, Roy peeled off toward the
school sign. I followed Pat into the foyer, reaching for my first
bottle of blood as I moved. Within two minutes we were in and
out of the place, having executed our plan without opposition.

However, we did make one exception to our original plan.
We decided not to use pig brains. They were too gross, too messy
to handle and dispense. Roy left the white letters on the SOA sign
dripping with blood then doused the front of the building and
dispensed poster pictures of the victims of the massacre about
the surrounding grounds. Pat and I left the inside of the building
looking like someone had exploded a grenade in a meat market.
(We did not realize the mess we had made until the prosecution
produced pictures at our trial.)

After smearing blood on ourselves, we played dead amidst
the posters, imitating the executed priests. Within minutes the
MPs arrived. Carefully avoiding contact with blood, they escorted us to the military police station.

Jail

We were placed in separate 8x10–foot adjoining cells furnished
with a wooden foldout bench attached to the wall, long enough
to lie down on. After a rather stressful morning, I was grateful for
the unintentional hospitality. Pat's new residence was immediately next door, equally salubrious, and convenient for communication through the open space at the top of the wall separating us.
Young, uniformed MPs watched us through steel bars to make
sure we were not up to mischief like defacing property as we had
done at the SOA headquarters.

Pat chose to sit down on his wooden bench and rest his head
against the cream-colored wall behind him, forgetting that he
had bloodied his head at the reenactment of the Jesuit massacre.
Without intending to do so Pat had defaced this sanitary wall
with the blood of activists substituted for the blood of the massacred victims.

The bloodstain stood out like a single star in the blackness of
night, moving the soldier who ordered it removed, to bellow:
"Just what the hell do you think you're doing, Mister, messing up
the wall? I'm bringing you a bucket of water to wash this wall
clean. I want it done immediately."

The soldier was obviously a man accustomed to giving orders and expecting his orders to be obeyed immediately. Pat did not respond. However, when the water, bucket, and rags arrived, Pat went to work with gusto, scrubbing the entire 8x10–foot wall. But he did not touch the blood stain. When the guard returned, he failed to appreciate Pat's creativity and angrily exclaimed in military intonation, "I told you to remove the blood, man. I did not say scrub the whole damn wall. Now wash off that blood!"

Pat calmly responded, "You told me to wash the wall, which I did." Then, pointing to the blood as if he were a docent in a museum explaining a work of art, he exclaimed, "This blood is a sacrament, a holy thing I cannot destroy." Dumbfounded, the guard departed, leaving Pat satisfied and the sacrament intact.

A peaceful silence followed the guard's departure, but not for long. A voice of outrage bounced off the cement walls and ceiling of the jail demanding attention: "I am not part of this group. I'm a journalist. Call my radio station. You are violating my constitutional rights."

I recognized the voice immediately and chastised myself for failing to consider the possibility that the photo-journalist might be regarded as an accomplice. His protestations eventually resulted in his release, but not without an admonition from a military judge advocate officer, "We are not done with you yet."

In addition to the journalist, I heard the distant sound of Roy's voice exclaiming the innocence of the man who did no more than drive us to the SOA headquarters.

After fingerprinting us, taking our mug shots, and conducting a preliminary interrogation, the police issued us a "ban and bar" letter that prohibited us from entering Fort Benning ever again. We were then released and given an arraignment date before the Muscogee County magistrate at the courthouse in downtown Columbus. Even though we had broken the law – trespassing on federal property with ill intent and defacing government property – we pled innocent to the commission of crimes.

To my mind we had performed a community service by exposing the existence of a school of dictators, assassins, and torturers on American soil. We were trying to prevent, rather than commit, crimes. We were trying to close an institution directly connected to the suffering and death of thousands of poor people. The gravity of what we did to the SOA headquarters cannot be compared to the crimes against humanity committed by the school's graduates.

Our defense was the age-old "defense of necessity," which allows for a breach of law in order to prevent a greater crime. However, rare is the judge who will permit a defense of necessity because it gives too much power to the people to suit most judges. And Judge Robert Elliot, a bigot and a bully, seated on a legal throne beneath a wood-carved sign that read "Lex et Justitia" (Law and Justice), was no exception. I decided to defend myself with no intention or illusion of winning. I felt that I could say things that a lawyer, bound by protocol, could not say.

I was new to the courtroom experience and the enormous power a judge exercises over a defendant. I presumed that I would at least have an opportunity to state the case against a military institution complicit in the murder and torture of innocent people. My presumption was dead wrong. When I tried to share a little of my military background with the judge, he bluntly told me my experience as a chaplain in Vietnam was irrelevant. "Judge, I was just trying to tell you who I am," I exclaimed.

"I know who you are. Your name is enough," he responded. He was not interested in me as a person. Discerning the futility of further communication with the judge, I opted out of any attempt to convince him that my background had any bearing on behavior he considered illegal. In effect, I dismissed myself without further comment.

Roy and Pat were defended by a bright, middle-aged lawyer who had traveled all the way from Minnesota to lend his expertise to our cause pro bono. While he was able to squeeze in more information about the SOA, his efforts went unrewarded. The three of us were found guilty as expected and sentenced to federal prison – six months for Pat and me, fourteen for Roy, due to his earlier convictions.

28

Allenwood Work Camp

So BUSY WAS THE COURT IN COLUMBUS, GEORGIA, that our sentencing for crimes against the U.S. government (illegal trespass with criminal intent and destruction of government property) did not take place until June of 1991, seven months after the action. Consequently, we had plenty of time to plan for imprisonment.

To its credit, the federal government tries to place convicted criminals close to their homes, unless circumstances warrant otherwise. Roy and I chose to enter prison immediately following sentencing, which meant transportation to the prison of the government's choice, at the government's expense, on the government's time schedule. Brother Pat chose to be released on his own recognizance and return to his residence in California and await notification of the government's prison of choice.

Initially, Roy and I were sent to a mammoth federal prison in Atlanta, Georgia, which included five levels of security from minimum to maximum. We were directed to a temporary holding center, until administrative powers could find a prison closer to our home of record.

After check-in, we were relieved of all clothing and personal items, given bright, roomy, orange jumpsuits (no underwear), and escorted to our respective four-person cells, furnished with two double-decker bunks and a sink. The heavy steel entrance door was locked from six at night to five in the morning. Common showers and toilets were midway down a long hallway running between cells.

For the novice like me, movies depicting prison life came to mind and I lived on high alert, especially in the shower. My fears were groundless. No one expressed any interest in my aging body.

Thrice daily hundreds of us were allowed to leave the building and walk to an enormous mess hall, stand in a long line, and wait for a turn to select bland food from a steam table. Standing in line for food when you're hungry is never a pleasant exercise. Some prisoners find it intolerable or beneath them and they try to forgo the experience by breaking line or claiming a place reserved by a friend.

The line breakers are usually big fellows who bully their way around until they are stopped by a bigger bully or by a prison guard unafraid to do his duty or by an inmate who refuses to be intimidated. I saw this happen when a fragile-looking old man refused to give way to a bully half again his size. When the bully elbowed his way into the space in front of the elderly inmate, the old man simply stepped out of line and without incident reentered in front of the bully.

I hoped I would be as brave in a similar situation. I hate bullies of any kind. Goes back to a first grade schoolyard experience, an altercation with a schoolyard bully that resulted in my first boxing lesson plus a stern admonition: "Never come home crying again," counseled my father. On occasion, as I have said, Dad was also a bully.

In a way hatred for bullies is responsible for my incarceration – the bully being my country, the victims being smaller countries possessing resources the United States wants to exploit, be it cheap labor or a commodity not abundantly available in the United States, like oil.

It seemed to me that the responsibility for maintaining order in the mess hall belonged to the guard on duty. I saw no reason to do his job for him and risk injury plus a trip to the "hole" (solitary confinement) as "a troublemaker."

But, before doing anything, I decided to confer with an older inmate seated alone at a nearby table. His gray disheveled hair, wrinkled face, and don't-mess-with-me body language indicated that he had traveled many prison miles and weathered many prison storms. Gingerly, I approached his table and said, "Excuse me sir, I have a question for you."

Looking at me quizzically he said in a tone lathered with annoyance, "What is it?"

"Well, I'm new here and I've noticed a few of the larger inmates breaking line in the presence of a guard on duty. It occurs to me that this could lead to trouble, especially in a racially mixed group."

Incredulously, he replied in a monotone, "Yes, it could."

"I'm thinking of speaking to the guard about it. What do you think?"

The old man's expression changed from agitation to concern, and he responded paternally as if he were counseling a child, "If you cause the guard any undue inconvenience, you will be labeled a troublemaker and they have a special way of dealing with troublemakers."

"Like what?" I asked. "The hole?"

"Something like the hole, but worse. It's called diesel therapy."

Ordinarily the word "therapy" is used to indicate positive treatment for a negative medical condition. I was puzzled by the use of the word "diesel" until this jailhouse professor explained. "When you make trouble for the guards, you will be removed from the prison population without notice and sent on a journey to nowhere by way of a prison diesel truck. No one, including you, will know where you are until you are returned to a prison of the Bureau of Prison's choice, which may or may not be here."

I did not feel like risking this form of extreme isolation. It was not worth the chance of infringing upon the guard's territory, especially since I was in a transition mode waiting for permanent prison assignment close to home. Disappearing without notice would also be difficult for Judy. Sadly, I let the line-breaking incident go and learned my first lesson in prison behavior and survival: sometimes you have to swallow hard and eat crow.

It took a month for the Bureau of Prisons to assign Roy and me to a penal institution within driving distance from our homes: Louisiana for Roy and Maryland for me. I would not see Roy again until the end of his fourteen-month sentence. Next to his sentence, mine was a breeze. He ended up in Tallahassee, Florida, in a mid-level security federal prison, far more restrictive than my work camp facility, in Allenwood, Pennsylvania, which reminded me of a recreational camp for big boys. I was lodged in a dormitory sectioned into cubicles by free-standing 6x6–foot portable particle walls, with no fences and no bars, and with telephone privileges every other day.

Inmates at Allenwood were for the most part white-collar criminals like stock brokers, accountants, drug dealers, and politicians – "gentlemen," for the most part. The prison was sometimes called the Federal Country Club.

The man in the cubicle next to mine was a sixty-ish German-born junk bond dealer, around 6'2", with a full head of pure white hair and a rich man's patina. Even in his prison jumpsuit, he looked like a rich aristocrat. He swore he had been misjudged and unjustly relieved of valuable goods and property. He was good looking and well groomed, and he walked and talked with the bearing of a person of importance, as if he were in charge of the place even though he was no more important in the prison population than the poorest among us.

He bragged that he was going to be picked up by a chauffeured limousine upon release and driven to the local airport where his private Leer jet would return him to New York, but not before buzzing the prison and performing a severe vertical climb, symbolic of the common middle finger gesture of disdain for a justice system that had failed him. He showed me pictures of his mansion in New York and his Rolls-Royce, both since confiscated by the government.

If there is a plus to prison life, it is the characters you meet and the temporary friends you make. Where else could an average person live next door to a millionaire? He did his best to maintain the privileged life he had enjoyed in the world beyond prison confines. He had enough money in his commissary account to hire a less fortunate inmate to do his laundry and cut his hair. Of course you could not legitimately use money as payment for service rendered. Typically, cigarettes and other goods purchased at the commissary served as tender for services. Come to think of it, I never saw him eat in the mess hall. He may have had his meals delivered. Class culture lives on in prison.

My dorm was in the smallest of three facilities serving a thousand inmates, four hundred more than normal capacity. I was fortunate to be assigned to a wing of a larger dorm holding only fifty inmates, most over fifty and as such, less likely to settle disagreements physically. Allenwood was a pleasant change after a month in the federal transition prison in Atlanta.

One unexpected pleasure was the acres of grass growing between several walkways that ran from the dorms to the mess hall. Walking on the grass constituted an infraction of rules for inmates, but local deer and hundreds of Canadian geese enjoyed free access to a bounty of lush green grass. The animals ate freely and pooped freely with no regard for sidewalks. Defecating with abandon, they left calling cards for inmate removal, providing demerit chores for inmates guilty of a minor infraction like failure to maintain a neat locker.

Every inmate in a work camp must work. Refusal results in transfer to a higher level of security and a considerable reduction in quality of life. I was assigned to the dishwashing room located next to the exit door of the dining room, large enough to accommodate a thousand inmates in shifts of three hundred. By the end of my six-month sentence, I had washed, dried, and stacked thousands of dishes, six to eight hours a day. It was mindless work, but time passed rapidly.

A special pleasure I had not enjoyed since college was the chance to play basketball in a first-class gymnasium. I was surprised to find that, despite my senior-citizen body, I could move and shoot well enough to compete with the younger boys, unaccustomed to 1940 basketball style: set, shoot, or fake and drive. A compliment I treasure was given to me by a young black player who cautioned a teammate guarding me too loosely, "You better watch out, Tyrone. That ole bastard will burn you." I did not burn him, but I relished the compliment.

Prison Life

All in all, prison was not that bad for me. Years of isolation in the seminary studying for the Catholic priesthood was in some ways more difficult for me than prison life. In both situations you are living in the exclusive company of men, devoid of ordinary privileges like visits and phone calls from loved ones. The absence of women in any culture takes its toll. Man was not meant to live alone and neither was it meant for him to live exclusively with other men. Problems related to choice of sexual partners do arise, but, thank God, no one found me attractive and I, being with wife, felt no inclination to "take a walk on the wild side."

I did not think about it at the time, but post-prison reflection tells me that Judy did the hard time. While I was in the big boys' camp feeling noble about resistance to injustice, she was holding down a full-time teaching job, spending her weekends driving up to prison for a few hours' visit, staying the night alone at a nearby motel, and returning home to resume teaching. I did not fully appreciate her support, focused as I was on the cause behind my incarceration. There is something sustaining about sacrificing one's self for a perceived good cause. But it doesn't do much for those who suffer the loss of a loved one, even a temporary six-month loss like imprisonment. Judy never complained; rather, she maintained a cheerful disposition and a devotion to satisfying my emotional needs.

Now, with the experience of prison behind me, I feel qualified to counsel anyone contemplating civil disobedience that could land them in prison. I would advise them to give as much consideration to those they are leaving behind as they do to the sacrifice they are making in the name of justice. I would not say, "Don't do it," because civil disobedience is a powerful nonviolent expression of denouncing injustice. But I would say, "Be aware of the sacrifice of those you leave behind who do not have the comfort of doing something noble."

My six-month sentence fulfilled, I stood on the hill outside my dorm looking down on the parking lot next to the administration building, waiting for Judy's arrival. She would be driving her mother's gray two-door Oldsmobile. It was a clear, cold, December 13th afternoon.

I had been waiting two hours for her arrival. When I saw the gray Olds pull into the parking lot and Judy walking to the office, my spirits ascended. I waited for another hour before hearing the sound of my name over the loudspeaker summoning me to the moment of my release. The order to report to the "Admin" building finally came.

Inmates inside and out of my dorm knew that one more of their own was taking the freedom walk. I dashed back to my locker, grabbed a plastic departure bag, and walked for the last time down the sidewalk and through the door to the room where I would exchange prison garb for a blue sweat suit and sneakers.

After hugs and kisses in the car, Judy produced a decorated paper bag containing the articles I had asked her to bring for the occasion: a fifth of Gordon's gin, another of Gallo vermouth, a small bottle of olives, and two martini glasses given to me by a friend. We postponed our toast to freedom until we reached a bed-and-breakfast lodge in a little town on the banks of the Susquehanna River that ran parallel to our road home.

29

Back to Fort Benning

A MILE FROM HOME Judy told me about a new resident, a female. "I hope you like her, Charlie. She was waiting for me in the driveway when I returned from your trial. She's an artistically marked, tan-and-white Calico cat. I named her 'CC', short for Calico Cuddles."

When we arrived home, CC was pacing around on the front door landing. She could not have been more than six months old. It was as if an angel had taken feline form to companion Judy while I was in prison.

Initially, Judy fed the cat outside. She was not yet a cat lover. She intended for CC to be an outside cat. CC had other plans. Gradually, she charmed her way into the house. Cats are not my favorite pets, but that does not deter them from insisting on my hospitality. Future strays would find their way to my door. Abandoned or dissatisfied with their owners, they homestead wherever hospitality is available. The first meal given is an invitation to stay forever. CC and Judy had bonded by the time I arrived.

CC was born to love and be loved. Her preferred place was the lap of any receptive person where she purred away her daily life for as long as the lap would have her. However, our initial too-close encounter did not go well. At three in the morning of my first night home from prison, as Judy and I rested peacefully after love revisited, CC joined us in a manner I then failed to appreciate.

Leaping from the floor on my side of the bed, she landed

with a thud on the quilt that covered my legs, awakening me to an imagined reality that I was lying on a prison cot shooing away a rat. This had actually happened to me in a county jail. Spooked, CC leapt over Judy and bolted into the darkness of the hallway.

I have to say, though, that CC was one of the blessings of my first prison sojourn. She was always there for Judy when I was elsewhere.

My release from prison freed Judy to fulfill her need to return to San Francisco and rejoin the church community she had been a part of for so long. I agreed with the move, but I still had the closing of the School of the Americas on my mind. Roy would remain in prison for at least eight more months.

So, after helping Judy resettle, I decided to take up residence in Columbus, Georgia, as close to Fort Benning as possible in order to establish a daily presence or a "vigil," in front of the entrance sign to the post. Donations from friends and activists made the move easy. Once the word spread that a vigil to close the SOA was beginning, activists from the West and East coasts began to give their time and money to support the effort.

Of particular note is a young woman from Syracuse, New York, who stayed for several months, sacrificing time with family and friends. Margaret, in her twenties, was as gutsy as women come, freely engaging off-duty soldiers in conversation about the SOA at the vigil site by day and in local bars at night. At times there were as few as the two of us and at other times I was alone.

We conceived the idea of making self-standing 3x4–foot signs emblazoned with the names of Salvadoran peasants (gold letters on black enamel) who had been murdered by SOA graduates and positioning the signs one after another on the side of the entrance road to Fort Benning. We never ran out of names. In particular were the names of the Salvadoran villagers of El Mozote. This entire village of around nine hundred men, women, and children, save one, was massacred.

Rufina Amaya, wife and mother of four small children, was the sole survivor. In the confusion of the soldiers gathering and killing the villagers, she hid herself in nearby bushes. She was not fleeing for her life. She sensed that someone had to witness the carnage. Stoically, she remained silent while soldiers shot or macheted her husband and children. She could hear her children crying for help. Someone needed to live to tell the story of the massacre at El Mozote.

Books have been written and accounts have been posted on

the Internet for anyone who cares to learn about the heroism of Rufina Amaya and the massacre in El Mozote led by officers trained and graduated from the School of the Americas. One day I would visit El Mozote and meet this incredible woman, who at great pain to herself, led a group of us activists to the burial site of her murdered loved ones.

Willa Elam

Some protesters act in groups; others do solos unannounced, surprising not only the military but friends as well. On Thanksgiving Day, November 1998, four days after a demonstration of thousands to close the SOA, the soldiers at Fort Benning and the students at the SOA were enjoying a quiet holiday and the traditional Thanksgiving meal. Protesters from around the country had gone home – all but one, Willa Elam, an African American fifty-five-year-old grandmother.

Patiently waiting out of sight for night to fall, Willa Elam was not giving thanks; rather, she was about to say, "No thanks" to the U.S. government for hosting the School of the Americas on the grounds of Fort Benning. She would do this in a way that the new SOA commandant would never forget.

Somehow, Willa made her way to the SOA building located inside the post. Avoiding discovery, she found or created a way to enter the building, a huge, three-story structure, recently renovated. Once inside, she proceeded to give the interior of the building a new look in keeping with its reputation for training dictators, assassins, and torturers.

From the first to the third floor, using indelible ink, she printed the names of atrocities committed by SOA graduates on the walls of the halls and classrooms. Scarcely a space was left untouched. On the entrance wall of the women's lavatory, she left a personal message for her own sex, "REAL WOMEN STOP MEN FROM GOING TO WAR." Sadly, real women like Willa are few, but their numbers are growing. They are popping up here and there like flowers in a cemetery, protesting their way into jail as their predecessors did to achieve equality and confront injustice.

Finished with her artistic effort, Willa entered the commandant's office and used his telephone to inform the military police of her presence. She could have departed the building as unknown as she arrived, but she was not trying to escape responsibility. When the MPs arrived, they discovered her sitting calmly at the commandant's desk. For all they knew she could have been the cleaning lady casually relaxing, but after a look around they escorted her to the brig.

From here she should have been taken to the county jail, arraigned, and scheduled for trial, but the Army wisely chose to release her, a political decision that overrode the illegal nature of her interior decoration. The Columbus paper, the *Ledger Enquirer*, quoted the commandant's reaction to Willa Elam's efforts to educate him. "I'm very saddened by this and I'm outraged. It's grossly unjust and it's outrageous that the American taxpayer has to clean up something like this." It's sad that the commandant missed the message of Willa's artwork, namely, her outrage over the injustice associated with the School of the America's complicity in life lost and suffering endured.

The Army wisely dropped charges against Willa Elam. She embarrassed the military by breaching security, and she frightened the SOA proponents with the threat of exposure. Willa Elam is a lawyer, a smart courageous woman who goes quietly about her quest for justice. She is apt to appear anywhere and say "No, not in my name" to one or another form of injustice. It would have been a treat to listen to her defend herself in a southern court of justice.

I continued making memorial panels for the vigil in front of the Fort Benning entrance sign. Had I continued, I'd still be there and the wall of signs with the names of SOA victims would easily have stretched for miles. But, after a couple of years I began to grow restless and desirous of doing something more contributive to the exposure of the School. However, I still envision a mile-long black-enameled wall – with the names of thousands of SOA victims imprinted in gold letters – stretching from the front gate of Fort Benning to the four-lane highway leading into Columbus. To what end? Would it close the school? No. But, it would serve as a daily symbolic reminder to all who enter and leave Fort Benning that the aims of the U.S. government are not as noble as we are led to believe.

SOA September Action

About this time, I received an invitation to be part of a group of activists intent on doing a significant public action to draw attention to the SOA. Seven of us met in Columbus: three women and four men – a nun from Kentucky; a potter from Georgia; two seasoned activists, male and female from New York; a Jesuit priest from Washington, D.C.; a college student from Oregon; and me.

Gathered in the front room of an apartment within walking distance of the Fort Benning front gate, we exchanged ideas and conceived two distinct plans. Five members of the group would concentrate on changing the message of the sign in front of Fort Benning from WELCOME TO FORT BENNING, U.S. ARMY, TO WELCOME TO FORT BENNING, HOME OF THE SCHOOL OF AMERICAS, with additional notations of SOA = TORTURE AND ASSASSINATION.

The ten-inch-tall black metal letters spelling out Fort Benning were firmly bolted in cement, necessitating considerable effort with crowbars to pry them loose. Each of two remaining members would climb two tall pine trees located conveniently behind the Benning entrance sign and hang a thirty-foot-wide banner from tree to tree. The banner would read "CLOSE THE SCHOOL OF THE AMERICAS." Chris, one of our group, and I chose to climb the trees and attach the sign. It would be an easy climb on a thirty-foot-tall ladder, and it could be done rapidly.

In addition to removing the metal lettering on the Benning sign with crowbars, the seven of us were to cover our hands with water-based red paint and imprint the off-white background of the sign with symbols of the bloody hands of SOA graduates.

At ten o'clock on the morning of September 29, 1997, the action was carried out as planned with one critical exception that may have saved me from prosecution, but it cost me regret that I feel to this day.

So focused was I on climbing the tree and securing my end of the sign that I forgot to immerse my hands in the paint and leave a print on the sign. No problem, I thought, I'll just pour the paint on myself once I'm comfortably positioned on the metal deer stand I planned to chain to the tree. (Deer hunters hide in such stands while they wait for their prey.) Halfway up the ladder, fear gripped my left leg and set it to trembling. I stopped climbing, took several deep breaths, and severely warned my leg to stop shaking, as if I were chiding an errant child. Strange as it may sound, the leg obeyed and I continued climbing to the top rung of the ladder where I could safely position myself and secure the deer stand.

My partner Chris did the same on the adjacent tree and within minutes a bright white, black-lettered sign reading "CLOSE THE SCHOOL OF THE AMERICAS" hung boldly behind Fort Benning's newly redesigned entrance sign. Perched on the deer stand I could comfortably stand or sit for hours, however long it would take for the MPs to arrive. Fifteen minutes after the completion of our action, squad cars loaded with MPs drove up and commenced to arrest the sign changers circled beneath our trees singing songs of peace and justice. Untypical of military police anywhere, the MPs did not rush upon the choral group to arrest and cuff them. Rather they positioned themselves behind the singers and waited for them to finish singing. One cannot say that the hearts of military people cannot be touched.

With no prior planning, I realized that the deer stand provided a perfect elevated pulpit for preaching a message about the immorality of the School of the Americas. I felt like a bishop preaching from a cathedral pulpit. Ideally, the congregation would have been instructors and students at the SOA, but protest circumstances are seldom ideal. I had to settle for a flock of MPs who were only indirectly associated with the school.

I could look directly down into the puzzled eyes of the MPs looking up at me as they thought about how to extricate an unwilling protester from his secure perch thirty-five feet from the ground. First they tried verbal means of persuasion. When that failed, they called for a cherry picker, equipment ordinarily used to make electrical repairs or rescue house-fire victims.

The effort at persuasion fell to a tall, stately, middle-aged black soldier, a uniformed MP sergeant wearing a Smokey the Bear hat. Craning his neck to look directly upward, he shouted, "Okay, you've made your point. Come down." My reply came rapidly without thinking, "Sir, would you have said to Martin Luther King Jr. in Birmingham, 'Martin, you've made your point. No need to continue protesting'." Without a word, the face of the black sergeant disappeared beneath the wide brim of his hat.

Finally, the cherry picker arrived, backed up to the base of my pine tree, and elevated a rectangular metal bucket to my side, close enough for an army firefighter to reach me. After exchanging pleasantries, I expected him to try to pry my hands loose from the heavy hemp security rope. But for some strange reason he decided to remove the deer stand with me still in it.

Maneuvering the bucket to the side of the tree, he began to cut the chain supporting the stand and me. What was obvious to me was not apparent to him. When he had successfully cut through half of the chain, I felt I needed to say, "Excuse me, sir, I want you to know that when you cut through the rest of that chain, this stand is going to drop beneath me, leaving me with nothing but this rope to hang on to."

After looking at the half-cut chain and the stand, he agreed and changed his method of extraction. He could see that I was firmly gripping the heavy hemp rope and that he was not in any position to loosen my grip. Moving the bucket to my right side, close enough for him to reach the rope, he pulled out a formidable pocket knife and unfolded the blade. I was anxious about what he intended to do with the knife.

Noticing the surprise in my eyes at the sight of his knife, the soldier advised me to remain calm and lean back. He then reached up, knife in hand, and slashed through the rope with a single fluid swipe, allowing me to free fall backwards, stiff as a corpse, into the bucket and the arms of his partner.

It was a cool move on the part of this pair of army firefighters. I respected them for being so professional and risking personal injury to avoid hurting me. But I did not appreciate the macho remark of the soldier just before he swiped his knife, "We're going to find out what you are made of." Reflecting on my reply, I wish I would have done better. I said, "I know what I'm made of," in my own macho tone. I wish I would have recalled the words for the nursery rhyme, relative to what boys are made of, "frogs and snails and puppy dog tails."

Once removed from the tree, I was driven in a squad car to the military police brig and ushered into a cell with my friends. After several hours, we were processed individually, given a citation, released, and told to expect notification of legal proceedings. A month passed before the summons to appear in court for trial arrived.

To my surprise, even though I had violated a permanent ban and entered Fort Benning, climbed a tree, refused to come down, and resisted arrest, I was passed over for prosecution. Likewise Chris, my fellow tree climber, was exempted. The five sign artists were tried, found guilty, and sentenced to eight to fourteen months in federal prisons for their crimes: trespassing and destroying government property.

My inner punishment was having to witness the trial and the sentencing of a group of friends I had intended to accompany to prison. Feeling left out, I began to tax my imagination for a way to join them in prison. Midway through the trial I conceived a plan.

I had heard that Vice President Al Gore was coming to town to recognize the efforts of educators at Columbus State University to address the problem of low-level education. As a high-ranking political figure, he would be flying in a military aircraft and landing at Fort Benning. The public was invited to greet his arrival. I decided to join the reception and present the vice president with an open letter urging him to investigate the morally low level of education given to foreign military students at the SOA.

My participation in the welcoming ceremony would necessitate violating a perpetual ban on my presence on the base. This would get me at least six months in prison and assuage my guilty feelings avoiding the earlier prosecution with my friends.

The hasty decision to invite the VP to investigate the SOA curricula caught me without proper attire for the occasion. All I had was white tennis shoes, blue-jeans, a jacket, and a floppy old fishing hat – not exactly the proper outfit for greeting political royalty. With no time to purchase dressier shoes, I decided to dye the tennis shoes black. With the dye still drying I hired a cab to drive me to the runway of Gore's arrival.

After successfully passing through a security checkpoint, I breathed easily and joined a crowd of around fifty greeters in a roped-off area at the end of the arrival runway. My intention was to join the reception line, shake the hand of the vice president, and give him this one-page, hastily written letter:

An Open Letter to Vice President Gore

Dear Mr. Vice President,

Welcome to Columbus, Georgia. Educators and concerned citizens from all over the United States applaud your efforts to address the serious problem of low-level education. We also recognize Columbus citizens who have made generous donations toward an enhanced education for their fellow Georgia residents. We wonder if you are aware of a different kind of education offered right here at Fort Benning.

It is hard to believe that a school that teaches the fine art of psychological warfare, which includes torture and assassination, is sponsored by the U.S. Army at Fort Benning, Georgia, and financed with U.S. tax dollars. Education that results in the suffering and death and oppression of poor people in Central and South America has no place in a democratic society that champions freedom and justice for all.

We appeal to you as a person deeply sensitive to the

sacredness of all life, to use your position and considerable influence to close this school of assassins, this school of torture known as the School of the Americas.

On this very day of March 2, 1998, as you travel through Georgia promoting education that leads to a better life, five U.S. citizens are on trial for trying to expose the kind of education offered by the SOA. Please add your voice to the chorus of people throughout the country and become a part of the historic closure of the SOA.

Signed,

Concerned Citizen for the Closure of the SOA

Standing alone in the crowd of Gore greeters, I tried to relax and look inconspicuous. I'm not sure what gave me away. Perhaps it was the shoes. I never asked.

The soldier who approached me from the rear nudged my right arm and said as politely as a maître d', "Excuse me, sir. What is your purpose here?"

"I'm here to welcome the vice president and give him a letter."

About this time, a big jet was landing and taxiing up the runway toward the roped-off area.

"Please wait here, sir," said the soldier as another young soldier moved to my left side.

Having no intention of going anywhere, I complied, deducing that I had probably been recognized and would soon be arrested. As the vice president and his entourage deplaned and headed toward the waiting crowd, a woman approached me and introduced herself as the personal secretary of Vice President Gore.

"I understand you have a letter for the vice president," she said with an engaging smile. "I will be happy to deliver it for you."

Now, flanked by two soldiers, I assumed they and the secretary had been instructed to avoid a confrontation with a stranger and a possible protester. So, I gave her the letter and thanked her.

She departed and soldier number one said, "Please come with me, Sir," as he and soldier number two led me away from the crowd toward a military squad car.

On the way soldier number two began to squeeze my arm to

pain level seven, moving me to counsel him, "I'm not going to run away." He continued squeezing in deadpan military fashion. Happily, the trip to the squad car was short.

Again, I was released without charge and given a ride to the entrance of the base without so much as an admonition not to return. My friends went to prison and I went home feeling bad about the failure of my effort to be a part of the prison witness team. The Army had passed me over twice without the courtesy of an explanation. I erroneously assumed that my exemption from prosecution was related to the Army's respect for the Medal of Honor.

This amounted to an inflated estimate of my importance. Subsequent reflections have led me to conclude that the Army's reticence to prosecute was based on the inconvenience of trying two cases at once. Since I was not part of desecrating the Fort Benning welcome sign, my tree climbing was a separate case evidently thought to be unworthy of prosecution.

30

Lompoc Federal Prison

PASSED OVER TWICE FOR PROSECUTION for the pine tree incident and illegal trespass, I was feeling the discomfort of discrimination. But two later crossings over the broad white line marking the outer limits of Fort Benning, while carrying a mock black-colored coffin, were enough to move the Army to prosecution. Convicted of two misdemeanors, I was sentenced to six months in federal prison for each offense. I felt good about the sentences and somewhat relieved of the guilt I still harbored about not having gone to prison earlier with friends.

I arrived at the federal prison complex in Lompoc, California, July 29, 2000 – emotionally prepared to make myself at home for a full year. My wife, Judy, and several friends from San Francisco accompanied me to the front gate of the huge, foreboding, cement-gray maximum security building. Judy chose not to walk me to the front door of the prison. She watched from the car outside the gate, while two friends accompanied me to the first of several prison doors.

Before entering, I turned and waved to Judy and friends, like a passenger on the deck of an ocean liner leaving port for the open sea.

This was not my first experience with incarceration. I knew what to expect: total depersonalization and near-total isolation. Separation from wife and friends would not be forever, I thought. I would see Judy again on the first visiting day of each month for the next twelve months. Friends from the church we attended in

San Francisco put together a fund to help Judy with travel and lodging expenses.

After fingerprints, mug shots, and an exchange of civilian for prison attire, I was given a ride from the maximum security building to the prison camp and introduced to the people who would control and monitor my life for the next 363 days. The administrator, his assistant, and a few guards were lounging about the dormitory office unconcerned over my arrival; just one more body to manage.

I was curious to see what kind of men served as caretakers for miscreants. The administrator was a man of imposing size, at least 260 pounds of muscle attached to a 6'4" frame. Though a mountain of a man, he did not look mean. He spoke calmly and clearly, yet with unmistakable authority.

People of his size so overshadow the rest of us that they do not have to pretend to be tough. Radiating patinas of importance related to their positions of control, the guards laid out a few house rules. Then one of the lower-level caretakers escorted me to an upper bunk and a locker in a room of a hundred of the same. The bunks were positioned side by side with enough room for standing in between, allowing access to one's meager supply of clothes and personal items, which were stored in a metal locker. This salubrious space would be my living quarters for most of my stay in Lompoc.

My immediate neighbors were mild-mannered, atlas-muscled black men who spoke African American English called Ebonics – not easily understood by non-blacks. They were on the last leg of their sentences, having good-behaviored their way down from higher-level incarceration to the work camp, where bad behavior is a ticket to ride.

Since I arrived too late for supper, my new space-mates supplied me with a portion of their stored commissary snacks: a bag of potato chips and a packaged piece of jellied sponge cake. This was the first of many expressions of human kindness I experienced in federal prison, contrary to the Hollywood depiction of prison life. An inmate once said to me: "To think I had to come to prison to experience the kindness of strangers." He was a Native American.

The following day I was assigned to a construction crew under the supervision of a local white man, a career state prison employee trying hard to be a no-nonsense tough guy. He made it clear that once assigned to his crew, requesting transfer was useless.

I had no plans for requesting a transfer until I learned that the building under construction was to be an armory, a storage place for the weapons of higher-level prison guards. This did not sit well with my sense of nonviolence; consequently, I refused to work on the weapons storage building on the premise that it was against my conscience.

The boss was upset, but he did not try to threaten me into compliance, which surprised me. He simply took the easy route to higher authority. When he returned he dismissed me without explanation and sent me to see the assistant director of the camp, who asked what I would like to do. "Anything but build a storage place for weapons," I replied.

For the next five months I attended a hands-on construction class that included lectures, reading, cement work, and gardening. This suited me just fine: a little work, a little class time, and the acquisition of a few new skills. It also gave me the opportunity to observe the character and personality of other inmates. People and their life stories interest me. I would have served the remainder of my sentence in the construction class had not an incredible opportunity arisen.

Religious Services

Federal law mandates provision of religious services for inmates; consequently, priests, rabbis, ministers, and Native American medicine men are allowed to conduct services for interested inmates. A small chapel built on work camp grounds accommodated Catholic, Protestant, and Jewish inmates.

Elsewhere, large log rounds piled six feet high surrounded a canvas-covered circle of saplings arranged like a turtle shell. This small structure served as a sweat lodge for Native American worship. Since a medicine man was not available to conduct the sweats, a Lakota Sioux inmate filled in. I was surprised to learn that by invitation, nonnatives were allowed to attend sweat lodge ceremonies. An inquiry led to an invitation to participate. In a spirit of curiosity I accepted and became a regular once-every-Saturday attendee.

The sweat lodge is well named because Native Americans and others who gather there for prayer sweat profusely. The heat in this little enclosure was intense enough to blister a half-naked novice like me, who did not know how to handle extreme temperatures. Pride enabled me to hold back a scream when steam from water poured over hot rocks wrapped around my shoulders and returned to blistering hot water.

Expecting a little sympathy, I showed my blisters to the lodge leader who shrugged indifferently and walked way. I quickly learned the trick of hugging the ground as the temperature rises. As time passed, I continued the sweat lodge worship and came to enjoy it more than my own Catholic brand of liturgy. It was a down-to-earth ceremony with immediately recognizable symbols like hot coals, water, and scents of smoking sage, along with personal rather than canned prayers, which participants offered spontaneously. God is the Great Spirit, Wakan Tanka.

His sentence completed, the resident lodge master recommended me as his replacement. I suppose it was due to my clerical background. The job meant maintaining the grassed and flowered grounds in and around the sweat lodge and preparing for the Native American religious ceremony every Saturday morning. It was a one-person job free of supervision at a location distant enough from the administration office to provide a modicum of privacy.

Aware that I was once a practicing Catholic priest, a guard cynically cautioned me to refrain from practicing black magic. He was trying to be funny in the presence of his fellows, but they did not respond. I did not immediately react to this blatant insult because I wanted the job. But, sensing that the man was familiar with the black arts, I replied, "Even though I've given up the practice of the priesthood, I still have the powers of the priesthood, which include placing a curse on someone or something." He fell silent and I left the room. I had no idea of the fear the threat of a curse could induce.

I could not have been happier with any other prison job: chopping wood for the fire to heat the ceremonial sweat lodge stones, tending to the flowers around the grounds, and enjoying the silence of the absent prison personnel. I was, so to speak, "far from the madding crowd." Occasionally, a guard dropped by the lodge, more to pass time than look for trouble. Most of the time there was no reason to be apprehensive, but a dicey situation did arise in the form of a favor I was asked to do by an inmate I did not know.

I did not want to build an in-house reputation for refusing a fellow inmate a favor just because of a little risk. He wanted me to barbecue around two dozen pork chops a guard at the big house (maximum security facility) had given to him as a reward for work his crew had completed. For all I knew he had stolen them from the prison employee mess, but I asked no questions. I had never seen such thick chops, in or out of prison. My compensation would be an adequate share of the goods, which I in turn could share with some of my friends. I had reservations about the origin of these rare delicacies. I could lose my coveted job if caught, but the rare pleasure of dining on inch-thick smoked pork chops overrode caution.

Around three o'clock on a clement, but windy afternoon, I began smoking the chops on a grill assembled from a rusty fifty-gallon drum pierced at the bottom for ventilation and covered with a discarded section of squared construction rebar, no doubt scrounged by my predecessor. This makeshift grill was perfect for smoking anything and large enough to accommodate half of the entrusted treasure. Engrossed in my new prison chef's role, I paid little attention to the wind blowing gently over the grill, carrying the rich scent of smoked pork directly into the prison compound.

When half the chops were done, I moved them to the top of a nearby stump to cool and began cooking the second batch, all the while looking about for unwanted visitors. In addition to providing a constant supply of oxygen to the coals, the wind cooled the finished chops sufficiently enough for me to store them in a purloined black plastic trash bag, which I had stashed beneath a pile of compost.

No sooner had I hidden the chops than I caught sight of a white-shirted figure, a hulk of a man, about fifty feet distant, walking in my direction. No question about his identity. There was no time to hide the chops from the administrator, but I thought I could guide him to the flower garden, away from my outdoor kitchen. No way! Like a bloodhound on scent he followed his nose to the source of the smoking meat. As he approached the site of a dozen plump pork chops ready to be plucked from the grill, neither he nor I spoke. I was lost for words, trying not to look sheepish. He stood six feet from the sizzling chops killing me with silence.

I was expecting a severe admonition and a statement of job termination. Neither came, nor did he ask about the origin of the chops. Instead, he calmly directed me to throw the pork chops over the fence and destroy the grill.

I should have complied immediately, but thinking only of the needless waste, I asked, "Are you sure you want me to do that?"

"On second thought," he replied, "Take the chops to the garbage bin next to the kitchen."

When he left, I chastised myself: "I could have rescued those chops, washed them clean and none of the recipients would have been the wiser."

Higher-Level Security

After the pork chop incident, the "main man" dropped in on me again and again, always unannounced, engaged in a little irrelevant conversation, looked around, and continued his inspection walk about the work camp. I was beginning to like my cushy job less and less.

From the edge of the lodge grounds, I could see the big house and the smaller, minimum-security compound, double-fenced around, and topped with razor wire. Considering that I had not experienced heavy-duty prison, I mused, "It's time for me to move up the security ladder at least one rung and acquire some real prison experience." So when the main man arrived for his next inspection visit, I requested a transfer to medium security.

"There is no such thing as a transfer to higher-level security," he informed me.

Pointing to the Federal Correctional Institution (FCI), a medium security building, one level above the work camp, I asked, "What do I do to get over there?"

Hastening to reply, he said, "I cannot have this conversation with you."

"Suppose I just walked out of here?" I continued.

"That would do it," he assured me.

His interpretation of our conversation surprised me when a guard came to my dormitory living space and ordered me to follow him to the admin office, where the administrator and his assistant questioned me about my plans to escape. Surprised, I explained that I had no immediate intention of leaving the camp, but if I chose to do so I would inform them. Failing to appreciate my sense of humor, they did not respond.

Free to go, I returned to my living space and began to change clothes for supper, but before I could dress, another guard appeared with a "Follow me!" message.

Back in the office, now crowded with guards, the main man informed me that I was under arrest and about to be transferred to FCI. "We have concluded that you are planning to escape," the main man said to me. I was amused, but recalling my pork chop indiscretion, I held my tongue, secretly reflecting on the anomaly that I was being gifted with exactly what I wanted, a transfer.

Cuffed and taken to a waiting pickup truck, I was driven to the FCI, where I met a new administrator who escorted me to a new residence. Still cuffed, I walked beside him to a separate building that housed inmates judged to need solitary confinement. On the way he asked me if I was still planning to escape. Feigning seriousness, I looked at the surrounding twelve-foot-tall fences capped with razor wire and said, "Escape would not be easy," but I did not deny the possibility.

The FCI administrator turned me over to a guard who led me to my cell. The cell door, which was made of steel, had a 4x8–inch peek-a-boo window and another smaller opening for the transfer of food. The door closed behind me, the keyed lock clicked, and I was face to face with two new cell mates young enough to be my sons.

After exchanging smiles and handshakes, they directed me to a pair of bunks at the far end of the cell. As a safety precaution, I chose the upper. The cell was further appointed with a stand-up shower, a stainless-steel sink, and a pressure-flushing commode, unencumbered by a toilet seat or privacy partitions. These stainless-steel necessities shone with meticulous care.

The place was just what I needed with the exception of the company. After eight months in a dormitory stuffed beyond capacity with men, lockers, and beds, I was hoping for complete privacy; however, I quickly adjusted to and enjoyed the company of the youngsters, who were in their early twenties, eager to share the stories that had led to their incarceration. From time to time my cell mates were moved, leaving me alone with the silence I craved.

Before I could settle in to my cozy new accommodations in what was not euphemistically called the "hole," I received two visitors: the main man and his assistant from the work camp. I felt a little silly bending over to talk through the small grated opening in the middle of the steel door.

"How's it going?" I was asked.

"Just fine. I'm very happy here," I replied.

"We will have you out of here and into population in a couple of days," they said in a somewhat apologetic tone. Sad to say I was not sympathetic to their concern for me.

"Oh no!" I said plaintively "I want to stay here. I'm very happy here." Then, with tongue in cheek I said to both of them, "I'm disappointed in you. You betrayed my trust. I told you I would not try to escape without telling you."

The assistant replied, "I was only following orders."

I retorted, "It seems to me I've heard that phrase before."

The two of them departed, leaving me in the peace of solitary confinement. I lived out the seventy remaining days of my incarceration reading, writing, and listening to stories of crime and punishment, anticipating better days to come. My hair grew, my beard grew, and I grew in appreciation for the love of my wife and friends whose unflagging support took the onus out of prison.

Judy would say, "When Charlie went to prison, I did too."

Released from Prison

On July 27, 2001, I walked through the exit door of Lompoc Federal Prison. Before release, I turned in my prison garb – a bright orange oversized jump suit; no shoes, socks, or underclothing – and selected a new outfit from a pile of mixed secondhand shirts and trousers stored in a small room near the exit. I suspected that this clothing had been taken from other miscreants on their way into prison or donated by the Salvation Army. I was allowed to keep my black rubber flip-flops, purchased at the canteen. Fortunately, Judy, brought along my pre-prison wardrobe.

Last stop, the final checkout window, where I was required to repeat my prison number printed on a plastic ID card before being given a 4x6–inch flyer imprinted with the figure of a hand gun, slash marked and circled in red indicating that I had no right to possess a weapon.

The room before the final exit door looked like an empty ballroom walled with curtain-less windows. On this day the room was, appropriately, sunlight bright. A lovely, lone woman stood in the middle of the room, arms outstretched as if she were beckoning me to dance. We embraced, slipped immediately into a dancing pose, waltzed our way across the empty room to the last prison exit door, and reentered a world I'd been away from for a year.

Freedom from the interior sounds and sights of prison was a sweet relief; heavy steel doors slamming shut, keys jingling, and uniformed care-less caretakers peering through a small peek-a-boo observation window to mark me present and accounted for.

You never get used to being watched. Makes you feel like a caged animal. Since prison, I've never been to a zoo.

My prison time was short in comparison with sentences given to other protesters like Father Roy Bourgeois, who totals over four years in four different heavy-duty prisons. He did not enjoy the luxury of work camps, with no bars or freedom of movement or unlimited phone calls.

In addition to a few good prison people, inmates and employees, two outsiders made my stay less odious. A friend, also a lawyer, and his teenage son heard about my intention to appeal my sentence and offered to help me prepare an appeal and present it to the Eleventh Circuit of Appeals, Atlanta. They would do this pro bono.

The appeal was denied, as was an attempt to present the case to the U.S. Supreme Court; hours of research and writing gone unrecognized by the power of legal titans, disinclined to consider a case based upon abuse of legal power. I felt badly for Harvey Harrison and his son, David, who, despite the counsel of a respected professor of law, lost the case.

Home again, I planned to continue protesting the existence of the School of the Americas. Twenty years beyond the first demonstration against the School, it still exists hidden within the bowels of Fort Benning, masquerading under a new name, Western Hemisphere Institute for Security Cooperation (WHINSEC), yet continuing to train military agents of oppression, protecting and doing the bidding of wealthy elites.

The SOA's new name, WHINSEC, does nothing to mask the decades-long history of atrocities by soldiers trained in state-of-the-art methods of controlling or eliminating revolutionary movements. It is the age-old story of oppression of the poor by the rich via the collusion and force of the military. It is a sad familiar story, but sadder yet is the fact that the government of my country supports the oppression of the poor in the name of freedom and democracy. Spokespersons for the newly named school claim that it no longer teaches torture and that its students no longer engage in terror tactics to suppress revolutions by the poor. I wish I could believe that.

My country, once a source of pride to me, has by training soldiers of oppressive governments become a deceitful purveyor of pseudo-democracy and a paragon of hypocrisy.

* * *

After leaving prison I received an invitation to talk about the reason for my imprisonment, namely, my illegal protest against the School of the Americas. The talk was scheduled in late September 2001, a month and a half after my release from Lompoc; the place, the University of Missouri (Columbia). Past experience made my preparation for the talk easy, but a shattering event two weeks prior to the scheduled talk overshadowed the importance of the topic.

Early in the morning of September 11, 2001, as Judy and I were waking to a new day, a friend called and urged us to turn on our TV. There was no need to select a specific channel; the event was on every major station. A commercial airliner had crashed into a tower of the World Trade Center in Manhattan.

We were too late to see the initial impact, but the immediate aftermath of smoke and flame and panic-stricken people running for their lives was a calamity in motion. Someone captured a perfect shot of the plane piercing the tower between the ninety-second and ninety-eighth floors. This picture was telecast around the world throughout the day.

Initially, I thought the crash was a tragic accident. Then a second plane slammed into the first tower's twin and media commentators began to use the word "terrorist." Before the day was over, two more hijacked commercial airliners had been used as missiles, one crashing into a field in Pennsylvania (evidently on its way to Washington, D.C.) and the other into the Pentagon.

Judy had to leave for work so she had to depend on the radio for more details, but I, like everyone with a TV set, remained fixed on the scene for the rest of a day that will always be remembered as 9/11. Did the terrorists chose 911, the national emergency number, to indelibly mark the date of their expression of hate for America? Mention 9/11 to anyone and he or she will know of what you speak. President Roosevelt might call it a second "Day of Infamy," after Pearl Harbor.

Together with all who witnessed the 9/11 attacks on TV, I was shocked and saddened by the loss of life; angry at the attackers, yet asking myself the "who and why" questions. Answers did not come immediately via the media or the press, but before day's end the identity, nationality, and methodology of the perpetrators were known. Nineteen Middle Eastern men had sacrificed their lives to make a point.

Some labeled it a religious point – jihad, the holy war against U.S. military forces stationed on Saudi Arabia's sacred ground.

Others said the reason was political: "blowback," a CIA term meaning retaliatory reactions against U.S. foreign policies, e.g., favoring Israel over Palestine. President George W. Bush said that the attackers were envious "of our freedom and prosperity," a patently absurd excuse and an insult to the intelligence of most Americans.

Reasons aside, the protective wall of distance proved to be made of glass, shattered forever in an instant. It did not take an intercontinental missile to do it, only a passion for vengeance rooted in religious belief. All wars are horrific, but religious wars are the worst. Human rights abuses are not even considered. Americans can never again take comfort in the security of distance – feeling impregnable to foreign attack.

Upon impact, the buildings burst into flame, belching pillowed plumes of smoke into a clear blue September sky. After an hour and a half of burning, the towers, as if by planned demolition, began to crumble, one floor collapsing successively upon another in perfect symmetry, leaving a pile of pulverized concrete, glass, twisted steel girders, and the cremated remains of thousands who were unable to escape.

Today, ten years after the event, questions raised about the attack by professional engineers and scientists remain unanswered. A government-appointed group comprised of former congressmen, lawyers, and businessmen failed to adequately explain the similarity of the crumbling towers to a professionally controlled demolition. Public demands for an independent investigation have gone unheeded.

Why the reticence? Do we have a government "for the people" or not? This failure to recognize the need of citizens to know casts a shadow of doubt and distrust upon a government floundering in a swamp of suspicion over issues like torture and the manufacture of weapons of mass destruction.

More money was spent in an investigation of President Bill Clinton's zipper problem, which hurt many but killed no one, than was spent answering questions related to the merciless murder of close to three thousand innocent victims of the 9/11 attacks.

Following the attack, I listened to the reactions of politicians, pundits, citizens, foreigners, and, of course, President Bush. When an aide announced the crash of the first plane into the north tower, the president was reading children's stories to a gathering of second graders in Sarasota, Florida. The president reportedly remained calm and continued reading "My Pet Goat," the story of a male goat that butted his way into heroic status.

When a second plane hit an adjacent tower, it was evident that this was a coordinated terrorist attack. The name of a Saudi Arabian, Osama bin Laden, was mentioned as a prime suspect. There was good reason to suspect him, but no solid proof. He had publicized his anger at the United States over its military presence in his country and its preferential treatment of Israel over Palestine.

The predictable political fallout of 9/11 began with President Bush that evening. Returning to Washington from his storytelling session with the second graders, the president gave the nation a brief account of the terrorist attack and told us that "our country is strong."

If we were so strong, how is it that we allowed four commercial airliners to be commandeered and used as weapons to snuff out thousands of innocent lives? Adding insult to injury, Bush continued: "We were attacked because we are the brightest beacon of freedom and opportunity in the world, and no one will keep that light from shining." Continuing with this pseudo-patriotic, fawning, pandering claptrap, the president of the United States assured us that we are "a great people moved to defend a great nation." My response to this remark is, "Mr. President, please define 'great'."

Nine days later, on September 20, 2001, President Bush addressed a joint session of Congress. Continuing his pandering palaver, he sought to assure us and reassure us with tributes to our greatness and strength. He finished with the politician's favorite word, "freedom." He then continued to beat the drums of vengeance against the "evil" that befell us, pledging relentless pursuit of the criminals who literally came crashing into our world, changing it for the foreseeable future.

I was in Columbia, Missouri, fulfilling a commitment to talk about the School of the Americas when President Bush addressed Congress. I knew very little then about U.S. involvement in the Middle East. My attention had been on U.S. policy in Central America. Feeling that I had to say something to my audience, I admitted my ignorance about the Middle East and pledged to begin course 101 on Middle East issues on 9/11. But, the annual fall demonstration to close the School of the Americas was approaching, and I wanted to be a part of it.

31

Witness in Iraq

ON THE WEEKEND FOLLOWING NOVEMBER 16, 2001, while watching thousands of protesters gathered in front of the main gate of Fort Benning, I remarked to one of the demonstration planners: "In comparison to 9/11, this is small potatoes. Atrocities connected to training given by the School of the Americas are minuscule in comparison to the trouble brewed by 9/11. An entire country was, is, and will be affected by these attacks for generations."

This younger man, by twenty years, hastened to correct me (paraphrased):

There is no triviality about the wanton killing of innocents, the criminals who do the killing, and the school that does the teaching. As long as U.S. institutions like the School of the Americas train foreign students who return to their country and employ the training received to oppress and kill their own people, the government of the United States betrays its claim to stand for human rights.

I did not immediately appreciate the younger man's insight. Elders seldom value the admonitions of the young. But truth gradually sidestepped pride, and I came to agree with him. It is important to address injustice wherever and whenever it happens.

Back home in San Francisco, I returned to writing this memoir and to reading about the continual failures of UN inspection teams to find weapons of mass destruction (WMDs) in Iraq and about the U.S. military's failure to find Osama bin Laden. Rumor had him fleeing to the mountains of Afghanistan. The news was full of fatuous information about Iraq's possession of WMDs and Saddam Hussein's failure to cooperate with WMD inspection teams.

After a year's worth of inspections by reputable international teams, no WMDs were found in Iraq. This was bad news for President Bush, who was on the hunt for a plausible excuse to invade Iraq. The discovery of WMDs would have been a publicly acceptable excuse to invade Iraq. To make matters worse, two of the principal weapons inspectors, Hans Blix from Sweden and Scott Ritter from the USA, resigned in protest.

I found myself wanting to go to Iraq to see traces of WMD evidence, but I had no idea how I would get there. Once again, just when I needed help, I received an invitation to join a group of activists and fly to Iraq on a fact-finding mission. The group was called Voices in the Wilderness [*Ed.:* Now known as Voices for Creative Nonviolence].

I was delighted, but feeling cautious about once again leaving Judy. We had been through a number of "social justice separations," but none carrying longtime jail sentences and heavy federal fines. My concerns were allayed when I asked for her opinion. She answered unequivocally, "I think you should go." Within two weeks I was boarding a plane with other activists flying to Amman, Jordan, where a hired Iraqi driver and van carried us over five hundred desert miles to Baghdad, Iraq.

We booked into a small hotel in Baghdad, the Al Finar, about five hundred yards east of the biblical Tigris River, with a mile-long view west across the river to one of Saddam Hussein's palaces that would become the post-invasion U.S. military security area called the Green Zone. (I have no idea why the color green was chosen. The palace is anything but ecological.) I was given a small, private, third-floor room on the south side of the hotel.

My lodging neighbor to the south was the palatial, eighteen-story Palestine Hotel. An easy walk led to a business district replete with bazaars, open-air markets, restaurants, and theaters. Heavy scents of meat grilling over charcoal hung in the air around bearded men turning lamb kebabs. Occasionally, a woman passed, covered from head to toe in black garb called a *burqa*. In some cases, the faces of the women were concealed behind a grill of braided black cloth; no visible flesh, nothing but dark eyes peering through the grill.

The men wore full-length alb-like white robes, topped with red-and-white turbans. Beardless and light skinned, dressed in a Western-style short-sleeved shirt and jeans, I stood apart from the black-and-white–clothed traffic of Iraqi men and women – drawing curious glances from passing Iraqis, some friendly and some with piercing eyes afire. Before going to Baghdad, I had memorized a few ice-breaking phrases in Arabic like *as-salaam-alaikum,* a genteel friendly greeting meaning "peace be with you." I used the greeting as often as my eyes met the eyes of an Iraqi, always a man, on the street or in the market. The recipient of the greeting invariably replied *wa-alaikum-salaam,* returning peace to me.

I used the phrase frequently and most often received a friendly response. But once I thoughtlessly replaced the Arabic word for peace, *salaam,* with the Hebrew word *shalom.* The middle-aged male recipient of my greeting, a burly, bearded mechanic, stopped working and began a slow, deliberate approach toward me. With the distance between him and me closing, I realized my verbal error in time to save my skull and replace the Hebrew *shalom* with the Arabic *salaam.*

The man stopped short, smiled, spun around, and returned my corrected greeting with the appropriate Arabic version. I had forgotten about the tense relations between Arabs and Israeli Jews. In the flash of an eye, I received a memorable, cultural language lesson. The majority of the Iraqi people were very friendly, even after discovering that I was an American, a man from a nation that had destroyed their electrical grids and water-purification plants and pushed the UN Security Council to impose an embargo that reportedly killed more half million Iraqi children.

To this day, the growing extent of infrastructural damage in San Francisco like potholes and neglected educational standards reminds me of Iraq. (Interesting how we, a nation in perilous debt, can spend billions killing people and destroying vital infrastructure while our potholes deepen, our people lose jobs, and our political leaders struggle to raise re-election money.)

I had no idea what I would do in Iraq given my lack of badly needed medical skills, but I reasoned that I could observe the human and material damage still evident ten years after the first Gulf War (1991) and share this information with people back home who had little access to unfiltered news. Curiously, Iraq's Ministry of Oil was left untouched by U.S. aerial attacks – one of the first recognizable on-site clues to Washington's reasons for attacking Iraq. After the merciless bombing of legally protected infrastructure, we (I hate to think this pronoun includes me) have, to this day, failed to repair or replace these critical resources.

On our second day in Baghdad, we began to make the rounds of places and people that would give us an idea of the results of the U.S. bombing of 1991 and the effects of ten years of sanctions. For a week we visited hospitals, damaged electrical stations, water-purification plants, and private homes. Ten years after the Gulf War, water plants, electrical grids, and public buildings had not yet been restored.

The blame for the slow-to-no repairs was placed on Saddam Hussein, who is alleged to have squandered the aid money. Perhaps he did, but ever since listening to U.S. State Department lies about Vietnam's alleged violations of international law I am left in doubt or in complete incredulity. The Iraqi people paid dearly for the damage their soldiers did to Kuwait, but they did not revolt against their iron-fisted dictator as U.S. warmongers expected they would.

I heard about a nearby orphanage a few blocks from my hotel run by the Sisters of Charity, the religious order founded by Mother Teresa, the internationally celebrated nun with a passion to help the poor. Five nuns tenderly cared for the basic needs of ten to fifteen abandoned Iraqi children, none of whom could care for themselves, none of whom looked older than five or seven.

Their deformities evoked revulsion and sadness. I wanted to leave the scene. The children were sitting or lying on a rug-covered tiled floor in a twelve-square-foot room, playing with toys or leafing through picture books.

All but one seven-year-old boy looked up at me, the stranger, as I entered the room. All but this one stone-faced child smiled infectiously like young children do, unaware of the ugliness of their abnormalities, their bodies, twisted bone and flesh, yet their faces angelic. I learned to look only at their faces.

The one sullen child looked as if life had been drained from his face. He made no sounds, just stared into space, oblivious of everything and everyone around him, a victim of more than physical deformity.

The contorted bodies of these children were not war injuries. They were fatalities of the negative side of nature, slipups of intelligent design, if there is such a thing. No efforts of mine or anyone could change the expression of gloom frozen on the face of this child. None of the children could walk; each one stricken by a debilitating disease like spinal bifida or polio. I left the orphanage short of breath and sick of heart, with no intention of returning.

But I was drawn back by the irresistible magnetism of love visible in the children and their caregivers, the white-robed, blue-and-white–veiled Sisters of Charity. I had come to Iraq to give what little love I had; instead, it was I who was given lessons in love indelibly imprinted on my memory. The experience makes me hope for a special place of health and happiness here-after for people like these children and the women who care for them.

Visa limitations required that I leave Iraq after eight weeks. Typical wartime propaganda blustered from the White House in-dicated that another attack on Iraq was in the planning. I felt like I was abandoning ship, leaving passengers who had no means of escaping the fate of death or injury. I had come to know a few Iraqi people personally, like storekeepers, barbers, taxi drivers, children, and the nuns. But there was no way of remaining. I left Iraq by a hired van – traveling the day-long desert route back to Amman, where I stayed for a week with friends.

By mid January, 2003, I was back in San Francisco, heavy of heart, painfully reliving my Iraqi experience and listening to news from Washington about the fictitious national security rea-sons for attacking Iraq: dethroning a dictator and eliminating weapons of mass destruction despite the assurance of reputable UN inspection teams that WMDs were nonexistent.

Return to Iraq, 2003

Safe but uncomfortable at home, I fretted and thought about the Iraqi people, especially the children. In mid February, 2003, an opportunity arose to return to Iraq to monitor the likely invasion that President Bush and company had been secretly planning as far back as months before 9/11.

Again with the support of Judy, I returned to Baghdad. I chose to settle into a tent inside the walls of a water-purification plant on the edge of the city. Damage from the first Gulf War had left the plant at only 50 percent capacity. I assumed that the plant would be bombed again and wanted to be there when the Ameri-can tanks came rolling in – presuming of course that I would sur-vive the bombing. I wanted to be a witness to another U.S. violation of international law, which forbids the destruction of a country's infrastructure.

Several other members of the Voices in the Wilderness Peace Team were willing to risk their lives to witness the destruction of the water plant. When the bombing began on March 19, 2003, the sky over Baghdad lit up like a Fourth of July celebration. Operation Shock and Awe (the macho title given to the U.S. attack by President Bush himself) was on.

As I lay in the tent listening to explosions across the Tigris River in the vicinity of Saddam's palace, I heard the sound of women's and children's voices passing on the road close to my tent. Pulling back the flap, I could just make out black-clad shadowy figures of women blending into the darkness of the night, herding their children toward the imagined safety of the plant administration buildings. These were the wives and children of the employees of the water-purification plant. As I emerged from the tent one of the women carrying an empty water bottle, approached me pointing to the bottle. Fortunately, I had a full bottle handy.

For forty-three days the bullets and bombs continued, ending on May 1. The plant was not hit again. The tanks did not come rolling in, nor did the American soldiers come marching in as I had presumed they would. I cannot say that I was disappointed.

I returned to the Al Finar hotel to find the streets around the adjacent Palestine Hotel blocked by U.S. tanks and personnel carriers. Life gradually returned to prewar normal, with the exception of looters running out of stores with stolen household goods. Initially, the U.S. invaders were welcomed with shouts of joy and waving hands of welcome, but that was soon to change.

The invasion over and the occupation begun, it was time for me to leave Iraq. But I did not want to leave before writing an open letter to the invader/occupier American troops – giving them the perception of a Vietnam veteran who had witnessed their triumphal entry into Baghdad.

An Open Letter to the U.S. Military that Attacked,
Invaded, and Now Occupies the Country of Iraq

Baghdad, Iraq – May 5, 2003

By way of introduction my name is Charlie Liteky, a U.S. citizen, a Vietnam veteran, and a Medal of Honor recipient who renounced the MOH on July 29, 1986, in opposition to the U.S. foreign policy in Central America. What the

United States was supporting in El Salvador and Nicaragua, namely, the savagery and domination of the poor, reminded me of what I was a part of in Vietnam fifteen years earlier.

I placed the medal at the apex of the Vietnam Memorial Wall onto which are etched the names of fifty-eight thousand young American men. In-depth study of the Vietnam War revealed political and military liars insensitive to the value of human life, inclusive of their own countrymen. The biggest liar was the commander and chief of U.S. armed forces, President Lyndon Johnson, who lied to Congress about the Gulf of Tonkin incident. It was this lie that motivated Congress to vote the money for the war. As a veteran of this ill-fated war [and] in the waning years of my life, I'd like to share some reflections on my country's attack on Iraq.

Once again, I find myself in protest of a U.S. military action that no court in the world will declare legal. Like Vietnam, the U.S. attack on the sovereign country of Iraq fails to meet any of the necessary provisions of a just war. In its attack on Iraq, the United States violated the UN Charter, international law, and universal standards of morality.

This is borne out by the worldwide condemnation of the U.S. attack by mainstream religious denominations and spiritual leaders.

Claiming liberation of the Iraqi people as a just cause for a war that killed thousands of innocents is hypocrisy at its worst. If liberation of an oppressed people were the real motive behind the invasion of Iraq, why did the United States wait twenty-five years to act? Why did the United States refrain from condemning Saddam Hussein's use of chemical weapons in its war with Iran in the eighties? Why did the United States fail to prevent chemicals critical to the production of biological weapons from reaching Iraq? How is it that what we condemn today we approved yesterday?

Many Iraqi people rejoiced at the sight of their American/British liberators, but many more did not, because they had no legs to walk to the sites of celebration, no arms to wave in jubilation, or they had no life left to celebrate. The sanitary military term for such people is "collateral damage."

I first went to Iraq in November of 2002 in response to the bellicose words of war coming from the president of the United States and his staff. When I think of war, I think first of children, the most vulnerable of the innocents. In my imagination I could hear them crying; I could see the terror in their eyes and faces as they heard the planes overhead, followed by bombs exploding. I hoped to be with them to offer some small comfort.

The cartoon below published in the Jordan Times on April 23, 2003, depicts what many Arab people believe is the U.S. motivation behind its attack on Iraq, namely, a deep-rooted, long-lasting presence.

Recently, newspapers have reported that plans are under way to establish four military bases in Iraq. Another gross indication of the U.S. intention to remain in Iraq is the recent completion of the largest embassy in the world at a cost of millions of taxpayer money.

What the cartoon does not include is the U.S. interest in and access to Iraq's immense oil reserves.

A two-time Medal of Honor recipient, General Smedley Butler, said that "War is a racket" and that he spent his thirty-three-year military career being a bodyguard for U.S. business interests. I submit that protecting U.S. business interests, sometimes called "national interest," is still the primary mission of the U.S. military. Again to quote Smedley, "War is a racket. It always has been. It is possibly the oldest, easily the most profitable, surely the most vicious. It is the only one international in scope. It is the only one in which the profits are reckoned in dollars and the losses in lives."

Too bad we no longer have military men of Smedley Butler's cut to enlighten us today and demand that we live up to humanitarian principles.

This letter containing some of my reflections is not meant to cast blame for an attack on Iraq on U.S. military personnel. I'm sure they believe that what they are a part of is right and just. I once believed the same of my participation in the Vietnam War.

Sincerely,

Charlie Liteky, Vietnam Veteran
San Francisco, California

I do not know that the letter was given to the company commander, but on the following day one young recipient of my letter informed me that his tank crew agreed with me. What a pleasant surprise to find soldiers, whom I had not credited with critical thinking, thinking.

I had not given pause to think when I was in Vietnam. It took the example of others less conditioned by pseudo-patriotic acculturation to awaken me to the U.S. motives underlying foreign policy. When I asked the soldier where his tank crew was from, he said "L.A."

A few days later I was on my way home again, feeling sad about the Iraqi innocents killed or wounded in the quest for oil behind the smokescreen of searching for Osama bin Laden.

32

Parting Thoughts

HOME AGAIN, I CONTINUED TO WRITE THIS MEMOIR, ever questioning the value of the effort and running low on writing fuel. It's time to end this task, reflect on what I've written, say thank you to friends, express my sorrow to all I've offended in and out of this story, and finally decide to or not to seek a publisher or self-publish a few copies for friends who have expressed interest or ask Judy to bury it at sea along with my ashes.

At this writing I've just passed my eighty-first year – walking once around the block for exercise, stopping to view the vast variety of flowers in front of neighbors' yards, disturbing dogs barking behind windows of homes they defend, and alarming house cats lounging on front-porch steps. I'm into a new life of old age, surprised to be here.

Thanks or no thanks to modern medicine, I'm living well beyond my parents, who both died of heart attacks at sixty-three. Bypass surgery was not there for them. Younger brothers, too, are gone, one leaving two sons and two grandsons.

I wonder how much longer I'll be here. I find it strange to be living as an old man, memory fading, people and names disappearing, steps growing shorter, hips hurting, and places I've known no longer known. Changes all around and within me, affecting what I see and how I feel; feeling more and more like a spectator of life than an active participant.

Despite these new debilities, however, I'm gradually beginning to enjoy this new beginning, the beginning of the end. I'm filled with curiosity. Hoping to be cognizant at the very end, feeling somewhat like a cosmonaut waiting for blastoff, destination unknown, a one-way, one-time, no-return journey. Hopefully, a little of the mystery of life will be revealed. I have no expectations about the existence of life hereafter, just curiosity. Part of me says there must be something just waiting for me to experience, and forever after, wow!!!

Little by little I've let the Roman Catholic faith of my birth slip away like a loosely held string tied to a balloon caught in the wind on a blustery day. I cannot say I have lost my faith. I simply let it go. The final release came on a second trip to Iraq when the leaders of the churches of the world failed to put their lives in the way of the invasive destruction of Iraq. The privilege and opportunity of martyrdom denied them, they talked the talk, but turned away from walking the walk.

In closing I want to say thanks for the memories and all the best.

Appendix 1

"A Matter of Honor: He gave back his Medal of Honor to risk his freedom in protesting his country's policies," by Michael Taylor. *San Francisco Chronicle*, March 13, 2000. © San Francisco Chronicle, 2000. Reprinted with permission.

FT. BENNING – Standing outside the gates of Fort Benning, Georgia, protesting a U.S. Army school that trains Latin American military officers, Charles Liteky is a paradox, a man equally respected by many in the Army he used to be part of and by the demonstrators who surround him.

Elite Army paratroopers and Navy commandos come out of the Fort Benning gates from time to time to shake Liteky's hand and talk to him, to ask him why he has spent years protesting the School of the Americas. Sometimes they simply want to talk to him about the war in Vietnam – in truth, about his war in Vietnam.

Liteky, who is now sixty-nine, can lay claim to a situation that, as far as anyone can tell, applies to only one other person: As an Army chaplain, Liteky was awarded the Medal of Honor, the nation's highest decoration for heroism in combat, and less than twenty years later, he gave it back and renounced all its privileges, including the lifetime, tax-free pension of six hundred dollars a month.

Today, this former Catholic priest, who spends half his time in San Francisco with his wife, Judy, is scheduled to go on trial in federal court in Georgia for trespassing at Fort Benning, a charge that he knows he will be convicted of and for which he thinks he will be sent to federal prison for as much as a year.

If he does go to prison, he might well be the only inmate with the nation's highest military decoration.

In American culture, the Medal of Honor is sacrosanct. Only 3,410 men and women have received it and there are only 150 living recipients. In the armed services, generals, admirals, and colonels are known to snap to attention when an enlisted man wearing the medal comes into the room.

When Lyndon Johnson draped the medal around Liteky's neck in November 1968, he said, "Son, I'd rather have one of these babies than be president."

Liteky's road from Army hero to lifelong protester is not as complicated as it might seem. Whatever drove him to drag twenty-three men to safety during a fierce firefight in Bien Hoa Province, he says, is probably what makes him now crusade against the Army training school, whose graduates, critics say, are responsible for the massacre of peasants and human rights workers in Central America.

"The reason I do what I do now is basically the same," he said in an interview recently. "It's to save lives. In the case of the School of the Americas, it's to stop training the military from the Third World, who take the training back and employ it in the oppression of their people."

In Vietnam, he said, "the situation was more immediate. People were getting blown up, shot and killed all around me. I didn't get hit, and there was nothing for me to do but help them. Some were dead. One young man died in my arms, breathing his last breath and just gasping for air. I held him for a bit, and then I gave him Last Rites. Then I moved on because there were other people crying for help."

The Army's official citation says that on December 6, 1967, when Liteky's company came under intense fire from an enemy battalion, he crawled through machine-gun fire and dragged his wounded comrades to the safety of a medevac helicopter landing zone. At one point, Liteky tried to lift a seriously wounded soldier. "Realizing that the wounded man was too heavy to carry," the citation read, "[Liteky] rolled on his back, placed the man on his chest and through sheer determination and fortitude crawled back to the landing zone using his elbows and heels to push himself along, pausing for breath momentarily."

Liteky grew up the son of a career Navy noncommissioned officer and says, "I was always very comfortable around service people, and it was easy for me to go into the service."

In 1966, six years after being ordained as a priest, Liteky answered an Army call for chaplains and was soon on his way to Vietnam.

"I was 100 percent behind going over there and putting those communists in their place," he says now. "I had no prob-

lems with that. I thought I was going there doing God's work."
He left the Army in 1971.

In 1975, "mainly because of celibacy," he left the priesthood
and in 1983, married former nun Judy Balch in San Francisco. She
introduced him to refugees from El Salvador, "teenagers, whose
fathers had been killed and tortured. I didn't believe it, but I kept
going to more and more of these meetings and it became clear
these people weren't blowing in the wind."

By 1986, Liteky was devoting as much time as possible to
demonstrating against U.S. policy in Central America and the
Reagan administration's support of the Contra rebels in Nicaragua. In July of that year, he removed his Medal of Honor –
awarded to him under the name of Angelo J. Liteky – and placed
it and a letter to President Ronald Reagan at the Vietnam Veterans' wall in Washington. The medal was retrieved by the National Park Service and is now on display at the National
Museum of American History in Washington.

Since then, Liteky has protested against the School of the
Americas and has been banned from Fort Benning because of the
many times he has invaded the post at the head of a column of
protesters.

So how does Charlie Liteky's life sit with other Medal of
Honor winners?

"When I look at Liteky, I have respect for the courage of his
views," says Paul Bucha, past president of the Congressional
Medal of Honor Society and himself a recipient of the medal for
his heroism as an Army captain in Vietnam. Bucha is now chair-
man of the board of Wheeling-Pittsburgh Steel Corp.

"It's difficult to be an iconoclast," Bucha says. "It's much easier to go along. Men like Liteky are people who should force us to
pause and think, they should not be ostracized and criticized.
They are entitled to their views, and perhaps if we listened we'd
be better off."

As for Liteky, it appears he may be having some effect. In
November, the Army said it would change its School of the
Americas curriculum, making more room for courses on democ-
racy and international law. And the other day, Major General
John Le Moyne, the post commander at Fort Benning, called up
Liteky and personally invited him to an annual symposium on
human rights.

Does Liteky think Le Moyne would have called him if he
didn't have the medal?

"No, I don't think he would have called," Liteky says. "And yes, I guess I did use the medal consciously. I didn't for a long time, but I see now that it provides me with a certain respectability even though I've renounced it."

Any regrets about giving it back in the first place?

"Not at all."

Appendix 2

"Army Hero Turned Activist Headed to Prison for Trespassing: Vet says protest against military school has been an 'act of conscience'," by Michael Taylor, *San Francisco Chronicle*, June 9, 2000. © San Francisco Chronicle, 2000. Reprinted with permission.

A federal judge sentenced Charles Liteky, a former Army chaplain and war hero turned lifelong demonstrator, to the maximum sentence of one year in prison yesterday, a term Liteky said he welcomed as a way of drawing attention to his cause.

Standing at the lectern in a Columbus, Georgia, courtroom, sixty-nine-year-old Liteky, who lives part-time in San Francisco, read a ten-minute statement to U.S. District Judge Hugh Lawson. The judge leaned forward and listened intently, clearly interested in hearing why one of 147 living recipients of the Medal of Honor would willingly spend a year of his life in prison.

Liteky got his one-year sentence and a fine of ten thousand dollars for two counts of illegally trespassing at Fort Benning, the sprawling Army infantry post that is home to the controversial School of the Americas, a training facility for Latin American military officers.

Liteky and other critics charge that many of the school's graduates have been responsible for massacres of peasants and human rights workers in Central and South America.

"I consider it an honor to be going to prison as a result of an act of conscience in response to a moral imperative that impelled and obligated me to speak for voices silenced by graduates of the School of the Americas, a military institution that has brought shame to our country and the U.S. Army," Liteky told Lawson.

Under terms of the sentence, Liteky, who is not in custody, will be notified by mail within six weeks about which federal prison he should report to. He said yesterday that he suspects he will be sent to Lompoc in southern California.

Liteky's years of protesting and his occasional appearances before federal judges – he did six months in prison ten years ago for the same offense – might well be overlooked had he not received the nation's highest award for bravery in combat. He then became one of only two of the 3,410 recipients of the Medal of Honor to give it back, again as an act of protest.

Liteky was awarded the medal (under the name of Angelo J. Liteky) for saving the lives of twenty-three soldiers during a fierce firefight in Vietnam in December 1967. At the time, he was a Catholic priest and was serving in the Army as a chaplain. He has since resigned from his religious order.

During the one-hour court session in Columbus, Lawson told Liteky that he did not understand "the connection between what is going on at the School of the Americas and this court."

Liteky said after sentencing that he intends to write Lawson from prison "because I want him to understand that connection."

"We're doing acts of civil disobedience in the tradition of our democracy," he said. "This has been going on for a long time. And in going to prison, I'm drawing attention to the issue. I'm happy with his ruling."

Liteky's wife, Judy, a former nun, joined him in court yesterday. "My main reason for being here," she said later, "was to be with Charlie. The sentence is longer than I thought it would be, so I'm going to have to take some time to get used to a whole year."

Correspondent Jason Miczek in Georgia contributed to this report.

Appendix 3

"Charles Liteky Sentenced to Lompoc Federal Correctional Institution," by Stephanie Salter. *San Francisco Examiner,* Saturday, July 22, 2000. Published courtesy of the *San Francisco Examiner.*

Next Valentine's Day, when Charlie Liteky turns seventy, it won't be with his wife of seventeen years in their home in San Francisco. Instead, the former Roman Catholic priest, Vietnam veteran and U.S. Medal of Honor winner will have to choose celebratory company from among the two hundred inmates he'll be living with in the minimum-security camp at Lompoc Federal Prison.

Liteky's sentence is one year, starting July 31. His crime: Two misdemeanor counts of trespassing during a protest march on the U.S. Army base at Fort Benning, Georgia.

Liteky (pronounced "LIT-key") was bearing a fake coffin and headed for the School of the Americas inside Fort Benning when he was arrested last November and again in December.

A controversial training center for what the federal government now calls "counterrevolutionary" education, the SOA was founded in Panama in 1946 and moved to Columbus, Georgia, in 1984. It was created by the United States to fight communism in Latin America. Along the way, though, it became the alma mater of hundreds of dictators, thugs, assassins, torturers, and military "strongmen" like former Panamanian general Manuel Noriega.

The late Roberto D'Aubuisson was another grad; he is generally credited with planning the 1980 assassination of El Salvador's archbishop, Óscar Romero.

Thanks in large part to the efforts of the Rev. Roy Bourgeois, a Maryknoll priest, and people like the Litekys, the SOA has become ground zero for a massive protest movement against U.S. social, political, and economic policies in Latin America.

In November, when Charlie picked up the first of his two trespassing arrests, more than 12,000 women, men, and children were in line behind him. Only ten of them are going to prison.

Among the ten are two retired ministers (Lutheran and Methodist), a Quaker, a Korean War vet and Sister Megan Rice, a seventy-year-old Baltimore nun who served for thirty-four years as a missionary in Nigeria and Ghana.

"Sister Megan got six months the last time, and six months this time – the maximum," said Liteky. "She's still in jail in Columbus, waiting transfer to a facility near her home. She said the hardest part of being in prison has nothing to do with her – it's witnessing the conditions of the other women inmates."

Charlie Liteky also got the maximum sentence: two six-month terms to be served consecutively, not concurrently.

To those of us outside the world of nonviolent civil disobedience, people like Megan Rice, Roy Bourgeois, and Charlie Liteky can seem a little nuts. Crisscrossing the country, getting themselves arrested or fasting to within a few days of death, they threaten their health, comfort, economic stability, and, sometimes – as the Litekys have learned – their closest personal relationships.

"On the one hand, I'm out here doing something I think is important, something I believe is bigger than me and my life," said Charlie. "On the other hand, there's this thing called love. And this person I love, who loves me, is suffering because of me. My pain is her pain, hers is mine."

It is no wonder that many of the most committed social justice activists are or were priests, nuns and ministers – people who once answered an ethereal call to service with vows of poverty, obedience and (for some) celibacy.

They deeply believe that sacrifice and personal suffering can bear rich fruit for the oppressed and marginalized. Like Mahatma Gandhi, there are many causes for which they might die, but none for which they'll kill.

Back in 1966, when Charlie Liteky, the priest, volunteered to be an Army chaplain in Vietnam, the notion of no-exceptions nonviolence was missing from his personal radar screen. The son of a career Navy noncommissioned officer, Liteky was comfortable with the military; he trusted its ways.

"I cannot believe the attitudes I had in '66, the things I believed," he said. "I'd been taught about the evils of communism and the just war theory. I had no problems with us being in Vietnam. I thought I was doing God's work."

To hear the survivors of a December 6, 1967, firefight in Bien Hoa Province tell it, Father Angelo (Liteky's ordination name) *did* seem to be working for a higher power. Crawling repeatedly through machine-gun fire, he dragged twenty-three wounded soldiers from his battalion to safety in a medical helicopter landing area.

Eleven months later, President Lyndon B. Johnson presented Liteky with this country's top award for heroism in combat, the Medal of Honor.

In July 1986, in protest of U.S. aid to the Contras in Nicaragua, Liteky gave the medal back – with a letter to President Ronald Reagan that he laid at the base of the Vietnam memorial in Washington, D.C.

"That was when Ronald Reagan was comparing the Contras to the moral equivalent of our founding fathers," said Liteky. "By then I'd begun to wake up about what my country was doing to Latin America. I'd studied the history and talked to refugees here in San Francisco.

"Then I had to go down and see for myself, to El Salvador, Nicaragua and Honduras. I was ashamed of my country. And I was ashamed I'd participated in the same thing in Vietnam."

Ironically (or inevitably), Liteky first met some of the casualties of U.S. Latin American policies through the woman who would become his wife.

An Immaculate Heart of Mary nun for thirteen years, Judy Balch had left her order for life in the laity in 1978 and moved from her native Los Angeles to San Francisco.

A year of teaching math to poor Latina students in the L.A. barrio had opened her eyes as a nun to the economic and social inequities suffered by many minorities. Social justice seminars, taught by fired-up Jesuits at the University of San Francisco, expanded her horizons and threw her into the company of anti-nuclear weapons activists and people in the "sanctuary movement" for Salvadoran refugees.

In 1980, learning that she was "ready to date," mutual friends picked out a candidate: a tall, Vietnam War hero who was working as a benefits counselor for the Veterans Administration. Like her, he'd changed his mind about how best to serve God; he'd left the priesthood in 1975.

"Right away, I figured she was the one," Charlie recalled last

week over a dinner of some of his favorite foods that Judy prepared in their modest Sunnyside neighborhood home.

"I'd had this physical vision in my mind of a tall, slim brunette – and there she was."

Judy had harbored no visions, but she knew at the end of
their first date that she wanted to see more of Charlie Liteky: "I
dropped him off near where he was living in the Tenderloin, and
I was so bold as to lean over and kiss him goodnight."

It would take more than two years for Judy to say yes to
Charlie's entreaties to marry. During that time he took his
wounded pride to a cabin in Colorado with the idea of writing a
novel, "But I ended up writing more love letters to her than I did
chapters of the book."

Finally, on October 22, 1983, the former nun and former
priest were married in Judy's parish church, St. John of God. The
bride was forty-one, the groom, fifty-two.

Three years later, Judy learned that being Charlie Liteky's
wife would be like no other challenge she'd ever imagined: He
told her he was going to Washington with another vet to protest
U.S. aid to the Contras with a water-only hunger strike on the
Capitol steps.

"That decision had a finished-product characteristic to it. I
had no impact on it," said Judy. "I do a little better when I have
time to reposition myself, when things unfold, like the stages of
this arrest and trial."

Said Charlie: "I don't know what I'd have done at that time if
she'd said no – I probably would have gone ahead. But she didn't.
She objected, but she was very good at listening to what was going on in my soul, and she honored that. She always has."

Honoring the goings-on in Charlie Liteky's soul would test
the boundaries of any wife's love and commitment. A math, science, and engineering teacher at Canada College in Belmont,
Judy has spent long stretches away from Charlie, earning the
bulk of the couple's income while he has been at the center of the
decades-old campaign to close the School of the Americas.

In addition to his dangerous 47-day fast, she endured Charlie's first trespassing prison sentence in 1990 – six months in the
federal pen in Allenwood, Pennsylvania.

Now, it's Lompoc for a year.

"Like going to war, going to prison as a protest is not a
self-contained experience," said Judy. "I get a year's sentence,

too."

It helps that she and Charlie still believe in a Creator whose son commanded his followers to love others without exclusion and to help the poor, enslaved, and oppressed.

It helps, too, that Judy has been an astute student of social justice politics. When the annual march on Fort Benning comes around in November, she'll be there without Charlie.

"The SOA movement has been an important one to both of us," she said. "I often think of those four Maryknoll nuns [*sic*] who were raped and murdered in El Salvador in 1980. I could imagine myself there, people like me being those women.

"I'm also aware that citizens' lobbying is not a sufficient way to change the U.S. government and its policies. The role of nonviolent protest is essential."

But, as both Litekys admit, political activism carries a high price.

"A year is a long time," Judy said, looking across the dining room table at Charlie. "He won't be home for dinner. I won't embrace him. So I am going to have to stretch and hope I'm going to learn what I need to learn while he's in prison."

Already, that stretching – and Barbara Sonneborn's documentary *Regret to Inform* – have led Judy to empathize with and connect spiritually to the actual widows of war.

"Women's way into the suffering of war has traditionally been through men," she said. "Wherever we met them, however we came to love them, we became their widow. In a sense, I'm learning what it is to be Charlie's Vietnam widow."

Perhaps the biggest help of all comes from the fact that Judy Liteky loves her husband with a quiet ferocity that can only come with long years and a shared mission.

"There is a history we can't take out of ourselves anymore. I can't not have known him this long," she said. "Through working with Charlie, I've had an incredible set of experiences, learning what it means for women to become a political voice.

"He's also shown me the importance of the symbol of witness – in prison or in crossing the line at Fort Benning. In a practical, greedy world, I believe it's important to all of us to surrender to such a symbol."

One break the Litekys will get in the coming year: Their seventeenth wedding anniversary falls on a Sunday. Judy will be permitted to visit Charlie in Lompoc.

"It won't be a consummated anniversary," Charlie joked.

"But I *will* be there," Judy said. "I promise."

Charles Liteky was released from the Lompoc Federal Correctional Institution in 2001.

Appendix 4

"A Tight Squeeze," by Kathy Kelly, Voices in the Wilderness.* Reprinted with permission from "Live from Baghdad," February 23–25, 2003.

Last night, while walking home along Abu Nuwas Street, Charlie Litkey and Jerry Zawada were met by two little boys who begged them for money, grabbed their hands, and then went for their wristwatches. The boys are seasoned little workers. After their father died some years ago, they moved in with their uncle's family. The uncle sends them out each day and night to beg on the streets. One of our team members recalls buying Saif and his brother bananas instead of giving them money. Both little boys were so hungry that they immediately ate the bananas, including the peels.

The tiny duo had spotted two of our "softies." Jerry, a Franciscan priest, is happiest when he is helping someone. Charlie, who towers over Jerry, is a former priest chaplain who returned the Medal of Honor awarded him for pulling soldiers off a battlefield in Vietnam. Like Jerry, he radiates quiet kindness. We had to chuckle over our two "Gentle Bens" being attacked by the charming but aggressive duo. The kids had just about scored two wristwatches when Charlie took matters in hand and tightly squeezed Saif's wrist until the watch dropped. Saif began to cry. Both watches were returned. This morning both Jerry and Charlie voiced their regrets. "I squeezed his hand pretty hard," said Charlie.

Squeeze. The word easily connotes gentle and helpful measures. You squeeze a loved one's hand in times of need. You squeeze an orange to make juice. But this morning, listening to several NGO workers try to work out how they might manage to distribute relief in the face of a "squeeze" planned by the U.S. Pentagon, the word sounds ugly and cruel. You squeeze a country to tighten the thumbscrews, exacerbate an already existing siege. You squeeze until civilians can't bear it any more. The squeeze means that people who are trapped without access to relief may panic. How will they find drinking water? How can they cook stored rations without water? How can they get medical care for the injured? Once the electricity goes down, how will they manage without refrigerators, lights, communication? Explosions, fires, shrapnel, destroyed buildings, maimed bodies, unburied corpses. Baghdad's residents have tasted all this before, but now comes anticipation of yet another agony: a squeeze that can cause chaos and panic to flow like lava.

I think most U.S. people can easily identify with Charlie's and Jerry's gentle, even affectionate regard for the little ones who so desperately "attacked" them last night. I think most would share Charlie's remorse over making little Saif wince. Charlie's regrets, compassion and courage are never more needed than now. War planners are readying a ghastly and protracted squeeze, designed to frighten, sicken and kill hundreds of thousands of vulnerable people.

*Voices for Creative Nonviolence: www.vcnv.org

Index